NATIONAL THEATERS IN THE LARGER GERMAN AND AUSTRIAN CITIES

NATIONAL THEATERS IN THE LARGER GERMAN AND AUSTRIAN CITIES

Wallace Dace

PUBLISHED BY
RICHARDS ROSEN PRESS, INC.
NEW YORK, N.Y. 10010

Published in 1980 by Richards Rosen Press, Inc.
29 East 21st Street, New York, N.Y. 10010

FIRST EDITION

Library of Congress Cataloging in Publication Data

Dace, Wallace, 1920–
    National theaters in the larger German and Austrian cities.

    Bibliography: p.
    Includes index.
    1. Theater and state—Germany, West. 2. Theater
and state—Austria. 3. Performing arts—Germany, West.
4. Performing arts—Austria. 5. Federal aid to the
performing arts. I. Title.
PN2044.G4D3   792'.0943   80-24785
ISBN 0–8239–0527–6

Manufactured in the United States of America

ABOUT THE AUTHOR

WALLACE DACE is Professor of Speech and Director of Graduate Studies in Theater at Kansas State University, Manhattan, Kansas. Educated at Illinois Wesleyan University, the Yale Drama School, and the University of Denver, he has been studying the public theaters in Austria and Germany for many years.

Other recent publications of his are an article, "The Failure of Public Funding" in *Performing Arts Journal* (Vol. IV, No. 1 and 2, May, 1979) pp. 167–176, and a book, *Proposal for a National Theater* (New York: Richards Rosen Press, 1978), in which he advocates a series of national theaters in the 50 largest cities of the United States similar to those described herein.

ACKNOWLEDGMENTS

I would like to acknowledge the valuable assistance I have received from theater colleagues in Europe and America in obtaining information, photographs, and drawings. I am especially indebted to the following:

Dr. Volker Bahn, Geschäftsführender Direktor, Schiller-Theater, Berlin
Ks. Judith Beckmann, soprano, Hamburgische Staatsoper
Wilhelm Berner, Dramaturgie, Düsseldorfer Schauspielhaus
Gretl Biedermann, Künstlerisches Betriebsbüro, Thalia Theater, Hamburg
Costanza Cuccaro, soprano, Deutsche Oper Berlin
Hildegard Gabbert, Verwaltung, Deutsches Schauspielhaus, Hamburg
Dr. Fritzdieter Gerhards, Dramaturgie, Bühnen der Stadt Köln
Ks. Donald Grobe, tenor, Deutsche Oper Berlin
Doris Hauns, Intendanz, Deutsche Oper Berlin
Barbara Hering, Dramaturgie, Hamburgische Staatsoper
William Ingle, tenor, Landestheater Linz
Brenda Jackson, soprano, Deutsche Oper Berlin
Dr. Peter Kerz, Chefdramaturg, Staatstheater am Gärtnerplatz, München
Ks. James King, tenor, Staatsoper Wien
Reg. Dir. Hanns Kirchner, Theaterreferent beim Senator für Kulturelle Angelegenheiten Berlin
Walter Kristoff, Waagner-Biró, A.G., Wien und Graz
Dr. Thomas-M. Langer, Dramaturgie, Deutsche Oper Berlin
Henriette Lloyd, Dramaturgie/Presse, Bayerische Staatsoper, München
Sigrid Lanzrath, Inter Nationes, Bonn
H. Lukas Lindenmaier, Ausstattung, Städtische Bühnen Nürnberg
Ks. Vera Little, mezzo-soprano, Deutsche Oper Berlin
Lesley Manring-Borchers, soprano, Wuppertaler Bühnen
Erika Mayer, Theaterleitung, Städtische Bühnen Nürnberg
Dr. Heinrich Minden, Betriebsdirektion, Städtische Bühnen Frankfurt am Main

William Murray, baritone, Deutsche Oper Berlin
John Neumeier, Ballettdirektor, Hamburgische Staatsoper
Dr. Gertrude Obzyna, Pressebüro, Österreichischer Bundestheaterverband, Wien
Gül Oswatitsch, Dramaturgie, Bayerisches Staatsschauspiel, München
Dr. Karl Richter, Dramaturgie, Bühnen der Stadt Köln
Irmgard Scharberth, Dramaturgie, Oper der Stadt Köln
Iri Seisser, Dramaturgie, Bayerisches Staatsschauspiel, München
Rolf Trouwborst, Chefdramaturg, Deutsche Oper am Rhein, Düsseldorf-Duisberg
Walter Tunk, Bayerische Verwaltung der Staatliche Schlösser, Gärten und Seen
Eberhard Uebe, Chefdramaturg, Landestheater Linz
Prof. Dipl.-Ing. Walther Unruh, Herausgeber, *Bühnentechnische Rundschau*
Christian M. Wackwitz, Inter Nationes, Bonn
Franz Wagner, Leiter des Abonnementbüros, Bayerische Staatsoper, München
Joachim Wenzel, Archiv, Hamburgische Staatsoper
Marion von Wille, Dramaturgie, Schauspiel Köln
Margot Wössner, Dramaturgie, Oper der Stadt Köln
Carol Wyatt, soprano, Deutsche Oper Berlin
Wolfgang Zimmermann, Dramaturgie, Münchner Kammerspiele

I am especially indebted to Ms. Darlene Wiley, who took time during her brief vacation from her strenuous schedule as a leading lyric coloratura soprano at the Staatstheater Darmsradt, to read and criticize the entire manuscript.

I am also indebted to David von Riesen, Director of Photographic Services at Kansas State University, and to Gene Guerrant, who prepared the negatives of all the drawings and charts that appear in this book.

Finally, special thanks go to Dr. Norma Bunton, Head of the Department of Speech at Kansas State University, for her encouragement and support while I was working on this project.

WALLACE DACE
Manhattan, Kansas

CONTENTS

ILLUSTRATIONS

INTRODUCTION

The passage of legislation in 1978 calling for a White House Conference on the Arts in 1979* has set in motion a great deal of inquiry and soul-searching regarding the state of American fine and performing arts organizations generally and especially those concerned with the production of serious drama, opera, and ballet. Since the establishment of the National Endowment for the Arts in 1965, many arts organizations have grown and developed remarkably, but among spoken and lyric drama companies signs of stagnation can be observed nearly everywhere. The spoken drama theaters do five or six plays a year on a winter stock production basis, with little or no possibility of growing into true repertory companies. The opera companies, with a few exceptions, produce four or five operas at three or four performances each per year, and ballet company production is even more sporadic. Everyone connected with performing arts companies believes that more support money is needed, and all eyes have turned toward Washington.

Staff members on Congressional committees and subcommittees concerned with the arts, in turn, have begun to study various techniques of arts support in foreign countries, especially in Canada, Great Britain, France, West Germany, and Austria. The latter two countries attract repeated scrutiny because of the public acceptance of the need for very large tax subsidies, an acceptance plainly based on the people's abiding satisfaction with the decentralization, the unified organization, and the variety of offerings made to them by their national theaters.

It has been argued that we already have national theaters here in America—the nonprofit professional resident companies—and all they need to grow into artistic maturity is more money from the National Endowment for the Arts every year. With more money the opera companies could increase their offerings, as could the ballet companies, and the theaters could try repertory.

Although it is true that more money can improve any company, doubts remain. The fragmentation of performing arts groups into separate drama, opera, and ballet

---

* Postponed by Congress to the 1980's.

companies, the lack of interest shown by the cities in their own theaters, and the current decline of support from foundations all point toward the conclusion that something is wrong with the American nonprofit theaters. One is led to ask, "What is the difference between European national theaters and American resident theaters?"

A national theater, as the term implies, is a theater supported by taxes collected on a national basis. It is a public theater, similar in scope and financing to a state university. It takes responsibility for all performance media—spoken drama, children's theater, opera, operetta, musicals, ballet, and modern dance. There is a unified management—one artistic direction group, one administrative setup, one box office and subscription department, one bookkeeping department, one publicity staff, one technical department, one complex of scene, costume, and property shops, one storage complex, and one house management. In the smaller cities, the company performs plays, operas, and ballets in one theater structure; in the medium-sized cities the company does operas, ballets, and large-cast plays in a large theater with an orchestra pit and does plays and chamber operas in a small theater. In the largest cities, there are three, four, or more theater structures in the national theater complex. The theaters perform nightly for a period of 42 to 46 weeks per year, and ticket prices are scaled so that anyone who wants to attend a performance can afford it.

These theater companies are managed by either city or state government agencies, and most personnel are government employees, enjoying the same pension benefits, health and accident insurance, and similar perquisites as other municipal and state employees. The theaters are subsidized in amounts that approach an average of 80 percent of the annual budget, so that only 20 percent has to be taken in at the box office, a practice that enables the managements to keep ticket prices exceptionally low.

The subsidies are taken from tax revenues, especially income taxes and value-added taxes. This latter tax is a federal levy on both industry and individuals and is collected all over the country. Unlike America, however, where all federal taxes are sent to Washington, the German cities and states are allowed to keep for their own needs a certain proportion of the income taxes and value-added taxes they collect. It is out of these funds that the states and cities support their educational and cultural institutions.

The feature that most distinguishes European national theaters from American resident theaters, however, is the principle of repertory production, an ideal established in European theatrical companies in the 18th century and maintained ever since. American companies, in general, mount a play or an opera for a specific run; in the case of plays, for about 15 to 20 performances, and in the case of operas, for about 3 to 8 performances. When the run is completed, the work is removed and a new work replaces it for a similar run. Performers are brought in for a particular work and are released when the run is over. The management is permanent, but many if not most of the performers are transients.

Zelda Fichandler, founder and director of Washington's Arena Stage, has commented in a published letter to W. McNeil Lowry on the advantages of repertory production if one is seeking "the very best that Theater can give." She points out that in repertory the actor or singer can develop a role over a long period of time, with alternating intervals of playing and gestation. Alvin Epstein, in an interview in a *Yale Drama Alumni Bulletin,* said much the same thing: "You never lose contact with the play if you perform it every three days or so; it's constantly alive and with you and it's also constantly let alone. It's very good to let a play simmer for a few days." Further, the actor can enrich a role like King Lear with material derived from playing Algernon in *The Importance of Being Earnest* the night before. The actor can find the common ground of the various historic acting styles by playing roles from all periods of the history of the theater. He can learn to knit his performance into the fabric established by his fellow performers as he gets to know them over some period of time. Finally, repertory is valuable for the management because good actors can be obtained for minor as well as major roles. A good actor would not agree to play 30 consecutive performances of a butler—even an interesting butler—but he might join a company that permitted him to play Macbeth on Monday, the butler on Tuesday, and Tony Lumpkin on Wednesday.

The repertory system improves standards of performance in spoken drama, opera, and ballet, and it also converts a national theater into an educational institution of a certain kind, an institution concerned with the education of feeling, that is, aesthetic education. Since the companies produce about 20 plays, about 20 to 25 operas, and 5 to 10 ballets in a given season, and since they change the bill every night, a subscriber can usually choose among several possible subscription plans. He can obtain a subscription to 10 plays, or 10 operas, or a combination of 15 of both, or a mixture of plays, operas, and ballets, or all ballets, depending on his personal preferences. By this means, a regular theatergoer receives, over a period of years, a wide variety of theatrical experiences in all the major performance media and from works of art from many cultures and time periods. Regular attendance at the theater, like regular attendance at a university, is the cornerstone of aesthetic education.

The following pages are devoted to a description of ten European national theater complexes, starting with one in a relatively small city, Linz (population 205,600), and concluding with the complex of theaters in West Berlin (population 1,950,000). In the smaller cities the theaters are grouped together into one architectural scheme. A large theater is usually connected to a small theater by shared scene and costume shops, the entire complex often facing a park or at least a sizable square. In the cities over a million population (Munich, Vienna, Hamburg, and Berlin), the buildings are more scattered. In Munich four of the six theaters are part of one building complex, but in Vienna all four national theaters are at some distance from one another.

All figures detailing budgetary information, ticket prices, attendance, personnel in the theaters, and numbers of performances given are taken, unless otherwise noted, from the annual issues of *Theaterstatistik,* published by the Deutscher Bühnenverein of Cologne. Information regarding theater buildings comes mainly from the *Deutsches Bühnen Jahrbuch,* published by the Genossenschaft Deutscher Bühnen-Angehörigen of Hamburg. Play and opera titles are cited in German unless the performance was in another language. Thus, *Der Troubadour* would indicate a performance in German and *Il trovatore* would mean the performance was sung in the original Italian. The original titles for British and American plays are listed in the *Glossary.*

NATIONAL THEATERS IN THE LARGER GERMAN AND AUSTRIAN CITIES

I. LINZ, AUSTRIA

Landestheater Linz

There are national theaters in all the major cities of Austria, and the Landestheater Linz provides a good example of the range of professional drama, opera, and ballet that is available ten months of the year at modest box office prices. The city is the capital of the state of Oberösterreich and has a population of 206,000.

The history of the Danube city of Linz can be traced to Roman times when the settlement was called Lentia, a name first recorded in 410 B.C. The city prospered as traffic along the Danube increased. Many churches were established, among which the Martinskirche is the oldest surviving building in Austria, dating from before 799.

The astronomer Johannes Kepler resided in Linz and completed there his *Harmonices mundi,* which was first printed in 1619. Mozart composed his Linz symphony there in 1783, Bruckner composed and played the organ in Linz from 1855 to 1868, and the novelist and playwright Hermann Bahr was born in the city. Another Austrian who finished his education in Linz and studied to become an architect between 1905 and 1908 was Adolf Hitler.

Unlike Vienna, Salzburg, or Innsbruck, the city of Linz was not the site of a permanent court that could establish and maintain a theater at court expense. Instead, the earliest theaters were developed by the citizens themselves in their schools. Between 1578 and 1595, a classics professor at the Landschaftschule, Georg Calaminus, wrote a number of plays in Latin, which were performed by his students. One of them, *Rudolphus et Ottocarus,* served Franz Grillparzer as inspiration for some portions of his own *König Ottokars Glück und Ende.*

The year 1803 marked the beginning of the modern theater tradition in Linz, when a new theater was planned for the city after a serious fire required that a major civic building project be undertaken. The theater was established on the site of the present Landestheater on Römerstrasse. The theater was destroyed in World War II but was rebuilt on the same site.

The company performs in three theaters, the Grosses Haus (opera, operetta, and ballet), the Kammerspiele (plays and children's pieces), and the Theaterkeller im Ursulinenhof (experimental plays). Technical aspects of these three theaters are as follows:

Grosses Haus

Seating capacity: 756 seats.
Architect: Professor Clemens Holzmeister.
Opened: December 20, 1958, with *Arabella,* opera by Richard Strauss and Hugo von Hofmannstahl.
Proscenium size: 9.60 meters wide by 7 meters high.
Stage size: 21 meters wide by 23 meters deep.
Technical equipment: Roll-up cyclorama, revolving stages, portal bridges with follow spots, 12 large scene projectors, control console with 120 dimmers (AEG).
Orchestra pit: 12.5 meters wide by 6 meters deep for 72 musicians.

Kammerspiele

Seating capacity: 421 seats.
Architect: Professor Clemens Holzmeister.
Opened: September 28, 1957, with *Paulus unter den Juden,* play by Franz Werfel.
Proscenium size: 7.6 meters wide by 6 meters high.
Stage size: 14 meters wide by 15 meters deep.
Lighting control: Console with 90 magnetic amplifier dimmers (Siemens).
Orchestra pit: 10 meters wide by 4.5 meters deep for 45 musicians.

Theaterkeller

Seating capacity: 100 (multiform).
Opened: November 30, 1973, with *Adam and Eva,* experimental play by Peter Hacks.

There are 16 visitor organizations in Linz with about 13,000 members who attend the theaters regularly. The company tours both plays and operas on a regular basis to the nearby cities of Wels (50,000), Steyr (43,000), and Gmunden (13,000).

The Generalintendant (artistic director) of the Landestheater Linz is Alfred Stögmüller. Personnel of the company number as follows:

Artistic direction	38
Principal singers	23
Actors and actresses	34
Chorus singers	36
Ballet dancers	16
Orchestra musicians	100
Technical personnel	107

Administrative and house personnel	78	
Guest performers	23	
Total	455	

During 1976–77 the Landestheater Linz offered the following variety of performances in its three theaters and on the road:

Grosses Haus

	PERFORMANCES	ATTENDANCE	PERCENT OF CAPACITY
Operas	95	51,945	
Operettas and musical comedies	94	58,995	
Adult and children's plays	48	27,878	
Performances on tour	23		
Totals	260	138,818	77.5%

Kammerspiele

Operettas and musical comedies	10	3,175	
Adult and children's plays	228	66,840	
Performances on tour	24		
Totals	262	70,015	69.3%

Theaterkeller

Operettas and musical comedies	53	4,577	
Adult and children's plays	98	6,573	
Performances on tour	3		
Totals	154	11,150	81.5%

The total attendance at the Linz national theaters during 1976–77 was thus 219,983, or about 107 percent of the population of the city.

During the 1977–78 season most of the operas and all of the plays were new productions. The operas, operettas, musicals, adult plays, and children's plays produced in the three theaters were as follows:

Grosses Haus

Operas	Mozart: *Così fan tutte*
	Smetana: *Die verkaufte Braut*
	Cornelius: *Der Barbier von Bagdad* (Revival)
	Kienzl: *Der Evangelimann*
	Puccini: *La Bohème* (Revival)
	Strauss: *Ariadne auf Naxos* (Revival)
	Strawinsky: *Oedipus Rex*
	Orff: *Die Kluge*
	Szokolay: *Bluthochzeit*
Operettas	Strauss: *Wiener Blut*
	Lecocq: *Giroflé-Girofla*
Musical	Leigh/Wassermann: *Der Mann von La Mancha*
Plays	Raimund: *Der Alpenkönig und der Menschenfeind*
	Zuckmayer: *Der Rattenfänger*
	Frisch: *Don Juan oder Die Liebe zur Geometrie*

Kammerspiele

Plays	Goldoni: *Der Diener zweier Herren*
	Goethe: *Iphigenie auf Tauris*
	Kleist: *Amphitryon*
	Labiche: *Der Florentinerhut*
	Gorki: *Feinde*
	Feuchtwanger: *Wahn, oder Der Teufel in Boston*
	Pagnol: *Das grosse ABC*
	Canetti: *Hochzeit*
	Flatow: *Vater einer Tochter*
	Wassermann: *Einer flog über das Kuckucksnest*

Theaterkeller

Plays	Buchrieser: *Das Produkt*
	Dorfer/Zettel: *Josef Lang, k.u.k. Scharfrichter*
	Enquist: *Die Nacht der Tribaden*
	Frank: *Der Spiegel*
	Genet: *Die Zofen*
	Müller: *Stille Nacht*
	Neumann: *Ich war Hitlers Schnurrbart*

In addition to direct box office sales, tickets were available from the Landestheater Linz in seven subscription series, as follows:

1. Ten premiers (Grosses Haus)	1st price range: S 1,382*
	2nd price range: S 992
	3rd price range: S 769
	4th price range: S 574
	5th price range: S 410
2. Ten premiers (Kammerspiele)	1st price range: S 856
	2nd price range: S 528
	3rd price range: S 352
3. Six Sunday afternoons (Grosses Haus and Kammerspiele)	1st price range: S 721
	2nd price range: S 502
	3rd price range: S 378
4. Ten Monday evenings (Grosses Haus)	1st price range: S 1,382
	2nd price range: S 992
	3rd price range S 769
	4th price range S 574
	5th price range S 410
5. Twenty Tuesday evenings (Grosses Haus and Kammerspiele) and	
6. Twenty Wednesday evenings (Grosses Haus and Kammerspiele)	1st price range: S 2,158
	2nd price range: S 1,440
	3rd price range: S 1,041
7. Ten Friday evenings (Kammerspiele)	1st price range: S 856
	2nd price range: S 528
	3rd price range: S 352

There follow drawings of the two theaters showing the seat prices for 1977–78 (Figs. 1 and 2, pp. 8–9).

The income and expenses of the Landestheater Linz in the calendar years 1969–77 are summarized in Fig. 3, p. 10. Average values for the Austrian schilling during this period varied as follows:

1969: 4.0¢	1972: 5.0¢	1975: 6.5¢
1970: 4.1¢	1973: 5.8¢	1976: 6.8¢
1971: 4.2¢	1974: 6.0¢	1977: 7.0¢

Scenes from productions of recent seasons by the Landestheater Linz are shown in Figs. 4–10, pp. 11–17.

---

* During 1977, one Austrian schilling averaged 7¢ in American currency.

Sitzplan Großes Haus

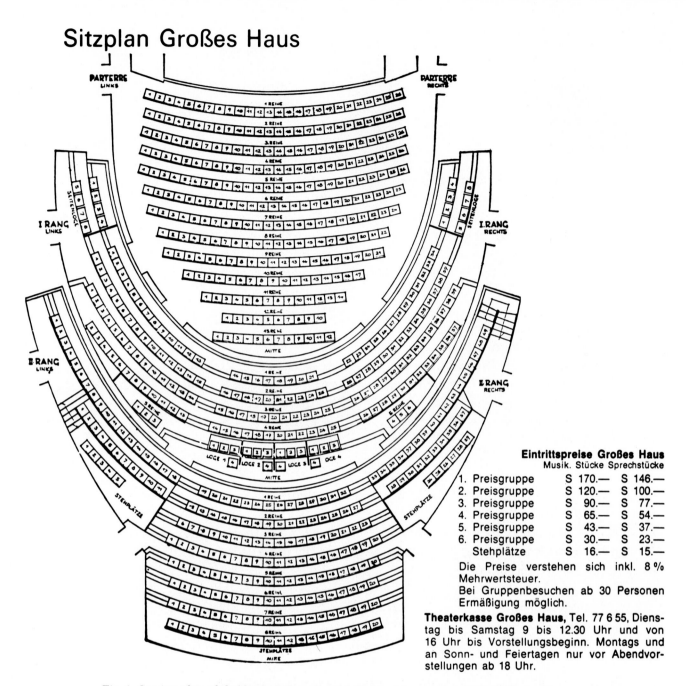

Eintrittspreise Großes Haus
Musik. Stücke Sprechstücke

	Musik. Stücke	Sprechstücke
1. Preisgruppe	S 170.—	S 146.—
2. Preisgruppe	S 120.—	S 100.—
3. Preisgruppe	S 90.—	S 77.—
4. Preisgruppe	S 65.—	S 54.—
5. Preisgruppe	S 43.—	S 37.—
6. Preisgruppe	S 30.—	S 23.—
Stehplätze	S 16.—	S 15.—

Die Preise verstehen sich inkl. 8 % Mehrwertsteuer.
Bei Gruppenbesuchen ab 30 Personen Ermäßigung möglich.

Theaterkasse Großes Haus, Tel. 77 6 55, Dienstag bis Samstag 9 bis 12.30 Uhr und von 16 Uhr bis Vorstellungsbeginn. Montags und an Sonn- und Feiertagen nur vor Abendvorstellungen ab 18 Uhr.

Fig. 1. Seating plan of the Grosses Haus, Landestheater Linz, season of 1977–78, together with single seat prices (Landestheater Linz)

Sitzplan Kammerspiele

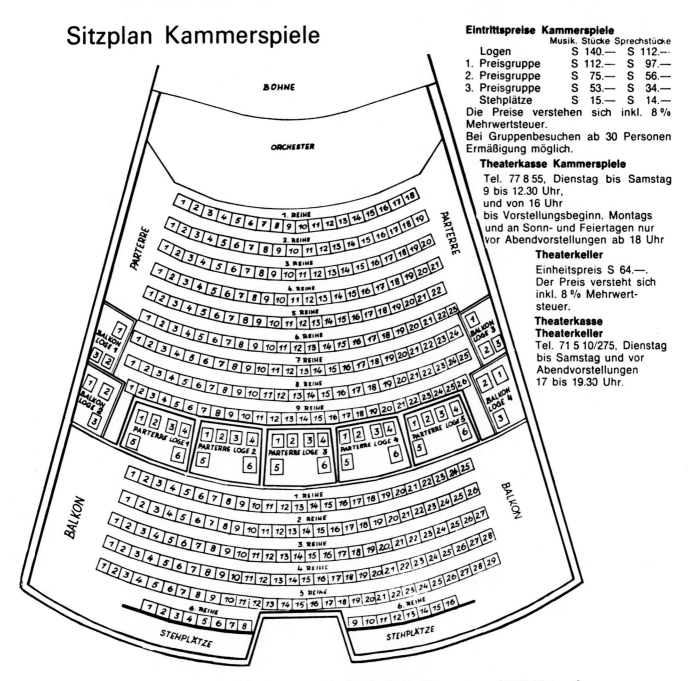

Eintrittspreise Kammerspiele

	Musik. Stücke	Sprechstücke
Logen	S 140.—	S 112.—
1. Preisgruppe	S 112.—	S 97.—
2. Preisgruppe	S 75.—	S 56.—
3. Preisgruppe	S 53.—	S 34.—
Stehplätze	S 15.—	S 14.—

Die Preise verstehen sich inkl. 8 % Mehrwertsteuer.
Bei Gruppenbesuchen ab 30 Personen Ermäßigung möglich.

Theaterkasse Kammerspiele

Tel. 77 8 55, Dienstag bis Samstag 9 bis 12.30 Uhr, und von 16 Uhr bis Vorstellungsbeginn. Montags und an Sonn- und Feiertagen nur vor Abendvorstellungen ab 18 Uhr

Theaterkeller

Einheitspreis S 64.—. Der Preis versteht sich inkl. 8 % Mehrwertsteuer.

Theaterkasse Theaterkeller

Tel. 71 5 10/275, Dienstag bis Samstag und vor Abendvorstellungen 17 bis 19.30 Uhr.

Fig. 2. Seating plan of the Kammerspiele, Landestheater Linz, season of 1977–78, together with single seat prices (Landestheater Linz)

YEAR	1969	1970	1971	1972	1973	1974	1975	1976	1977
VALUE OF SCHILLING	4.0¢	4.1¢	4.2¢	5.0¢	5.8¢	6.0¢	6.5¢	6.8¢	7.0¢
EXPENSES									
Salaries and performance fees	S 30,733,000	S 33,029,000	S 37,876,000	S 44,077,000	S 50,671,000	S 54,683,000	S 60,331,000	S 69,811,000	S 76,992,000
Scene and costume design costs	1,513,000	1,724,000	1,963,000	2,145,000	3,143,000	3,393,000	3,572,000	11,573,000	4,040,000
Other costs	4,118,000	3,625,000	4,444,000	5,001,000	5,693,000	10,551,000	12,056,000	4,000,000	12,989,000
TOTAL	S 36,364,000	S 38,378,000	S 44,283,000	S 51,223,000	S 59,507,000	S 68,627,000	S 75,959,000	S 85,384,000	S 94,021,000
INCOME									
Single ticket and subscription sales	S 7,781,000	S 8,558,000	S 8,868,000	S 9,750,000	S 9,879,000	S 12,818,000	S 13,612,000	S 14,876,000	S 15,804,000
Cloakroom and program sales	599,000	418,000	399,000	597,000	612,000	669,000	607,000	772,000	749,000
Other income	208,000	---	---	699,000	779,000	875,000	868,000	1,132,000	1,129,000
TOTAL	S 8,588,000	S 8,976,000	S 9,267,000	S 11,046,000	S 11,270,000	S 14,362,000	S 15,087,000	S 16,780,000	S 17,682,000
TAX SUBSIDY	S 27,776,000	S 29,402,000	S 35,016,000	S 40,177,000	S 48,237,000	S 54,265,000	S 60,872,000	S 68,604,000	S 76,339,000
SUBSIDY PERCENTAGE	76.4%	76.6%	79.1%	78.4%	81.1%	79.1%	80.1%	80.3%	81.2%

Fig. 3. Expenses and income for the Landestheater Linz, 1969–77 (Deutscher Bühnen-verein, Köln)

Fig. 4. Eugene O'Neill's *Der Eismann kommt.* Left to right: Engelbert Jirak, Gisela Siemann, Michael Pawlik, and Ulrich G. Hoffmann (Martin Schindelar/Landestheater Linz)

Fig. 5. *Die Kassette* by Carl Sternheim; Silvia Glogner and Hubert Mann (Martin Schindelar/Landestheater Linz)

12 • NATIONAL THEATERS IN GERMAN AND AUSTRIAN CITIES

Fig. 6. Ödön von Horváth's bitter play *Geschichten aus dem Wienerwald*. In the fore-ground: Ernst Zeller, Walter Hirt and Edith Hieronimus (Martin Schindelar/Landes-theater Linz)

Fig. 7. Vanessa Foster, Teddy Keller, Anna Stewart-Lynton, Sally Angus, Sylvia von Reh-
berg, and Margit Neubauer kick up their heels in Leonard Bernstein's musical, *West
Side Story* (Martin Schindelar/Landestheater Linz)

Fig. 8. Federico García Lorca's tragedy *Yerma,* with Barbara Blume in the title role, Günther Panak, and Kurt Schossmann (Martin Schindelar/Landestheater Linz)

Fig. 9. Wagner's *Lohengrin* at the Landestheater Linz. Maria Slatinarn as Elsa and William Ingle as Lohengrin (Martin Schindelar/Landestheater Linz)

Fig. 10. Hans Pfitzner's musical legend *Palestrina;* William Ingle as Palestrina and Rudolf Holtenau as Kardinal Borromeo (Landestheater Linz)

II. NUREMBERG, GERMANY

Städtische Bühnen Nürnberg

It is often suggested that the reason the German and Austrian national theaters are so well attended and subsidized lies in the tradition of the court theaters, supported by dukes, princes, and kings all over central Europe. When the kings were deposed in 1918, the state governments simply continued the services to which the people were accustomed.

Although it is true that some of the famous theaters, such as the Burgtheater in Vienna and the Nationaltheater in Munich, began as princely institutions, a surprising number of German theaters grew up without royal patronage of any kind. Particularly in the free imperial cities, which were not under the protection of a princely family, the people themselves founded and subsidized their theaters. Often the city built a theater and leased it to a private manager, although sometimes the managers themselves were able to put up the buildings out of their profits.

Although Nuremberg was founded around 1050 by the Hohenstaufen Emperor Henry III and still keeps up a large castle erected at the time for its defense, the collapse of the Hohenstaufen dynasty at the end of the 13th century caused the abrupt departure of the military garrison, and the town was left to shift for itself as a free imperial city. Both the opera house and the playhouse were established originally by the people of Nuremberg; only gradually did they change over from the status of privately supported theaters whose deficits were made up by donations from citizens and business, to that of public, tax-supported institutions.

In the 19th century, the Nuremberg Schauspielhaus was situated on the Lorenzerplatz in the heart of the old part of the city, and the Opernhaus was just outside the city walls, near the railroad station. During World War II the Schauspielhaus was destroyed in a bombing raid, but the Opernhaus was not seriously damaged. It was decided after the war to build a new playhouse next to the opera house and connect the two theaters with a building that could house scene and costume shops, office space for the administration, and rehearsal areas. This policy was adopted in several other German cities such as Kassel, Frankfurt am Main, Mannheim, and Cologne that had also lost their theaters in the war. Thus the two-theater complex, connected by shop and office structures and situated usually in a park or on a large square, became the usual plan for national theater structures in modern Germany. Only in the very largest cities, where new theaters were rebuilt on the ruins of the old ones to save space and maintain traditions, are the constituent units of the national theaters scattered about.

Nuremberg is in northern Bavaria and has a population of 492,447. The Städtische Bühnen consist of the Opernhaus, the Schauspielhaus, and the Kammerspiele. The opera house orchestra, which is also the Philharmonic Orchestra of the city, gives eight concerts a year in the Meistersinger Halle, which is not part of the theater complex.

Technical aspects of the three theaters are as follows:

Opernhaus

Seating capacity: 1,456 seats.
Opened: September 1, 1905, with a special play by Bürgermeister von Jäger, *Im neuen Haus,* followed by the Festwiese scene from Act III of Wagner's *Die Meistersinger.*
Proscenium size: 11.4 meters wide by 7.5 meters high.
Stage size: 18.5 meters wide by 16.5 meters deep.
Technical equipment: Rundhorizont, double-decked lighting bridge, cyclorama lighting bridge, fluorescent cyc lighting units, several large scenic projectors, and a control console that programs 120 magnetic amplifier dimmers.
Orchestra pit: 13.5 meters wide by 6.5 meters deep for 80 musicians.

Schauspielhaus

Seating capacity: 924 seats.
Architect: Kurt Schneckendorf.
Opened: September 9, 1959.
Proscenium size: 9.5 meters wide by 6.5 meters high.
Stage size: 20 meters wide by 14.8 meters deep.
Technical equipment: Rundhorizont, double-decked lighting bridge, cyclorama light bridge, scene projectors, and lighting control for 140 magnetic amplifier dimmers.
Orchestra pit for 36 musicians.

Kammerspiele (in the Schauspielhaus)

Seating capacity: 197 seats.
Architect: Kurt Schneckendorf.
Opened: July 28, 1962.
Proscenium size: 11.5 meters wide by 3 meters high.

Stage size: 11.5 meters wide by 10.5 meters deep.
Technical equipment: Standard counterweight system and lighting control for 48 Bordoni dimmers.

The principal block booking organization in Nuremberg is the Fränkischer Besucherring, which numbers about 9,000 members. The theater and opera companies tour to various towns in the vicinity and regularly play the Bergwaldtheater in Weissenberg, one of the most impressive open-air theaters in Europe.

Fig. 11. The old Schauspielhaus on the Lorenzerplatz, which was opened October 1, 1833, and destroyed in World War II (Städtische Bühnen Nürnberg)

Fig. 12. The new Schauspielhaus, erected next to the Opernhaus on Richard-Wagner-Platz. A building for shops, offices, and rehearsal rooms connects the two theaters at rear (Städtische Bühnen Nürnberg)

Fig 13. Recently completed outdoor lounging area in front of the Schauspielhaus (Städtische Bühnen Nürnberg)

Fig. 14. New underground parking area for the two theaters (Städtische Bühnen Nürnberg)

Fig. 15. The old Opernhaus, dating from 1905 (Städtische Bühnen Nürnberg)

The Städtische Bühnen Nürnberg are directed by a three-person management team instead of the earlier, all-powerful Generalintendant. Several years ago, the subject of Mitbestimmung, or equal voice in management decisions by various members of the company, became a widely debated issue in the German, Austrian, and German-speaking Swiss theaters. The most important set of decisions in any repertory company is the choice of the repertory for the following season. A balance should be maintained between old and new works, between works in the native language of the audience and those from other languages and cultures, and between conservative and experimental production styles. The staff directors all have favorite plays they want to stage, and the conductors lean toward operas and operettas they think they do especially well. The singers and actors all have their favorites, and the dancers, too, have some say in the music theater productions. A further complicating factor is the use of guest directors, with their demands and special ideas that the company may not be used to. Nuremberg uses a few guest stage directors each season to stage opera productions, among whom have been Hans Neuenfels *(Der Troubadour)*, Hans Neugebauer (*Wozzeck* and a new *Ring* cycle), and Hans Hollmann *(Die Hochzeit des Figaro)*.

Since the choice of the repertory determines the lion's share of the annual budget, financial restrictions—to which every theater in the world is subject—pose another collection of problems. If several agreed-on productions prove to be too expensive for the predicted budget, someone has to give up his cherished project and do something else that is cheaper.

At Nuremberg, therefore, it was decided some years ago to establish a management team consisting of Hans Gierster, director of the music theater division and conductor of the Nuremberg Philharmonic; Hansjörg Utzerath, director of the spoken drama division, and Willi Eck, director of the business and finance department. This triadic leadership has worked very successfully for the Städtische Bühnen, and the policy is to be continued. In the United States the Metropolitan Opera Association has also gone over to this form of management with good results. Many other repertory theaters, however, both here and in Europe, continue to operate under the leadership of a single artistic director.

Personnel of the Städtische Bühnen Nürnberg numbered during the season 1976–77 as follows:

Artistic direction	54
Principal singers	39
Actors and actresses	39
Ballet dancers	25
Chorus singers	54
Orchestra musicians	85
Technical personnel	261
Administrative personnel	40
House personnel	42
Total	639

During the 1976–77 season the Städtische Bühnen Nürnberg made performances available to the public as follows:

Opernhaus

	PERFORMANCES	ATTENDANCE	PERCENT OF CAPACITY
Operas	128	120,350	64.6%
Ballets	19	19,750	59.0%
Operettas	67	73,519	75.4%
Musicals	13	14,699	77.7%
Guest companies	4	(included above)	
Totals	231	228,318	69.2%

Schauspielhaus

Adult plays	192	85,401	79.2%
Children's plays	84	32,679	72.2%
Guest companies	8	(included above)	
Totals	284	118,080	75.7%

Kammerspiele

Ballets	2	309	78.4%
Adult plays	173	29,185	84.2%
Children's plays	29	4,910	85.9%
Guest companies	5	(included above)	
Totals	209	34,404	82.8%

The total attendance during 1976–77 thus was 380,802, or about 77.3 percent of the population of the city.

During the season 1978–79, the following productions were mounted in the three theaters:

Opernhaus

New Productions

Borodin: *Fürst Igor*
Zeller: *Der Vogelhändler*
Mascagni: *Cavalleria rusticana,* and Leoncavallo: *Der Bajazzo*
Monteverdi: *Die Heimkehr des Odysseus*
Ballet Evening
Debussy: *Pelléas et Mélisande*

	Verdi: *Rigoletto*
	Benatzky: *Im weissen Rössl*
	Ravel: *Die spanische Stunde*, and Puccini: *Gianni Schicchi*
	Wagner: *Die Walküre*
Revivals	Verdi: *Othello*
	Wagner: *Der fliegende Holländer*
	Lohengrin
	Die Meistersinger von Nürnberg
	Das Rheingold
	Tannhäuser
	Saint-Saëns: *Samson und Dalila*
	Strauss, R.: *Ariadne auf Naxos*
	Der Rosenkavalier
	Donizetti: *Viva la Mamma*
	Lortzing: *Zar und Zimmermann*
	Humperdinck: *Hänsel und Gretel*
	Smetana: *Die verkaufte Braut*
	Prokofieff: *Cinderella* (ballet)
	Strauss, J.: *Die Fledermaus*
	Eine Nacht in Venedig
	Millöcker: *Der Bettelstudent*
	Kalmán: *Gräfin Mariza*
	Lehár: *Das Land des Lächelns*
	Künneke: *Der Vetter aus Dingsda*
	Loewe: *My Fair Lady*

Schauspielhaus

New Productions	Ibsen: *Gespenster*
	Schiller: *Kabale und Liebe*
	Wedekind: *Frühlings Erwachen*
	Fleisser: *Fegefeuer in Ingolstadt*
	Thoma/Schneyder: *Mich hätten Sie sehen sollen*
	Zuckmayer: *Der Hauptmann von Köpenick*
	Nestroy: *Der Talisman*
	Hauptmann: *Der Biberpelz*
Revivals	Sternheim: *Bürger Schippel*
	Horváth: *Der jüngste Tag*

Kammerspiele

All Productions New	Hacks: *Das Jahrmarktsfest zu Plundersweilern*
	Kroetz: *Mensch Meier*
	Mrozek: *Tango*

Kishon: *Der Trauschein*
Shaffer: *Revanche*

Subscription opportunities for the Nuremberg theaters are detailed in Figs. 16 and 17, pp. 31–33.

The financing of the German national theaters is based on box office income (and other earned income) and tax support. Since tax support makes up between 60 percent and 80 percent of the budget of the average theater, a brief examination of the German tax structure may be helpful. As indicated in the tables below, reproduced from the *Monthly Report of the Deutsche Bundesbank* (Vol. 31, No. 1, January 1979, in English), the largest single source of revenue in Germany, as in the United States, is income taxes. The Germans have only federal income taxes, however; they do not permit state or city income taxes. To compensate the states and cities for this, they divide their tax revenues as follows: wage tax and assessed income tax revenues—43 percent to the federal government, 43 percent to the state governments, and 14 percent to the cities; corporation tax and investment tax income—50 percent to the federal government and 50 percent to the state governments. Thus, in 1977, the cities received DM 17,679,000,000 as their calculated share of the income tax pie and could budget expenditures accordingly, since they knew in advance about how much they would probably receive.

Another shared tax is the value-added tax (VAT) or turnover tax, as the Germans call it. This tax is allocated according to a distribution key that varies from year to year. In 1978 the federal government kept 67.5 percent and the states got 32.5 percent of the income. The tax is placed on the value that a manufacturer adds to raw materials as he refines them into a finished product. The manufacturer of ball bearings, for example, buys steel for a certain price and sells the ball bearings he has made for a higher price. The tax is paid on the difference between these two prices. In the case of imported goods, the importer pays VAT on the difference between what he pays for the goods and what he sells them for. In general, it may be said that this tax corresponds to some extent to American sales taxes, but it covers every part of a manufactured product instead of just the final price, and it is collected as a federal tax only—there are no local or state value-added taxes.

Other taxes are not shared. The federal government receives all the revenue from income tax surcharges, gasoline taxes, tobacco taxes, liquor taxes, and capital transaction taxes; the states receive all the revenue from taxes on beer, personal and corporate property, and motor vehicles; and the cities tax trade, local wages paid, and land and buildings within their city limits.

During 1976–77 the Städtische Bühnen Nürnberg received a total of DM 29,042,000 in subsidies—DM 30,000 from the federal government, DM 6,790,000 from the state of Bavaria, DM 22,221,000 from the city of Nürnberg, and DM 1,000 from private sources.

Figs. 18 and 19, pp. 34 and 35 show various kinds of taxes collected in West Germany.

There follows a summary of the expenses and income for the Städtische Bühnen Nürnberg from 1969 through 1977. During this period the yearly average value of the West German mark in relation to American money varied approximately as follows:

1969: 28¢	1972: 34¢	1975: 44¢
1970: 29¢	1973: 40¢	1976: 48¢
1971: 30¢	1974: 42¢	1977: 50¢

Scenes from plays and operas recently performed by the Städtische Bühnen Nürnberg are shown in Figs. 21–31, pp. 36–47.

Fig. 16. Seating plan and subscription arrangement for the Opernhaus Nürnberg (Städtische Bühnen Nürnberg)

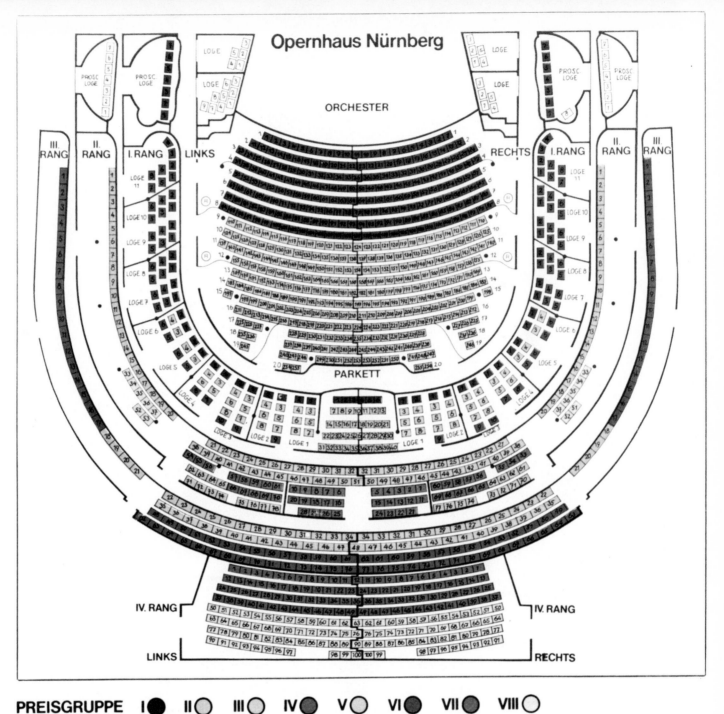

Opernhaus Nürnberg

PREISGRUPPE I ● II ○ III ○ IV ◐ V ○ VI ◐ VII ◐ VIII ○

● **Musiktheater-Abonnement**
(Oper, Operette, Ballett, Musical)

Serie A oder D   Platzmietetag   Dienstag
Serie E   Platzmietetag   Mittwoch
Serie C oder F   Platzmietetag   Donnerstag

30% Preisermäßigung

● **Musiktheater-Familienabonnement** (Oper, Operette)
Serie G   Platzmietetag Sonntag – nur nachmittags

● **Opern-Abonnement** (Oper, Ballett, klassische Operette)
Serie U   Platzmietetag Sonntag – nur abends

25% Preisermäßigung · 8 Vorstellungen im Opernhaus

OPER · OPERETTE · BALLETT · MUSICAL
10 Vorstellungen im Opernhaus

Preis-gruppe	Tages-kassenpreis	Abonnementspreis		
		1 Vorst.	10 Vorst.	Raten
I	29,—	20,90	209,—	1 x 71,— / 2 x 69,—
II	25,—	18,10	181,—	1 x 61,— / 2 x 60,—
III	20,—	14,60	146,—	1 x 50,— / 2 x 48,—
IV	17,—	12,50	125,—	1 x 43,— / 2 x 41,—
V	13,—	9,70	97,—	1 x 33,— / 2 x 32,—
VI	10,—	7,60	76,—	1 x 26,— / 2 x 25,—
VII	8,—	6,20	62,—	1 x 22,— / 2 x 20,—
VIII	5,50	4,45	44,50	1 x 16,50 / 2 x 14,—

Preise einschl. aller Abgaben und Garderobe

OPER · OPERETTE / nachmittags
OPER · KLASSISCHE OPERETTE · BALLETT / abends

Preis-gruppe	Tages-kassenpreis	Abonnementspreis		
		1 Vorst.	8 Vorst.	Raten
I	29,—	22,25	178,—	1 x 60,— / 2 x 59,—
II	25,—	19,25	154,—	1 x 52,— / 2 x 51,—
III	20,—	15,50	124,—	1 x 42,— / 2 x 41,—
IV	17,—	13,25	106,—	1 x 36,— / 2 x 35,—
V	13,—	10,25	82,—	1 x 28,— / 2 x 27,—
VI	10,—	8,—	64,—	1 x 22,— / 2 x 21,—
VII	8,—	6,50	52,—	1 x 18,— / 2 x 17,—
VIII	5,50	4,65	37,20	1 x 13,20 / 2 x 12,—

Preise einschl. aller Abgaben und Garderobe

Fig. 17. Seating plan and subscription arrangement for the Schauspielhaus Nürnberg
(Städtische Bühnen Nürnberg)

Schauspielhaus
Nürnberg

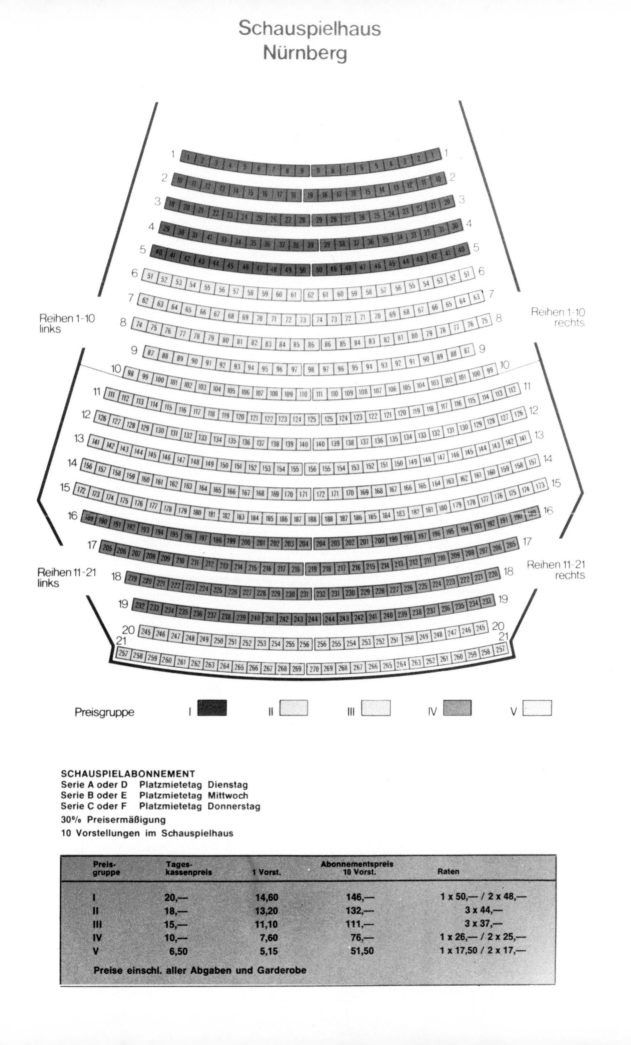

Reihen 1-10 links

Reihen 1-10 rechts

Reihen 11-21 links

Reihen 11-21 rechts

Preisgruppe   I ■   II ☐   III ☐   IV ▨   V ☐

SCHAUSPIELABONNEMENT
Serie A oder D   Platzmietetag Dienstag
Serie B oder E   Platzmietetag Mittwoch
Serie C oder F   Platzmietetag Donnerstag
30% Preisermäßigung
10 Vorstellungen im Schauspielhaus

Preis-gruppe	Tages-kassenpreis	1 Vorst.	Abonnementspreis 10 Vorst.	Raten
I	20,—	14,60	146,—	1 x 50,— / 2 x 48,—
II	18,—	13,20	132,—	3 x 44,—
III	15,—	11,10	111,—	3 x 37,—
IV	10,—	7,60	76,—	1 x 26,— / 2 x 25,—
V	6,50	5,15	51,50	1 x 17,50 / 2 x 17,—

Preise einschl. aller Abgaben und Garderobe

2. Breakdown by type of tax

DM million

| Period | Total 1 | Joint taxes | | | | | | | | Share in trade tax 4 | Taxes accruing entirely to | | EEC share in customs duties | Memo item |
| | | Income taxes 2 | | | | | Turnover taxes 3 (including EEC share) | | | | | | | Local authorities' share in income taxes |
		Total	Wage tax	Assessed income tax	Corporation tax	Investment income tax	Total	Value-added tax	Turnover tax on imports		Federal Government 5	Länder Governments 5		
1970	141,230	61,824	35,086	16,001	8,717	2,021	38,125	26,791	11,334	4,355	27,396	9,531	—	7,152
1971	158,240	70,384	42,803	18,340	7,167	2,074	42,896	30,868	12,028	5,157	29,556	10,247	—	8,560
1972	180,399	83,594	49,770	23,140	8,495	2,189	46,981	34,153	12,828	5,851	31,549	10,883	1,541	10,207
1973	205,885	100,617	61,255	26,452	10,887	2,024	49,486	34,922	14,563	7,023	35,111	11,485	2,163	12,279
1974	219,346	111,731	71,960	26,793	10,403	2,574	51,170	32,853	18,317	7,345	34,550	11,790	2,761	13,826
1975	221,393	111,491	71,191	28,001	10,054	2,246	54,082	35,722	18,361	6,888	33,611	12,143	3,177	13,887
1976	244,456	125,622	80,609	30,860	11,840	2,313	58,459	36,559	21,900	7,319	35,646	13,788	3,620	15,606
1977	273,671	146,492	90,773	35,508	16,830	3,381	62,684	39,357	23,327	8,741	37,131	14,983	3,641	17,679
1977 1st qtr	61,856	33,102	20,014	8,793	3,557	738	16,210	10,546	5,664	348	7,558	3,705	932	4,033
2nd qtr	62,451	31,940	19,690	7,752	3,640	858	14,950	9,044	5,906	2,003	8,853	3,723	982	3,842
3rd qtr	68,535	37,442	23,136	8,809	4,382	1,115	15,022	9,254	5,768	2,073	9,455	3,666	876	4,472
4th qtr	80,830	44,008	27,934	10,153	5,251	670	16,503	10,514	5,989	4,316	11,263	3,889	851	5,332
1978 1st qtr	68,074	35,653	20,361	9,705	4,888	699	19,965	13,631	6,334	178	7,670	3,746	863	4,209
2nd qtr	66,394	32,931	19,226	8,571	4,254	880	17,228	10,543	6,685	2,044	9,495	3,800	896	3,892
3rd qtr	72,443	38,921	23,579	9,110	4,818	1,413	17,206	10,686	6,520	2,199	9,539	3,700	878	4,577
1977 Oct.	20,439	9,319	7,656	913	363	388	5,216	3,268	1,948	1,605	3,047	966	286	1,200
Nov.	20,031	8,423	7,451	607	243	121	5,578	3,575	2,004	585	3,222	1,932	290	1,128
Dec.	40,360	26,266	12,827	8,634	4,645	161	5,708	3,671	2,038	2,126	4,994	991	274	3,004
1978 Jan.	20,517	10,620	8,461	1,197	635	327	7,216	5,197	2,019	11	1,298	1,076	296	1,352
Feb.	20,526	7,723	6,369	908	274	173	7,458	5,280	2,178	114	3,309	1,646	277	1,019
March	27,030	17,310	5,532	7,600	3,979	199	5,292	3,154	2,137	53	3,063	1,023	289	1,839
April	18,363	6,993	5,826	728	147	292	5,509	3,223	2,286	1,528	2,998	1,022	313	918
May	18,892	7,124	6,134	506	262	222	5,993	3,805	2,188	508	3,221	1,757	288	930
June	29,140	18,814	7,266	7,337	3,845	365	5,725	3,515	2,210	8	3,276	1,021	295	2,044
July	22,399	10,230	8,311	773	288	857	5,934	3,711	2,223	1,597	3,335	1,006	297	1,272
Aug.	20,600	8,815	7,682	431	232	471	5,759	3,599	2,161	597	3,406	1,737	285	1,136
Sep.	29,444	19,876	7,586	7,906	4,298	85	5,513	3,376	2,136	5	2,798	957	295	2,169
Oct.	21,898	9,318	7,811	825	568	113	5,939	3,704	2,236	1,633	3,665	1,039	305	1,209
Nov. p	21,360	8,588	7,676	487	331	94	6,449	3,996	2,453	579	3,609	1,804	332	1,143

1 Excluding special anticyclical taxes. — 2 Since 1970 the yield of wage tax and assessed income tax has been distributed among the Federal and Länder Governments and local authorities in the ratio 43 : 43 : 14, and the yield of corporation tax and investment income tax between the Federal and Länder Governments in the ratio 50 : 50. —

3 1970 and 1971: Federal Government = 70 %, Länder Governments = 30 %; 1972 and 1973: Federal Government = 65 %, Länder Governments = 35 %; 1974: Federal Government = 63 %, Länder Governments = 37 %; 1975: Federal Government = 68.25 %, Länder Governments = 31.75 %; 1976 and 1977: Federal Government = 69 %, Länder Governments = 31 %; 1978: Federal Government = 67.5 %, Länder Governments = 32.5 %; as from 1975 the EEC share must be deducted from the Federal Government share stated. — 4 Federal Government and Länder Governments 50 % each. — 5 For breakdown see Table VII, 3. — p Provisional.

Fig. 18. Types of taxes collected in West Germany. (From *Monthly Report of the Deutsche Bundesbank,* Vol. 31, No. 1, January, 1979, p.56)

3. Individual taxes of central, regional and local authorities

DM million

Period	Federal taxes						Länder taxes				Local authority taxes			
	Income tax surcharge	Petroleum tax	Tobacco tax	Spirits tax	Capital transaction taxes 1	Other Federal Government taxes 2	Beer tax	Property tax	Motor vehicle tax	Other Länder Government taxes	Trade tax 3	Tax on total wages paid	Tax on land and buildings	Other local taxes 4
1970	949	11,512	6,537	2,228	1,224	4,947	1,175	2,877	3,830	1,650	10,728	1,389	2,683	879
1971	1,100	12,417	6,863	2,403	1,483	5,290	1,226	3,123	4,156	1,742	12,313	1,805	2,801	967
1972	1,406	14,227	7,826	2,870	1,654	3,566	1,250	2,994	4,722	1,917	14,847	2,176	3,004	1,049
1973	1,854	16,589	8,872	3,175	1,675	2,946	1,269	3,234	4,989	1,993	17,777	2,535	3,209	1,122
1974	2,160	16,052	8,952	3,288	1,615	2,483	1,262	3,410	5,159	1,958	18,774	2,794	3,521	1,228
1975	695	17,121	8,886	3,122	1,743	2,043	1,275	3,339	5,303	2,227	17,898	2,998	4,150	1,276
1976	762	18,121	9,379	3,367	1,850	2,168	1,317	3,917	5,630	2,925	20,113	3,221	4,800	1,485
1977	241	19,184	9,803	3,743	1,980	2,179	1,287	4,995	5,929	2,771	23,028	3,454	5,291	1,397
1977 1st qtr	94	3,196	1,771	1,305	600	593	283	1,170	1,518	735	5,408	919	1,189	416
2nd qtr	60	4,646	2,369	742	472	565	323	1,174	1,538	689	5,594	796	1,292	356
3rd qtr	47	5,001	2,643	800	458	508	351	1,236	1,444	634	5,926	887	1,510	319
4th qtr	40	6,342	3,021	897	450	513	331	1,415	1,429	713	6,099	853	1,301	307
1978 1st qtr	39	3,417	1,813	1,171	664	565	276	1,144	1,566	759	5,635	967	1,232	381
2nd qtr	29	4,889	2,607	921	494	555	320	1,102	1,699	679	5,890	754	1,406	431
3rd qtr	34	4,876	2,705	909	499	516	354	1,101	1,493	752	5,910	817	1,558	357
1977 Oct.	13	1,636	836	254	154	154	116	139	493	217	.	.	.	.
Nov.	15	1,747	851	292	151	166	103	1,100	471	257	.	.	.	.
Dec.	12	2,959	1,333	351	146	192	111	176	464	240	.	.	.	.
1978 Jan.	18	305	231	367	152	224	109	115	602	250	.	.	.	.
Feb.	11	1,628	742	417	336	175	80	876	441	249	.	.	.	.
March	10	1,484	839	387	176	166	87	154	524	258	.	.	.	.
April	8	1,449	877	310	180	173	100	92	604	225	.	.	.	.
May	11	1,699	868	294	164	186	104	896	536	221	.	.	.	.
June	9	1,741	862	317	151	196	116	114	559	232	.	.	.	.
July	16	1,718	946	330	145	179	122	83	553	248	.	.	.	.
Aug.	9	1,766	961	296	210	164	104	880	470	284	.	.	.	.
Sep.	9	1,393	798	283	144	172	128	139	469	221	.	.	.	.
Oct.	6	2,129	892	298	153	186	101	116	562	260	.	.	.	.
Nov. p	5	1,853	1,078	298	175	201	104	929	496	275	.	.	.	.

1 Capital transaction taxes (stock exchange turnover tax, company tax), insurance and bill taxes. — 2 Other excise taxes, road haulage tax, transport tax and, until 1971, all customs duties received; from 1972 including the Federal Government's residual share in customs duties received (1977: DM 104 million). — 3 On returns and capital. — 4 From 1974 including tax-like receipts. — p Provisional.

Fig. 19. Special taxes collected respectively by the federal government, the states, and the cities. (From *Monthly Report of the Deutsche Bundesbank,* Vol. 31, No. 1, January, 1979, p.57)

YEAR	1969	1970	1971	1972	1973	1974	1975	1976	1977
VALUE OF DEUTSCHE MARK	28¢	29¢	30¢	34¢	40¢	42¢	44¢	48¢	50¢
EXPENSES									
Artists' salaries	DM 7,563,000	8,402,000	9,906,000	10,393,000	11,068,000	11,931,000	13,894,000	14,269,000	14,734,000
Technical salaries	3,870,000	4,330,000	5,123,000	5,240,000	7,275,000	6,850,000	7,717,000	7,935,000	7,908,000
Administration	765,000	880,000	963,000	889,000	1,272,000	1,081,000	961,000	1,183,000	1,338,000
Other personnel	136,000	172,000	130,000	---	---	61,000	57,000	73,000	63,000
Pension funds	822,000	880,000	981,000	1,056,000	---	3,284,000	2,343,000	2,751,000	2,922,000
Production costs	2,391,000	2,643,000	3,026,000	2,775,000	2,946,000	3,400,000	3,844,000	3,834,000	4,078,000
Loan payments	621,000	606,000	590,000	566,000	548,000	1,595,000	285,000	2,021,000	2,522,000
Building maintenance	159,000	314,000	112,000	42,000	135,000	242,000	---	---	---
TOTAL	DM 16,327,000	DM 18,227,000	DM 20,831,000	DM 20,961,000	DM 23,242,000	DM 28,444,000	DM 29,101,000	DM 32,066,000	DM 33,565,000
INCOME									
Single tickets	DM 687,000	DM 622,000	DM 814,000	DM 741,000	DM 1,023,000	DM 736,000	DM 723,000	DM 896,000	DM 743,000
Subscriptions	606,000	528,000	407,000	382,000	318,000	373,000	383,000	515,000	595,000
Children's theater subscriptions	312,000	367,000	355,000	347,000	216,000	159,000	202,000	39,000	152,000
Visitor groups	933,000	735,000	728,000	771,000	535,000	632,000	615,000	749,000	784,000
Cloakroom charges	1,000	1,000	2,000	1,000	76,000	172,000	170,000	196,000	241,000
Radio and TV fees	7,000	---	11,000	---	---	---	---	---	---
Touring	139,000	110,000	203,000	54,000	95,000	262,000	109,000	42,000	75,000
Guest performances by other companies	---	10,000	---	---	---	111,000	36,000	112,000	48,000
Program sales	44,000	26,000	18,000	7,000	7,000	---	268,000	283,000	337,000
Other income	427,000	340,000	303,000	245,000	194,000	1,659,000	329,000	192,000	951,000
TOTAL	DM 3,156,000	DM 2,739,000	DM 2,841,000	DM 2,548,000	DM 2,464,000	DM 4,104,000	DM 2,835,000	DM 3,024,000	DM 3,924,000
TAX SUBSIDY	DM 13,171,000	DM 15,488,000	DM 17,990,000	DM 18,413,000	DM 20,778,000	DM 24,340,000	DM 26,266,000	DM 29,042,000	DM 29,641,000
SUBSIDY PERCENTAGE	80.7%	84.9%	86.4%	87.8%	89.4%	85.6%	90.3%	90.5%	88.3%

Fig. 20. Expenses and income, Städtische Bühnen Nürnberg, 1969–77 (Deutscher Bühnenverein, Köln)

Fig. 21. *Josef Lang, k.u.k. Scharfrichter* by Gerhard Dorfer and Anton Zettel, directed by Hans Dieter Schwarze. Anton Pointecker in the title role and Dieter Hebecker as the violinist (H. Lukas Lindenmaier/Städtische Bühnen Nürnberg)

Fig. 22. George Bernard Shaw's *Die heilige Johanna,* directed by Paul Bösiger. From left, Ingris Braun (Johanna), Jochen Kuhl (de Courcelles), Fridolin Eppe (de Stogumber), Leo Bieber (Cauchon), Kurt Mestrijk (Inquisitor), Wolfgang Sembdner (Ladvenu), and Anton Pointecker (D'Estivet) (H. Lukas Lindenmaier/Städtische Bühnen Nürnberg)

Fig. 23. Wolfram Mehring's production of Shakespeare's romantic comedy *Was ihr wollt*. Bernhard Letizky as Orsino and Elizabeth Volkmann as Viola (H. Lukas Lindenmaier/ Städtische Bühnen Nürnberg)

Fig. 24. *Clownspielen,* with Johanna Bucher (Clown) on the touring truck stage of the Nuremberg theater company (H. Lukas Lindenmaier/Städtische Bühnen Nürnberg)

Fig. 25. *Mord,* by Hans Peter Renfranz, on the Theaterwagen in a public square in Nuremberg. From left, Peter Loth, Johanna Bucher, Kristin Lentz, and Elmar Roloff, the narrator and one-man band (H. Lukas Lindenmaier/Städtische Bühnen Nürnberg)

Fig. 26. Scenes from a Freudian version of Verdi's *Der Troubadour,* directed by Hans Neuenfels, designed by Klaus Gelhaar, and conducted by Hans Gierster. Ferrando (Andreas Camillo Agrelli) relates the complex history of the Luna family from his wheelchair. The porcelain dogs suggest the savagery of Luna and his men . . . (Peter Ruprecht/Städtische Bühnen Nürnberg)

Fig. 27. . . . Manrico (Sandor Arisz) confronts Count Luna (Barry Hanner) in the garden of Leonore (Maria de Francesca-Cavazza). At the right, Ruiz (Norbert Orth) stands near a porcelain horse, symbol of the freedom of the gypsy life to which Manrico would lead Leonore. The peacocks suggest the empty life of luxury led by the heroine . . . (Peter Ruprecht/Städtische Bühnen Nürnberg)

Fig. 28. . . . The gypsy camp. Azucena (Dunja Vejzovic) sings of the death of her mother by torture. A dove of peace hovers over the encampment . . . (Peter Ruprecht/Städtische Bühnen Nürnberg)

44 • NATIONAL THEATERS IN GERMAN AND AUSTRIAN CITIES

Fig. 29. . . . Azucena's tent. The bed to the left hints at the erotic attachment she has for Manrico, who is not her true son . . . (Peter Ruprecht/Städtische Bühnen Nürnberg)

Fig. 30. . . . Count Luna's torture chamber. Leonore prepares to submit to him to save
Manrico's life . . . (Peter Ruprecht/Städtische Bühnen Nürnberg)

Fig. 31. . . . Luna's dungeon. Azucena, her head shaved, anticipates death and revenge
(Peter Ruprecht/Städtische Bühnen Nürnberg)

III. STUTTGART, GERMANY

Württembergische Staatstheater

The city of Stuttgart was established about 1160 on a site that had been used to breed horses; hence the city's emblem—a black horse on a field of gold. By the 13th century the Margraves of Württenberg had made Stuttgart their residence, and through the years the family went from the status of dukes to electors to kings in 1806. In 1918 the kingdom became a state, and in 1953 it received its present designation as the state of Baden-Württemberg, with Stuttgart (population 590,135) as its capital.

Today the city is well known in foreign countries for its quality automobiles. Still preserved is the small workshop that Gottlieb Daimler established near his estate in 1882, where several valuable inventions were made. In the summer of 1883 he constructed the first fast-running gasoline engine, and in 1886 his experiments led to the first automobile. Many of the early Daimler-Benz cars are on display in Stuttgart's automobile museum.

Theater activity also was flourishing in the city at that time. The kings of Württemberg prided themselves on the cultural atmosphere of their capital city and supported institutions devoted to the theater, opera, ballet, painting, and sculpture out of the royal treasury. After 1918 the state government continued the subsidies in response to the people's wish to go on enjoying their arts institutions.

Perhaps the city's best-known cultural institution today is the Stuttgart Ballet, which has toured many countries to critical acclaim. Like all other major European ballet companies, the Stuttgart group is part of a national theater complex—in this case, the Württembergische Staatstheater—and not an independent entity as are the dance companies in the United States. Ballet companies need a home, a theater building they can call their own. Constant touring does not improve the quality of any performing arts group, and the fact that only one American company, the New York City Ballet, works in its own theater—the New York State Theater at Lincoln Center—is a depressing comment on the status of the art of ballet in the United States.

The European solution to the ballet problem is to establish the dance companies in the opera houses of the national theater complexes. Thus, the Royal Ballet works with and is considered a part of the Royal Opera at Covent Garden in London. It performs in the Covent Garden Opera House, its scenery and costumes are made in the opera workshops, and most of the corps dancers dance in the opera ballets, although the principals usually do not. The same may be said of the Bolshoi Ballet, which is part of the Bolshoi Opera, or the Kirov Ballet, which is part of the Kirov Opera. The leading ballet companies in Germany and Austria are associated with and perform in the theater buildings of the Deutsche Oper Berlin, the Hamburgische Staatsoper, the Deutsche Oper am Rhein, the Bayerische Staatsoper, the Staatsoper Wien, and the Württembergische Staatstheater.

Employment of dancers on a year-round basis thus makes economic sense, as their services are in continuous demand by the company performing the operas and operettas of the repertory. The beginning dancers are used in all the lyric theater productions that need them, and the solo roles are danced by the members of the corps who are designated as having "solo responsibilities." The principal dancers, however, dance only in the ballets, as a rule. Ballets are given on what are designated "ballet evenings" during the regular ten-month opera/operetta season in the Grosses Haus of the complex. There is usually one ballet evening per week, making about 40 performances per year in the average theater. The largest theaters also stage a Ballet Woche every year as well, an eight- to ten-day period in which nothing but ballet is done and the opera singers take a rest. It is often during the theater's ballet week that new productions are given premiere performances. The largest companies thus average about 50 ballet performances per year, with Stuttgart the German leader at 65 performances, and Hamburg second with 64 (1976–77).

The emergence of the Stuttgart Ballet into the first rank of world dance ensembles came about with the acceptance of the directorship of the ballet company by the South African choreographer John Cranko in 1961. The Generalintendant, Walter Erich Schäfer, gradually increased the budget and the number of performances per year, and Cranko developed an ensemble of remarkable dancers—among them Richard Cragun and John Neumeier, both Americans, the Brazilian Marcia Haydée, and Egon Madsen from Denmark—into a first-rank company. The dancers in the 1960's came from 14 countries. Communication was as varied as the performers' backgrounds: ballet positions were in French, counting was done in German, and stage directions and praise were conveyed in English.

Cranko's principal achievement at Stuttgart, in addition to forging a superb interpretive instrument, was the creation of several short and at least four full-length new ballets that have entered the repertories of the world's leading dance companies. Until Cranko's appearance on the world stage as a choreographer, the attitudes of George Balanchine toward story ballets had prevailed everywhere. Balanchine thought that the old plot ballets such as *Giselle, Swan Lake,* and *Nutcracker* intruded on literature in the sense that the ballet form could not improve on the original story, play, or poem. Also, most of the ballets related simpleminded fairy tales best suited to the tastes of children, and relying on a plot structure to develop a series of dances had to run into a dead end sooner or later. John Cranko challenged this belief, however, and in such masterpieces as his *Romeo and Juliet* (music by Prokofiev), *The Taming of the Shrew* (music by Scarlatti), and *Onegin* (music by Tschaikovsky, but not from his opera of the same name) he demonstrated that the story ballet form has been anything but exhausted and, in fact, may well be the form that holds the most promise for the future of ballet.

The Grosses Haus and Kleines Haus of the Stuttgart complex in the Oberer Schlossgarten were opened in 1912. One of the earliest performances in the intimate Kleines Haus was the original version of the Strauss/Hofmannsthal *Ariadne auf Naxos*, which was designed as a one-act opera to follow a performance of Molière's play *Le bourgeois gentilhomme* in a German adaptation. During World War II the Kleines Haus was destroyed, but the Grosses Haus was damaged only slightly and performances continued almost uninterrupted through the air raids. The Kleines Haus was rebuilt on the same site, and a large office and scene shop wing was added to connect the two theaters along Konrad-Adenauer-Strasse.

Technical aspects of the theaters are as follows:

Grosses Haus

Seating capacity: 1,400 seats.
Opened: September 15, 1912.
Proscenium size: 11.2 meters wide by 7.5 meters high.
Stage size: 17.5 meters wide by 19 meters deep. Two side stages and one rear stage triple the main stage area.
Technical apparatus: Rundhorizont, three wagon stages, and large light bridge with platform tormentors.
Orchestra pit: 74 square meters for 85 musicians.
Kammertheater seating 400 is located on the third floor of the Grosses Haus; opened December 22, 1946.

Kleines Haus

Seating capacity: 841 seats.
Opened: September 16, 1912. Destroyed in World War II; rebuilt and reopened October 5, 1962.
Architects: H. Volkart, K. Pläcking, B. Perlia.
Technical consultants: Th. Münter and R. Biste.
Proscenium size: 12 meters wide by 7 meters high.
Stage size: 16 meters wide by 18 meters deep. Two side stages and one rear stage nearly triple the main stage area.
Technical apparatus: Two wagon stages, a revolve unit on the main stage with three lifts, lighting control console with 200 magnetic amplifier dimmers (ELA-Anlage).
Orchestra pit: Two lifts to accommodate 40 musicians.

The principal Besucherorganisation is the Volksbühne des Deutschen Gewerkschaftsbundes, with about 18,000 members.

Fig. 32. Aerial view of the Stuttgart national theater complex in the Oberer Schlossgarten. The Kleines Haus is to the left and the Grosses Haus to the right. The scene shop–administration wing connects the two theaters at rear. A surprising architectural harmony exists between two buildings that were designed 50 years apart (Württembergische Staatstheater)

Fig. 33. The upper lobby of the Kleines Haus. The windows look out on the park with
its small lake and fountain (Württembergische Staatstheater)

Fig. 34. Interior of the Kleines Haus auditorium. The forestage is being used for part of the stage design in a production of the chamber opera *Ariadne auf Naxos,* by Richard Strauss (Württembergische Staatstheater)

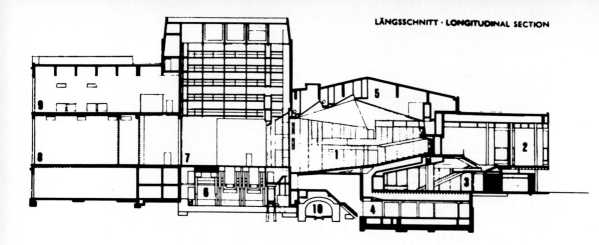

LÄNGSSCHNITT · LONGITUDINAL SECTION

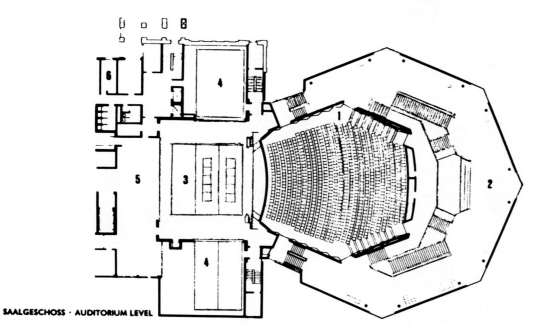

SAALGESCHOSS · AUDITORIUM LEVEL

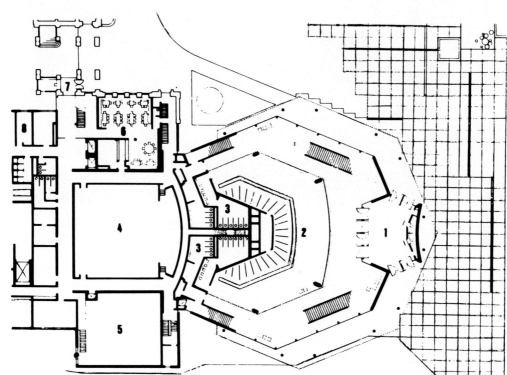

SOCKELGESCHOSS · BASEMENT

MASSSTAB 1 : 600 · SCALE 1 : 600

Fig. 35. Plans and elevation of the Kleines Haus, Stuttgart (Württembergische Staatstheater)

The Generalintendant of the Württembergische Staatstheater is Hans Peter Doll. The personnel of the companies numbered, during the Spielzeit 1976–77, as follows:

Artistic direction	59
Principal singers	44
Actors and actresses	45
Ballet dancers	61
Chorus singers	122
Orchestra musicians	108
Technical personnel	401
Administrative personnel	66
House personnel	103
Total	1,009

During the same season the theater companies made available to their public performances of lyric and spoken drama as follows:

Grosses Haus

	PERFORMANCES	ATTENDANCE	PERCENT OF CAPACITY
Operas	208	278,147	88.9%
Ballets	65	93,555	95.3%
Guest companies	16	(included above)	
Totals	289	371,702	92.1%

Kleines Haus

Operettas	14	8,786	74.6%
Plays	281	213,957	85.9%
Guest companies	15	(included above)	
Totals	310	222,743	80.3%

Kammertheater

Operettas	69	12,834	40.1%
Plays	71	14,576	45.0%
Guest companies	21	(included above)	
Totals	161	27,410	42.6%

The total attendance at the Stuttgart public theaters during 1976–77 thus came to 621,855, or about 105.4 percent of the city's population.

During the 1978–79 season the Stuttgart opera, ballet, and spoken drama companies performed the following works:

Grosses Haus

Operas

New Productions Wagner: *Die Walküre*
                          Siegfried
                   Verdi: *Rigoletto*
                   Penderecki: *Das verlorene Paradies* (first performance in Germany)
                   Mozart: *Così fan tutte*
Revivals   Tschaikowsky: *Pique Dame* (newly restudied)
                   Beethoven: *Fidelio*
                   Bizet: *Carmen*
                   Donizetti: *Don Pasquale*
                   Händel: *Achill unter den Mädchen*
                   Humperdinck: *Hänsel und Gretel*
                   Kodály: *Háry János*
                   Lehár: *Die lustige Witwe*
                   Lortzing: *Der Wildschütz*
                   Monteverdi: *Die Krönung der Poppea*
                   Mozart: *Die Entführung aus dem Serail*
                          Die Hochzeit des Figaro
                          Die Zauberflöte
                   Offenbach: *Orpheus in der Unterwelt*
                   Puccini: *La Bohème*
                          Tosca
                          Madame Butterfly
                          Turandot
                   Smetana: *Die verkaufte Braut*
                   Strauss, R.: *Salome*
                          Der Rosenkavalier
                          Ariadne auf Naxos
                   Tschaikowsky: *Eugen Onegin*
                   Verdi: *Der Troubadour*
                          La traviata
                          Ein Maskenball
                          Don Carlos
                   Wagner: *Der fliegende Holländer*
                          Tannhäuser
                          Lohengrin

Tristan und Isolde
Die Meistersinger von Nürnberg
Das Rheingold
Götterdämmerung
Parsifal

Ballets

New Productions
Chopin/Neumeier: *Kameliendame* (world premiere)
Henze/Forsythe: *Orpheus* (world premiere)
Tschaikowsky/Cranko: *Schwanensee* (restudied)

Revivals
Adam/Wright: *Giselle*
Berio/Tetley: *Laborintus*
Bizet/Balanchine: *Sinfonie in C*
Brahms/Cranko: *Initialen R. B. M. E.*
Bruckner/Montagnon: *Innere Not*
Chausson/Helliwell: *Ballade vom Meer und der Liebe*
Copland/Neumeier: *Der Fall Hamlet*
Debussy/Cranko: *Brouillards*
Dvořák/Forsythe: *Daphne*
Fauré/MacMillan: *Requiem*
Fortner-Steinbrenner/Cranko/Haydée: *Carmen*
Händel/Forsythe: *flore subsimplici*
Janáček/Helliwell: *Concertino*
Janáček/Kylián: *Rückkehr ins fremde Land*
Ligetti/Forsythe: *In endloser Zeit*
Mahler/Béjart: *Lieder eines fahrenden Gesellen*
Mahler/Forsythe: *Urlicht*
Mahler/MacMillan: *Das Lied von der Erde*
Martin/Helliwell: *Mirage*
Martin/MacMillan: *Las Hermanas*
Martinu/MacMillan: *Anastasia*
Mozart/Cranko: *Konzert für Flöte und Harfe*
Nordheim/Tetley: *Greening*
Penderecki/Forsythe: *Traum des Galilei*
Poulenc/Tetley: *Voluntaries*
Prokofieff/Cranko: *Romeo und Julia*
Prokofieff/Ursuliak: *Therese*
Rachmaninow/Montagnon: *Glocken*
Ravel/Balanchine: *La Valse*
Ravel/Tetley: *Daphnis und Chloë*
Scarlatti/Stolze/Cranko: *Der Widerspenstigen Zähmung*
Schubert/Montagnon: *Der Tod und das Mädchen*
Schönberg/Webern/MacMillan: *Mein Bruder und meine Schwestern*
Skrjabin/Cranko: *Poème de l'extase*

Strawinsky/Balanchine: *Apollo*
Strawinsky/Cranko: *Jeu de cartes*
Strawinsky/Tetley: *Sacre du Printemps*
Subotnik/Tetley: *Arena*
Tschaikowsky/Stolze/Cranko: *Onegin*
Tschaikowsky/Petipa/Hightower: *Dornröschen*
Vivaldi/Cranko: *L'Estro Armonico*
Webern/Cranko: *Opus 1*

Kleines Haus

New Productions	Goethe: *Torquato Tasso*
	Molière: *Der Menschenfeind*
	Kleist: *Der zerbrochene Krug*
	Tschechow: *Drei Schwestern*
	Jarry: *König Ubu*
	Bernhard: *Die Milchkanne* (world premiere)
	Strauss, B.: *Gross und Klein*
Revivals	Goethe: *Faust I*
	Faust II
	Iphigenie auf Tauris
	Shakespeare: *Ein Sommernachtstraum*
	Kleist: *Das Käthchen von Heilbronn*
	Hauptmann: *Der Biberpelz*
	Wedekind: *Frühlings Erwachen*
	Nestroy: *Der Zerissene*
	Goldoni: *Der Diener zweier Herren*
	Troll: *Der Entaklemmer*
	Molière: *Tartuffe*
	Ibsen: *Der Wildente*
	Brecht: *Die Mutter*
	Anouilh/Jensen/Koch: *Das Orchester*
	Elvis Presley Memorial
	Bernhard: *Minetti*
	Immanuel Kant

Kammertheater

New Productions	Dario Fo: *Bezahlt wird nicht*
	Einer für alle, alle für einen! Aber Verzeihung, wer ist hier eigentlich der Boss?
	Brecht: *Die heilige Johanna der Schlachthöfe*
Revivals	Hölderlin: *Antigonae*
	Achternbusch: *Ella*

Brecht: *Hauspostille*
Heine: *Deutschland*
Ein Wintermärchen

Single-ticket and subscription price lists for the Grosses Haus and the Kleines Haus during 1978 are shown in Figs. 36 and 37, p. 60.

Fig. 38, p. 61, shows a nine-year financial summary for the Württembergische Staatstheater.

Scenes from productions during recent seasons by the spoken drama company, the opera company, and the ballet company of the Württembergische Staatstheater appear in Figs. 39–46, pp. 62–72.

Opernmiete-Serie	A, D, G, K	N, O, P, R	B, E, H, L	C, F, J, M	S	T, U, V, W
Vorstellungstag	Dienstag	Mittwoch	Donnerstag	Freitag	Samstag	Sonntag

Preis-gruppe	Platzgattung	Tageskassenpreise[1] A	B	C	D	E	Opernmiete Preis für 1 Vorst.	Preis[2] für 9 Vorst.	Ratenzahlg. 25. 8.78 25.11.78 25. 3.79	Wahlmiete „Großes Haus" Preis[2] für 20 Gutscheine „Großes Haus"	Ratenzahlg. 25. 8.78 25.11.78 25. 3.79
I	Parkett 1.-8. Reihe I. Rang Logen I-VIII und Mittelloge I. Rang Sperrsitz Mitte	36,-	40,-	45,-	50,-	60,-	25,50	234,-	je 78,-	649,50	je 216,50
II	Parkett 9.-15. Reihe I. Rang Logen IX-XIV, A-F I. Rang Sperrsitz Seite	32,-	35,-	40,-	45,-	54,-	22,50	207,-	je 69,-	577,50	je 192,50
III	Parkett 16.-21. Reihe II. Rang Mitte 1.-4. Reihe	29,-	32,-	34,-	40,-	48,-	20,50	189,-	je 63,-	523,50	je 174,50
IV	II. Rang Halbmitte	24,-	25,-	29,-	34,-	41,-	17,-	157,50	je 52,50	433,50	je 144,50
V	II. Rang Seite 1.-3. Reihe III. Rang 1. Reihe ganz (ohne Seitenlogen) III. Rang Mitte 2. und 3. Reihe	20,-	21,-	23,-	27,-	33,-	15,-	139,50	je 46,50	361,50	je 120,50
VI	III. Rang Mitte 4. und 5. Reihe III. Rang Seite 2.-4. Reihe	15,-	16,-	18,-	21,-	25,-	11,-	103,50	je 34,50	271,50	je 90,50
VII	III. Rang Mitte 6. und 7. Reihe III. Rang Seite 5.-7. Reihe	10,-	11,-	12,-	14,-	17,-	7,-	67,50	je 22,50	181,50	je 60,50
VIII	III. Rang Seitenlogen	6,-	6,-	7,-	8,-	9,-	Keine Mieten			Keine Mieten	

In sämtlichen Preisen sind Garderobengebühr, Urheberabgabe und Altersversorgungsabgabe enthalten.

[1]) Bei besonderen Vorstellungen können abweichende Tageskassenpreise angesetzt werden. [2]) Einschließlich Jahresbeitrag.

Fig. 36. Ticket prices in the Grosses Haus, 1978 (Württembergische Staatstheater)

Schauspielmiete-Serie	I, IV, VII	X, XI, XII	II, V, VIII	III, VI, IX	XIII	XIV, XV, XVI
Vorstellungstag	Dienstag	Mittwoch	Donnerstag	Freitag	Samstag	Sonntag

Preis-gruppe	Platzgattung	Tages-kassen-preise[1] A	B	Schauspielmiete Preis für 1 Vorst.	Preis[2] f. 9 Vorst.	Ratenz. 25. 8.78 25.11.78 25. 3.79	Lerntheater Schauspiel Preis für 1 Vorst.	Preis[2])[3]) für 9 Vorst. und 5 Sonderveranst.	Ratenz. 25. 8.78 25.11.78 25. 3.79	Wahlmiete „Kleines Haus" Preis[2]) für 10 Gutscheine „Kl. Haus"	Ratenz. 25. 8.78 25.11.78 25. 3.79	Preis für 1 Vorst.
I	1.- 7. Reihe Logen	21,-	23,-	17,-	157,50	je 52,50	17,-	181,50	je 60,50	190,50	je 63,50	19,05
II	8.-13. Reihe	19,-	21,-	15,-	139,50	je 46,50	15,-	163,50	je 54,50	172,50	je 57,50	17,25
III	14.-17. Reihe	18,-	20,-	14,50	135,-	je 45,-	14,50	159,-	je 53,-	163,50	je 54,50	16,35
IV	18.-20. Reihe	16,-	18,-	13,-	121,50	je 40,50	13,-	145,50	je 48,50	145,50	je 48,50	14,55
V	21.-23. Reihe	13,-	15,-	10,-	94,50	je 31,50	10,-	118,50	je 39,50	118,50	je 39,50	11,85
VI	24.-26. Reihe	8,-	9,-	6,-	58,50	je 19,50	6,-	82,50	je 27,50	73,50	je 24,50	7,35

In sämtlichen Preisen sind Garderobengebühr, Urheberabgabe und Altersversorgungsabgabe enthalten.

[1]) Bei besonderen Vorstellungen können abweichende Tageskassenpreise angesetzt werden. [2]) Einschließlich Jahresbeitrag.
[3]) Im Mietegesamtpreis „Lerntheater Schauspiel" ist ein Unkostenbeitrag von 24,- DM für 5 Sonderveranstaltungen enthalten.

Fig. 37. Ticket prices in the Kleines Haus, 1978 (Württembergische Staatstheater)

YEAR	1969	1970	1971	1972	1973	1974	1975	1976	1977
VALUE OF DEUTSCHE MARK	28¢	29¢	30¢	34¢	40¢	42¢	44¢	48¢	50¢
EXPENSES									
Artists' salaries	DM 10,839,000	DM 12,629,000	DM 14,693,000	DM 16,894,000	DM 17,697,000	DM 19,524,000	DM 21,448,000	DM 21,822,000	DM 23,897,000
Technical salaries	5,579,000	6,639,000	9,183,000	10,028,000	11,980,000	13,808,000	14,384,000	16,034,000	16,648,000
Administration	2,014,000	1,857,000	1,125,000	1,319,000	1,678,000	1,888,000	2,408,000	1,882,000	2,528,000
Other personnel	234,000	290,000	181,000	576,000	460,000	535,000	825,000	328,000	310,000
Pension funds	1,232,000	1,170,000	1,332,000	1,118,000	1,103,000	1,258,000	1,648,000	1,438,000	1,370,000
Production costs	4,924,000	5,249,000	6,441,000	6,007,000	5,956,000	6,272,000	7,600,000	7,629,000	10,040,000
Loan payments	---	---	---	---	---	159,000	52,000	977,000	568,000
Building maintenance	766,000	2,047,000	3,043,000	750,000	909,000	1,504,000	2,786,000	1,590,000	1,855,000
TOTAL	DM 25,588,000	DM 29,881,000	DM 35,998,000	DM 36,692,000	DM 39,783,000	DM 44,948,000	DM 51,151,000	DM 51,700,000	DM 57,216,000
INCOME									
Single tickets	DM 2,955,000	DM 3,290,000	DM 3,188,000	DM 3,423,000	DM 3,384,000	DM 2,797,000	DM 3,929,000	DM 4,294,000	DM 4,218,000
Subscriptions	2,289,000	2,102,000	2,635,000	2,666,000	2,618,000	3,390,000	2,903,000	3,350,000	3,110,000
Children's theater subscriptions	283,000	336,000	220,000	260,000	278,000	329,000	---	---	---
Visitor groups	619,000	583,000	508,000	533,000	521,000	615,000	582,000	200,000	175,000
Cloakroom charges	192,000	176,000	158,000	200,000	174,000	181,000	170,000	200,000	118,000
Radio and TV fees	267,000	118,000	130,000	248,000	184,000	34,000	145,000	440,000	118,000
Touring	1,522,000	1,346,000	1,395,000	200,000	704,000	875,000	1,678,000	700,000	2,173,000
Guest performances by other companies	---	---	697,000	1,300,000	1,081,000	---	---	660,000	---
Program sales	318,000	322,000	311,000	356,000	326,000	358,000	354,000	411,000	469,000
Other income	394,000	431,000	414,000	182,000	327,000	397,000	309,000	402,000	1,128,000
TOTAL	DM 8,839,000	DM 8,704,000	DM 9,656,000	DM 9,368,000	DM 9,597,000	DM 8,976,000	DM 10,070,000	DM 10,457,000	DM 11,391,000
TAX SUBSIDY	DM 16,749,000	DM 21,177,000	DM 26,342,000	DM 27,324,000	DM 30,186,000	DM 35,972,000	DM 41,081,000	DM 41,243,000	DM 45,825,000
SUBSIDY PERCENTAGE	65.5%	70.9%	73.2%	74.5%	75.9%	80.0%	80.3%	79.8%	80.1%

Fig. 38. Expenses and income for the Württembergische Staatstheater, 1969–77 (Deutscher Bühnenverein, Köln)

Fig. 39. *Die Dreigroschenoper* by Bert Brecht and Kurt Weill, directed by Peter Palitzsch and designed by Wilfried Minks (Madeline Winkler-Betzendahl)

Fig. 40. A modern version of Goethe's *Faust II,* directed by Claus Peymann and designed by Achim Freyer. Martin Luttge as Faust and Branko Samarowski as Mephistopheles (Madeline Winkler-Betzendahl)

Fig. 41. The murder scene from Alban Berg's opera *Wozzeck,* directed by Günther Rennert.
Maria Kinas as Marie and Toni Blankenheim as Wozzeck (Madeline Winkler-Betzendahl)

Fig. 42. Carl Orff's musical setting of *Oedipus der Tyrann* by Sophocles, directed by Günther Rennert and designed by Casper Neher. Gerhard Stolze as Oedipus and Astrid Varnay as Jokasta, with the male chorus (Madeline Winkler-Betzendahl)

Fig. 43. John Neumeier's *Kameliendame,* choreographed to music by Frederic Chopin, conducted by Stewart Kershaw and designed by Jürgen Rose. Marcia Haydée as Marguerite Gautier and Egon Madsen as Armand Duval (Madeline Winkler-Betzendahl)

Fig. 44. The ballet *Romeo und Julia,* with music by Prokofieff, choreography by John Cranko, and scenery by Jürgen Rose. John Neumeier as Romeo and Christine Schwerdt-feger as Lady Capulet (Madeline Winkler-Betzendahl)

Fig. 45. Two scenes from John Neumeier's conception of *Der Fall Hamlet,* with music by Aaron Copland. Marcia Haydée as Gertrud pauses near the spirit of her dead husband (Reid Anderson) . . . (Madeline Winkler-Betzendahl)

Fig. 46. . . . and dances a pas de deux with Claudius (Richard Cragun) (Madeline Winkler-
Betzendahl)

IV. DÜSSELDORF, GERMANY

Deutsche Oper am Rhein, Düsseldorf-Duisburg

Düsseldorf developed in the vicinity of a Benedictine monastery founded about 700 A.D. and was first mentioned by name in official records dating from 1135. The settlement was named a city in 1288 by Count Adolf von Berg, and by 1520 it had become the capital of the duchies of Jülich, Cleves, and Berg and the counties of Marck and Ravensberg. The Dukes of Berg ruled their domains from their Residenz in Düsseldorf until 1918, when Germany became a democracy. In 1946 the city became the capital of the new state of Nordrhein-Westfalen, and by 1976 the population had reached 615,494.

In the 17th and 18th centuries troupes of traveling comedians had played Düsseldorf in the Giesshaus am Markt, and in 1818 this theater became an official city theater with a modest subsidy from the Duke, although the manager was expected to earn most of his annual budget at the box office. Under the management of Karl Immermann, from 1832 to 1837, the theater developed a national reputation with its productions of Italian, French, and German opera and plays by Goethe, Schiller, Kleist, Shakespeare, Goldoni, Grillparzer, and Nestroy. The citizens were pleased with their city theater and by 1875 had added a second building, an opera house, which was erected in the garden of the Royal Palace.

During the 1920's the city of Düsseldorf formed a partnership with the nearby city of Duisburg for the joint management of a large opera company that could play in both cities. This company became the Deutsche Oper am Rhein, with financial support from both municipalities. In 1924 a Kleines Haus was opened for plays so that opera production and play production could be handled in separate theaters. Today the opera company performs in the rebuilt Opernhaus in Düsseldorf and in the Theater der Stadt Duisburg, and the drama company plays in the Grosses Haus and Kleines Haus of the new Düsseldorfer Schauspielhaus.

Technical aspects of the opera house are as follows:

Seating capacity: 1,342 seats.
Architect: Professor Ernst Giese, Dresden.

Fig. 47. The Marktplatz in Düsseldorf with the Immermann Theater to the left, about 1835 (Düsseldorfer Schauspielhaus)

Opened: November 29, 1875. Damaged during World War II and reopened April 22, 1956, with Beethoven's *Fidelio,* conducted by Eugen Szenkar.

Proscenium size: 11.4 meters wide by 7 meters high.

Main stage size: 22.5 meters wide by 14.75 meters deep.

Side stage size: 15.5 meters wide by 15 meters deep.

Rear stage: 22 meters wide by 14 meters deep.

Technical equipment: Rear stage wagon with a turntable 9.8 meters in diameter mounted on it, side stage wagon and five stage lifts that occupy the playing area of the main stage. The tormentor platforms and lighting bridges support

10 KW scene projectors and some Xenon projectors. The large lighting installation makes use of magnetic amplifier dimmers.

Orchestra pit: Two lifts, one of which can be used as a forestage. In forestage position, the pit holds about 50 musicians; in full orchestra pit position, over 90 musicians.

The principal Besucherorganisationen are the Düsseldorfer Volksbühne and the Theatergemeinde Düsseldorf e.V., with about 28,000 members.

The Generalintendant of the Deutsche Oper am Rhein is Grischa Barfuss. Personnel of the company during the Spielzeit 1976–77 numbered as follows:

Artistic direction	71
Principal singers	62
Ballet dancers	69
Chorus singers	88
Orchestra musicians	107
Technical personnel	231
Administrative personnel	35
House personnel	78
Total	741

Public performances, attendance, and percentages of capacity were as follows:

	PERFORMANCES	ATTENDANCE	PERCENT OF CAPACITY
Operas	239	297,375	92.7%
Ballets	45	57,477	95.2%
Totals	284	354,852	94.0%

During the season 1977–78 the following opera and ballet productions were offered to the public:

Operas

New Productions	Mozart: *Die Entführung aus dem Serail*
	Verdi: *Der Troubadour*
	Offenbach: *Orpheus in der Unterwelt*
	Bizet: *Carmen*
	Strauss, R.: *Die Frau ohne Schatten*
	Honegger: *Johanna auf dem Scheiterhaufen*
	Orff: *Der Mond*
	Kelterborn: *Ein Engel kommt nach Babylon*
Revivals	Cavalieri: *Rappresentazione di anima e di corpo*

Fig. 48. Opera House of the Deutsche Oper am Rhein in the Hofgarten, Düsseldorf, rebuilt
after the war and opened in 1956 (Deutsche Oper am Rhein)

Mozart: *Die Hochzeit des Figaro*
Don Giovanni
Così fan tutte
Beethoven: *Fidelio*
Donizetti: *Der Liebestrank*
Lucia di Lammermoor
Don Pasquale
Rossini: *Die Italienerin in Algier*
Der Barbier von Sevilla

La Cenerentola (Aschenbrödel)

Graf Ory

Lortzing: *Zar und Zimmermann*

Nicolai: *Die lustigen Weiber von Windsor*

Wagner: *Der fliegende Holländer*

Tannhäuser

Lohengrin

Tristan und Isolde

Die Meistersinger von Nürnberg

Das Rheingold

Die Walküre

Siegfried

Götterdämmerung

Parsifal

Verdi: *Rigoletto*

La traviata

Don Carlos

Othello

Falstaff

Smetana: *Die verkaufte Braut*

Tschaikowsky: *Pique Dame*

Dvořák: *Rusalka*

Humperdinck: *Hänsel und Gretel*

Janáček: *Jenufa*

Die Ausflüge des Herrn Brouček

Katja Kabanowa

Das schlaue Füchslein

Die Sache Makropulos

Aus einem Totenhaus

Mascagni: *Cavalleria rusticana*

Leoncavallo: *Der Bajazzo*

Puccini: *La Bohème*

Tosca

Madame Butterfly

Turandot

Strauss, R.: *Salome*

Elektra

Arabella

Die schweigsame Frau

Capriccio

Giordano: *André Chénier*

Pfitzner: *Palestrina*

Berg: *Wozzeck*

Schönberg: *Moses und Aron*

Orff: *Die Kluge/Carmina burana*
Zimmermann, B.: *Die Soldaten*
Britten: *Bettleroper*
       Der Tod in Venedig

Ballets

New Productions	Herold-Lanchberry/Ashton: *La Fille mal gardée*
	Sibelius/Walter: *Kalevala*
Revivals	Monteverdi/Walter: *L'Orfeo*
	Vivaldi/Walter: *Die vier Jahreszeiten*
	Albinoni/Walter: *Hommage à Albinoni*
	Beethoven/Walter: *Klaviertrio D-dur op. 70 Nr. 1*
	Weber/Fokine: *Der Geist der Rose*
	Schubert/Walter: *Der Tod und das Mädchen*
	Adam/Mazalova-Walter: *Giselle*
	Berlioz/Walter: *Symphonie fantastique*
	Chopin/Fokine: *Les Sylphides*
	Tschaikowsky/Mazalova-Walter: *Schwanensee*
	Tschaikowsky/Walter: *Dornröschen*
	Dvořák/Walter: *Cellokonzert h-moll*
	Minkus/Petipa: *La Bayadère*
	Saint-Saëns/van Manen: *Septet Extra (Septett op. 65)*
	Saint-Saëns/Fokine: *Der sterbende Schwann*
	Janáček/Walter: *Streichquartett Nr. 1*
	Debussy/Nijinsky: *Der Nachmittag eines Faun*
	Strauss/Walter: *Josephslegende*
	Satie/van Manen: *Squares*
	Skrjabin/Walter: *Dritte Sinfonie*
	Bartók/Walter: *Der hölzerne Prinz*
	Bartók/Walter: *Der wunderbare Mandarin*
	Bartók/Walter: *Musik für Saiteninstrumente, Schlagzeug und Celesta*
	Bartók/Walter: *Divertimento für Streichorchester*
	Strawinsky/Walter: *Le Sacre du Printemps*
	Strawinsky/Walter: *Pulcinella*
	Webern/Cranko: *Opus 1*
	Prokofieff/Walter: *Romeo und Julia*
	Prokofieff/Walter: *Die steinerne Blume*
	Cohen/Joos: *Der grüne Tisch*

Subscription series are available on every night of the week in 23 different combinations, most of which are for ten performances and a few for six. The price reduction comes to 40 percent of the single-ticket prices. Price ranges are as follows:

	TEN PREMIERES	TEN EVENINGS	SIX AFTERNOONS
First price range	DM 400	DM 168	DM 90
Second price range	350	144	78
Third price range	300	129	66
Fourth price range	250	108	54
Fifth price range	200	90	48
Sixth price range	160	66	36
Seventh price range	130	54	30

These prices include DM 0.30 coat room charge and DM 0.20 for the theater's pension fund. Special prices at reduced rates are made available to visitor organizations and youth groups that buy tickets in quantity.

Fig. 49, p. 80, shows a nine-year summary of the finances of the Deutsche Oper am Rhein.

Scenes from productions of recent seasons appear in Figs. 50–59, pp. 81–90.

Düsseldorfer Schauspielhaus

The Immermann years at the Düsseldorfer Schauspielhaus were followed by a period of sporadic development through the rest of the 19th century, and on October 28, 1905, a new theater was opened on Karl-Theodor-Strasse with Hebbel's *Judith*. The new house was managed by the team of Louise Dumont and Gustav Lindemann until 1932. During this period the Schauspielhaus consolidated its international reputation with productions of the classics together with new works by Kaiser, Hauptmann, Tolstoi, and Bahr. After the Nazi period Gustaf Gründgens was Generalintendant of the Schauspielhaus, and when he took over the Deutsches Schauspielhaus in Hamburg in 1955 he was followed at Düsseldorf by Karl Heinz Stroux. In 1970 Stroux presided over the opening of the new building on Bleichstrasse, one of the most interesting and well-equipped playhouses of the postwar period in German theater architecture. The opening festivities were marked by new productions of two classics, *Dantons Tod* by Büchner (the same piece that was used to open the Vivian Beaumont Theater in New York), and *Die Bacchantinnen* by Euripides, followed by world premieres of three new plays, *Trotzki im Exil* by Peter Weiss, *Der Clown* by Heinrich Böll, and *Der Triumph des Todes* by Eugène Ionesco. All five premieres took place within a space of nine days in January, 1970.

Technical aspects of the Düsseldorfer Schauspielhaus are as follows:

Grosses Haus

Seating capacity: 1,036 seats.
Architect: Bernhard Pfau.
Technical consultant: Willi Ehle.
Opened: January 16, 1970, with Büchner's *Dantons Tod,* directed by Karl Heinz Stroux.

YEAR	1969	1970	1971	1972	1973	1974	1975	1976	1977
VALUE OF DEUTSCHE MARK	28¢	29¢	30¢	34¢	40¢	42¢	44¢	48¢	50¢
EXPENSES									
Artists' salaries	DM 8,878,000	DM 10,186,000	DM 12,805,000	13,606,000	14,758,000	DM 13,682,000	DM 18,131,000	DM 19,002,000	DM 20,729,000
Technical salaries	4,376,000	4,612,000	5,179,000	5,591,000	6,252,000	7,382,000	8,929,000	8,395,000	8,866,000
Administration	1,241,000	1,064,000	1,351,000	1,381,000	1,483,000	1,767,000	2,012,000	2,041,000	2,180,000
Other personnel	59,000	155,000	70,000	877,000	1,330,000	1,500,000	1,576,000	1,826,000	1,894,000
Pension funds	467,000	371,000	488,000	456,000	563,000	251,000	252,000	263,000	565,000
Production costs	3,021,000	3,212,000	3,496,000	4,164,000	3,715,000	4,081,000	3,946,000	5,520,000	6,486,000
Loan payments	238,000	240,000	1,951,000	602,000	95,000	---	23,000	1,080,000	985,000
Building maintenance	515,000	447,000	240,000	477,000	1,479,000	3,208,000	5,154,000	---	441,000
TOTAL	DM 18,795,000	DM 20,287,000	DM 25,580,000	DM 27,154,000	DM 29,675,000	DM 31,871,000	DM 40,023,000	DM 38,127,000	DM 42,146,000
INCOME									
Single tickets	DM 801,000	DM 731,000	DM 850,000	DM 900,000	DM 847,000	DM 1,371,000	DM 1,108,000	DM 1,078,000	DM 1,325,000
Subscriptions	879,000	953,000	1,038,000	1,099,000	1,104,000	1,135,000	1,288,000	1,391,000	1,358,000
Children's theater subscriptions	78,000	72,000	75,000	66,000	53,000	70,000	---	---	---
Visitor groups	410,000	416,000	499,000	572,000	552,000	530,000	643,000	825,000	782,000
Cloakroom charges	98,000	101,000	---	---	---	---	---	---	---
Radio and TV fees	28,000	---	---	---	---	---	---	---	---
Touring	693,000	372,000	513,000	951,000	622,000	318,000	224,000	400,000	---
Guest performances by other companies	---	45,000	5,000	---	---	---	37,000	---	5,000
Program sales	127,000	129,000	133,000	137,000	147,000	165,000	271,000	228,000	219,000
Other income	367,000	468,000	1,182,000	1,152,000	1,422,000	67,000	195,000	1,979,000	903,000
TOTAL	DM 3,481,000	DM 3,287,000	DM 4,295,000	DM 4,877,000	DM 4,747,000	DM 3,656,000	DM 3,766,000	DM 5,901,000	DM 4,592,000
TAX SUBSIDY	DM 15,314,000	DM 17,000,000	DM 21,285,000	DM 22,277,000	DM 24,928,000	DM 28,215,000	DM 36,257,000	DM 32,226,000	DM 37,554,000
SUBSIDY PERCENTAGE	81.5%	83.8%	83.2%	82.0%	84.0%	88.5%	90.6%	84.5%	89.1%

Fig. 49. Expenses and income for the Deutsche Oper am Rhein, 1969–77 (Deutscher Bühnenverein, Köln)

Fig. 50. The Chopin ballet *Les Sylphides,* with choreography by Michel Fokine, scenery by Jürgen Dreier, and costume designs following those by Léon Bakst. Paolo Bortoluzzi with the Corps de Ballet (Deutsche Oper am Rhein/Fred Kliché)

Fig. 51. Offenbach's operetta *Orpheus in der Unterwelt*—the cancan scene. The production was directed by Bohumil Herlischka, choreographed by Erich Walter, and designed by Ruodi Barth (Deutsche Oper am Rhein/Fred Kliché)

Fig. 52. *Die Ausflüge des Herrn Brouček* by Leoš Janáček, part of a cycle of all the major operas of the modern Czech composer currently in the repertory of the Deutsche Oper am Rhein. This production was directed by Bohumil Herlischka and designed by Ruodi Barth. From left, Rachel Yakar as Malinka, Peter van der Bilt as the Sakristan, Wolfgang Witte as Mazal, Udo Holdorf as Herr Brouček, and Jaroslav Stajnc as Würfl (Deutsche Oper am Rhein/Fred Kliché)

Fig. 53. *Das schlaue Füchslein,* another opera in the Janáček cycle currently being performed in Düsseldorf and Duisberg, also directed by Bohumil Herlischka, with scenery and costumes by Ruodi Barth and conducted by Peter Schneider. From left, Trudeliese Schmidt as the sly Vixen, Peter van der Bilt as the Förster, Alfons Holte as Dackel, and Margrit Caspari as the Försterin (Deutsche Oper am Rhein/Fred Kliché)

Fig. 54. Ravel's comic opera *Die spanische Stunde,* directed by Otto Schenk, choreographed by Erich Walter, and designed by Günther Schneider-Siemssen. From left: Alfred Kuhn as Gomez, Helmut Pampuch as Torquemada, Oskar Czerwenka as Ramiro, Emily Rawlins as Concepcion, and Michael Rosness as Gonzalvo (Deutsche Oper am Rhein/Fred Kliché)

Fig. 55. The Deutsche Oper am Rhein presents a cycle of modern operas each year, and one of its most striking productions has been that of the staggeringly difficult *Die Soldaten* by the Cologne composer Bernd Alois Zimmermann. Based on a play of the same name from the German *Sturm und Drang* period by Jacob Michael Reinhold Lenz, the opera relates the story of the hopes of a middle-class girl, Marie, for a better life as a gnädige Frau, and the degradation that comes to her when she takes the "easy way" to her goal. The opera calls for a huge orchestra and many electronic devices intended to envelop the audience in what Zimmermann thought of as Total Musiktheater. Many scenes take place simultaneously: to the left, both the inside and outside of Marie's house can be seen as Baron Desportes (Anton de Ridder) makes advances to Marie (Catherine Gayer). In the center, Wesener's mother (Henny Ekström) sings of her past life while on the right Stolzius (Peter-Christoph Runge) broods over a letter from Marie as his mother (Gwynn Cornell) watches . . . (Deutsche Oper am Rhein/Fred Kliché)

Fig. 56. . . . Marie's father, Wesener (Marius Rintzler), warns his daughter not to trust the French officers, especially Baron Desportes . . . (Deutsche Oper am Rhein/Fred Kliché)

Fig. 57. . . . The officers of *Die Soldaten* gather in a coffee house in Armentières for drink and conversation. The projections come from the rear of the three screens. The production was directed by Georg Reinhardt, conducted by Günther Wich and designed by Heinrich Wendel . . . (Deutsche Oper am Rhein/Fred Kliché)

Fig. 58. . . . In Act III of *Die Soldaten,* the Countess de la Roche (Faith Puleston) upbraids her son (Nicola Tagger) for his love affair with Marie. Again, both the inside of a room in her manor house and views of her estate are seen at the same time. Actions in the left and center scenes occur both before and after the action in the right scene. . .(Deutsche Oper am Rhein/Fred Kliché)

Fig. 59. . . . In the final scene of the opera, the sounds of marching men are heard over amplifiers, military commands are given in many languages, and, in a deserted street, Wesener fails to recognize his daughter Marie (Deutsche Oper am Rhein/Fred Kliché)

Proscenium size: 10 meters to 15 meters wide by 8 meters high.

Main stage size: 24.3 meters wide by 20.5 meters deep; with rear stage, depth is 34.5 meters. Two side stages triple the stage width.

Technical apparatus: Revolving stage cylinder 18.3 meters in diameter and 8 meters deep, in which are installed four double-decked stage lifts; two side stage wagons and one rear stage wagon capable of adjustment for raked stages; double-decked light bridge, and platform tormentors with 25 scene projectors. The stage lighting console controls 240 dimmers that can be preset with the Siemens card system. A D.C. system is installed for Xenon projectors.

Orchestra pit: 17 meters wide by 4.8 meters deep for 55 musicians.

Kleines Haus

Seating capacity: as arena theater, 309 seats;

as thrust stage theater, 219 seats;

as proscenium theater, 307 seats.

Stage size: 14 meters wide by 7.3 meters deep; as arena stage, the depth is 13.5 meters.

Technical equipment: Two lifts that can form a raked stage and a 72-dimmer control board for lighting equipment (Siemens).

The principal visitor organizations in Düsseldorf are the Theatergemeinde der Gesellschaft für christliche Kultur e.V. and the Düsseldorfer Volksbühne e.V. The company tours various cities in the state of Nordrhein-Westfalen.

The Generalintendant of the Düsseldorfer Schauspielhaus is Günther Beelitz. Personnel of the company numbered, during the Spielzeit 1976–77, as follows:

Artistic direction	34
Actors and actresses	73
Technical personnel	202
Administrative personnel	25
House personnel	53
Total	387

Public performances, attendance, and percentages of capacity were as follows:

	PERFORMANCES	ATTENDANCE	PERCENT OF CAPACITY
Adult plays	521	288,318	78.1%
Children's plays	222	79,775	87.2%
Guest companies	13	(included above)	
Totals	756	368,093	82.7%

Fig. 60. The Düsseldorfer Schauspielhaus at night. The architect was Bernhard Pfau, and the stage areas were designed by the theater consultant Willi Ehle (Düsseldorfer Schauspielhaus)

Fig. 61. The theater from overhead. The many curved surfaces are a reaction against the foursquare, box design of most theater buildings (Düsseldorfer Schauspielhaus)

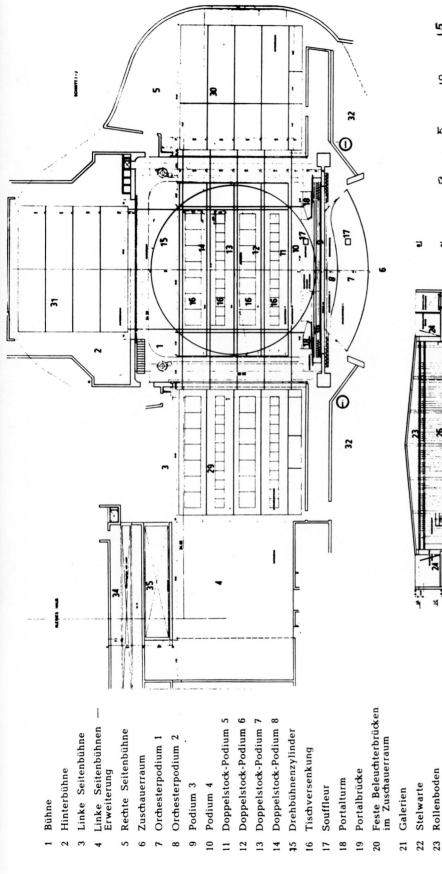

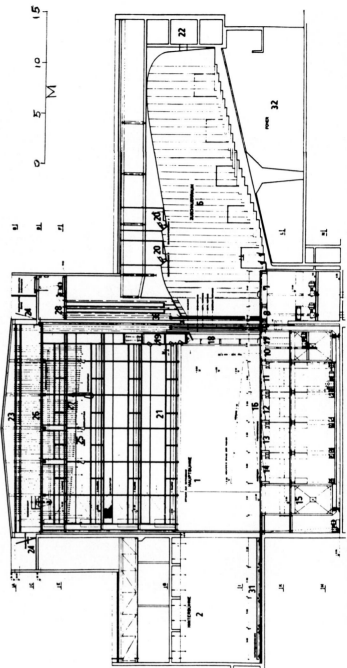

1 Bühne
2 Hinterbühne
3 Linke Seitenbühne
4 Linke Seitenbühnen — Erweiterung
5 Rechte Seitenbühne
6 Zuschauerraum
7 Orchesterpodium 1
8 Orchesterpodium 2
9 Podium 3
10 Podium 4
11 Doppelstock-Podium 5
12 Doppelstock-Podium 6
13 Doppelstock-Podium 7
14 Doppelstock-Podium 8
15 Drehbühnenzylinder
16 Tischversenkung
17 Souffleur
18 Portalturm
19 Portalbrücke
20 Feste Beleuchterbrücken im Zuschauerraum
21 Galerien
22 Stelwarte
23 Rollenboden
24 Rauchklappen Bühne
25 Maschinenzüge
26 Schnürboden
27 Prospektzüge
28 Schnürboden über der Vorbühne
29 Linker Seitenbühnenwagen
30 Rechter Seitenbühnenwagen
31 Hinterbühnenwagen
32 Foyer
33 gr. Probebühne
34 Prospektmagazin
35 Hebebühne
36 Vorhanggasse

Fig. 62. Plan and section of the Grosses Haus. Full stage wagons can move scenery onto the main stage from either of the two side stage areas or the rear stage. The double-decked lifts revolve within a huge stage cylinder, making an elevated stage possible at any angle to the audience. The surfaces of the lifts can be raked to form a raked stage that rises in any direction preset by the position of the cylinder (Bühnentechnische Rundschau)

Altogether, the two national theaters in Düsseldorf played to a total of 722,945 persons, or 117 percent of the population of the city.

During the 1978–79 Spielzeit the Düsseldorfer Schauspielhaus produced the following plays in its two theaters:

Grosses Haus

New Productions	Bernhard: *Immanuel Kant*
	Camus: *Die Gerechten*
	Molière: *Don Juan oder Der steinerne Gast*
	Schnitzler: *Das weite Land*
	Offenbach: *Pariser Leben*
	Schiller: *Die Räuber*
	Kleist: *Das Käthchen von Heilbronn*
	Tschechow: *Die Möwe*
	Shakespeare: *König Lear*
	Brecht: *Schweyk im zweiten Weltkrieg*
Revivals	Schiller: *Kabale und Liebe*
	Shakespeare: *Mass für Mass*
	Horváth: *Der jüngste Tag*
	Lorca: *Bernarda Albas Haus*

Kleines Haus

New Productions	Laube: *Der erste Tag des Friedens* (world premiere)
	Kroetz: *Mensch Meier* (first German production)
	Ionesco: *Die Stühle*
	Keefe: *Barbaren* (first German production)
	Baumgart: *Jettchen Geberts Geschichte*
Revivals	Valentin: *Das Leben ist wie eine Lawine, einmal rauf und einmal runter*
	Sartre: *Die schmutzigen Hände*
	Beckett: *Warten auf Godot*
	Dyer: *Unter der Treppe*
	Dorst: *Auf dem Chimborazo*

Prices for subscriptions and single tickets are shown in Figs. 63–65, pp. 97–99.

Subscriptions are available on the basis of 12 performances, 2 in the Kleines Haus and 10 in the Grosses Haus, at prices of DM 236, DM 216, DM 186, DM 156, and DM 108. Premieres and guest and special performances are not included in the subscription prices.

Fig. 66, p. 100, shows a nine-year financial summary.

Scenes from recent Düsseldorfer Schauspielhaus productions follow in Figs. 67–69, pp. 101–103.

Die Eintritts- preise

Großes Haus

Platzgruppe	Premieren- preise	Kassen- preise
Orchester Reihe 1—9	31,—	25,—
I. Parkett Reihe 1—6	28,—	22,—
I. Parkett Reihe 7—10	25,—	19,—
II. Parkett Reihe 1—5	21,—	16,—
II. Parkett 6—9	16,—	13,—
II. Parkett Reihe 10	10,—	7,—

Kleines Haus

Preisgruppe	Premieren- preise	Kassen- preise
I	28,—	22,—
II	21,—	16,—
III	16,—	13,—

● Für Gastspiele und Sonderveranstaltungen gelten Premieren-preise, wenn keine geänderten Preise bekanntgegeben werden.

● Schüler, Studenten, Lehrlinge, Wehrpflichtige und Schwerbe-schädigte erhalten gegen Vorlage entsprechender Ausweise eine Preisermäßigung von etwa 50%. Diese Ermäßigung gilt nicht für Premieren, Gastspiele und Sonderveranstaltungen.

● Für Vorstellungen mit besonderem Aufwand werden Preis-änderungen rechtzeitig bekanntgegeben.

Fig. 63. Single-ticket prices for the Grosses Haus and the Kleines Haus. The premiere price also applies to productions by guest companies and to special performances. Special rates are available to students, apprentices, servicemen, and the handicapped

Großes Haus

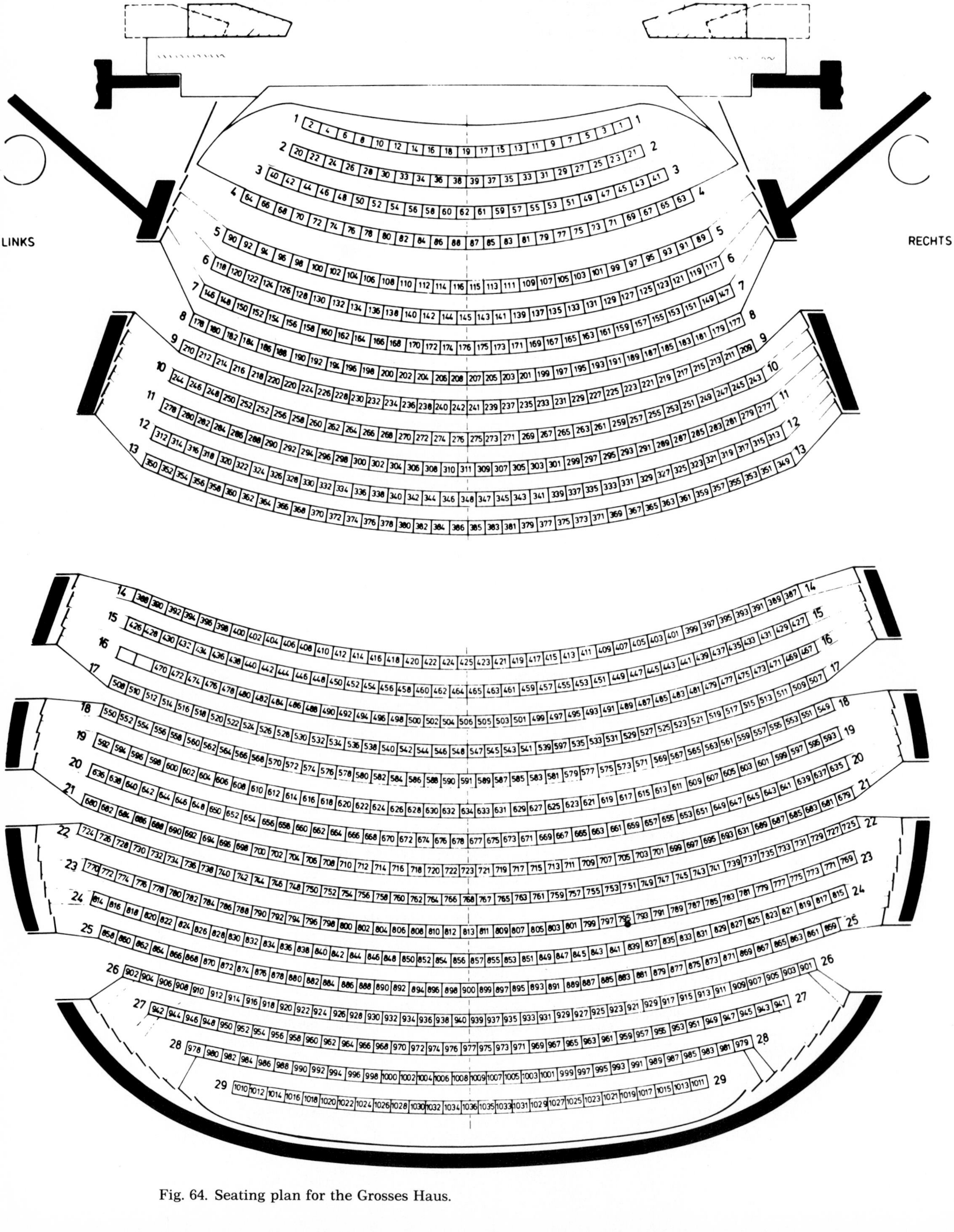

Fig. 64. Seating plan for the Grosses Haus.

Kleines Haus

Das Kleine Haus besitzt eine variable Bühne, die mit ihren technischen Möglichkeiten einmalig im deutschsprachigen Theater ist. Sie kann — je nach den Anforderungen der Inszenierung — verlegt werden, auch mitten unter die Zuschauer. Deshalb entspricht die Angabe der Reihe auf den Eintrittskarten nicht immer der üblichen Preisgruppe; also kann z. B. die 8. oder 19. Reihe die 1. Reihe an der Bühne sein. Die Zuweisung der Eintrittskarten erfolgt in der Preisgruppe, die der Entfernung Ihres Platzes von der Bühne entspricht.

Vier Beispiele der variablen Bühne:

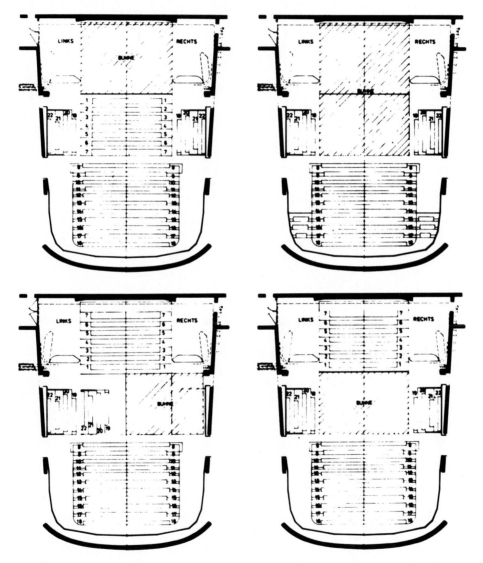

Fig. 65. Seating plan for the Kleines Haus, showing the four possible audience–playing area relationships.

YEAR	1969	1970	1971	1972	1973	1974	1975	1976	1977
VALUE OF DEUTSCHE MARK	28¢	29¢	30¢	34¢	40¢	42¢	44¢	48¢	50¢
EXPENSES									
Artists' salaries	DM 4,170,000	DM 3,947,000	DM 4,171,000	DM 4,983,000	DM 5,400,000	DM 6,063,000	DM 5,830,000	DM 6,866,000	DM 7,020,000
Technical salaries	3,659,000	4,162,000	4,793,000	6,241,000	6,916,000	7,849,000	8,065,000	8,926,000	9,660,000
Administration	934,000	1,166,000	1,361,000	1,734,000	1,913,000	2,194,000	2,150,000	2,345,000	2,367,000
Other personnel	1,027,000	1,114,000	1,381,000	276,000	252,000	110,000	89,000	95,000	101,000
Pension funds	---	---	---	---	---	38,000	39,000	41,000	42,000
Production costs	2,537,000	3,135,000	4,167,000	3,561,000	3,394,000	4,058,000	4,172,000	5,110,000	5,271,000
Loan payments	---	23,000	4,000	---	---	201,000	288,000	224,000	380,000
Building maintenance	---	---	---	---	153,000	---	---	---	---
TOTAL	DM 12,327,000	DM 13,547,000	DM 15,877,000	DM 16,795,000	DM 18,028,000	DM 20,513,000	DM 20,633,000	DM 23,607,000	DM 24,841,000
INCOME									
Single tickets	DM 747,000	DM 804,000	DM 788,000	DM 545,000	DM 541,000	DM 703,000	DM 787,000	DM 1,158,000	DM 1,243,000
Subscriptions	1,510,000	1,568,000	1,444,000	1,322,000	860,000	812,000	950,000	935,000	982,000
Children's theater subscriptions	44,000	149,000	148,000	204,000	235,000	327,000	---	---	---
Visitor groups	405,000	492,000	675,000	627,000	584,000	650,000	616,000	640,000	687,000
Cloakroom charges	135,000	157,000	155,000	152,000	131,000	137,000	119,000	270,000	270,000
Radio and TV fees	77,000	---	---	---	---	---	---	---	---
Touring	1,628,000	1,634,000	1,958,000	1,563,000	1,657,000	1,963,000	1,942,000	2,181,000	2,399,000
Guest performances by other companies	---	19,000	---	32,000	224,000	103,000	110,000	146,000	70,000
Program sales	156,000	192,000	141,000	190,000	161,000	162,000	151,000	155,000	168,000
Other income	340,000	334,000	418,000	404,000	344,000	335,000	276,000	755,000	348,000
TOTAL	DM 5,042,000	DM 5,349,000	DM 5,727,000	DM 5,039,000	DM 4,737,000	DM 5,192,000	DM 4,951,000	DM 6,240,000	DM 6,167,000
TAX SUBSIDY	DM 7,285,000	DM 8,198,000	DM 10,150,000	DM 11,756,000	DM 13,291,000	DM 15,321,000	DM 15,682,000	DM 17,367,000	DM 18,674,000
SUBSIDY PERCENTAGE	59.1%	60.5%	63.9%	70.1%	73.7%	74.7%	76.0%	73.4%	75.2%

Fig. 66. Expenses and income for the Düsseldorfer Schauspielhaus, 1969–77 (Deutscher Bühnenverein)

Fig. 67. In Thomas Bernhard's new comedy *Immanuel Kant,* the philosopher (Karlheinz Böhm) focuses his powers of concentration on the thigh of a millionairess (Joana Maria Gorvin) while the steward (Helmut Everke) looks the other way, during a voyage to America. (Kant never visited America). The play was directed by Volker Hesse and designed by Franz Koppendorfer (Lore Bermbach)

Fig. 68. The populace awaits Judgment Day in Michael Gruner's production of Ödön von Horváth's *Der jüngste Tag* (Lore Bermbach)

Fig. 69. Federico García Lorca's tragedy *Bernarda Albas Haus* was directed by Valentin Jeker and designed by Bernd Holzapfel. Bernarda (Ingeborg Lapsien) confronts four of her daughters (Veronika Bayer, Gudrun Gabriel, Charlotte Schwab and Angela Müthel) as La Poncia (Ingeborg Engelmann) watches with amusement (Lore Bermbach)

V. FRANKFURT AM MAIN, GERMANY

Städtische Bühnen Frankfurt am Main

The area around the Main River that became modern Frankfurt am Main was settled at least as far back as the Stone Age. By 794 A.D. the name of the city had appeared on an official document drawn up by Charlemagne to proclaim the convening of a holy synod. Frederick Barbarossa was elected King of the Germans here in 1152, and in 1352 Frankfurt was confirmed as the place of election of all German kings and emperors by the "Golden Bull" of Charles IV. Twenty years later Frankfurt was declared a free imperial city since there was no prince in residence, and the city had to look to its defenses. As in other free cities of the Holy Roman Empire of the German Nation, the citizens took a lively interest in touring companies, especially English comedians, who were drawn to the city during trade fairs and imperial coronation ceremonies.

By the 18th century the city was wealthy enough to sustain a private theater company in a leased building, the Komödienhaus, which was erected in 1782. The first performance of Schiller's *Kabale und Liebe* took place there in 1784, and Goethe enjoyed two successes, *Clavigo* and *Götz von Berlichingen,* in that theater. After some years as a private theater, the Komödienhaus was reorganized as a national theater, and in 1792 it received a regular subsidy from the city.

In the next century, the citizens of Frankfurt occupied themselves with a really grand opera house, an edifice to rival those of Paris and Vienna. The city council appropriated 6.8 million marks, and private individuals contributed 850,000 more. The theater was built over an eight-year period on one of Frankfurt's grandest squares. It was designed in the style of Semper and Schinkel by the architect Richard Lucae, and it opened on October 20, 1880, with a gala performance of *Don Giovanni,* conducted by Otto Dessoff. The Emperor Wilhelm I is said to have remarked, "In Berlin, we can't afford this!"

The Frankfurt Opera House became one of the important centers of activity in Europe. Under the leadership of the conductor Clemens Krauss and the stage director Lothar Wallerstein, there were many exemplary productions of works by Wagner, Richard Strauss, Hugo Wolf, Max von Schillings, Franz Schrecker, and the standard French and Italian composers. Later there were world premieres of Carl Orff's *Die Kluge* and *Carmina burana*, Werner Egk's *Die Zaubergeige* and *Columbus,* and Hermann Reutter's *Odysseus.* In March, 1944, the house was hit by fire bombs and the entire interior was burned out. The shell of the theater remained, however, and today, its exterior scrubbed clean, work is progressing slowly on turning it into a large concert hall.

After the war the problem of rebuilding Frankfurt's public theaters was studied in the light of the recent tendency to concentrate theater buildings into one set of connected structures that would include not only the performing units but scene and costume shops, storage areas, office space, and other service areas as well. The site of the old Schauspielhaus, which had also been destroyed, seemed large enough to accommodate a structure that could house three theaters, and it was decided to utilize the space for a new Opernhaus, a Schauspielhaus, and a Kammerspiel. The Generalintendant, Harry Buckwitz, liked the idea of a site that was surrounded by the city, by buildings, traffic, and people. The theater should be readily available to pedestrians walking by, he thought, and not removed to a park or other isolated area. Thus, there grew up a Theaterinsel or island of theater on Untermainanlage, which draws it vitality directly from the city's 645,867 inhabitants, and which has become one of the more significant of the German-language theater complexes.

German theaters have shown some interest in giving first hearings to American playwrights and opera composers. Edward Albee was first performed by the Schiller-Theater, and the Deutsche Oper Berlin performed Roger Sessions' opera *Montezuma* for the first time in 1964. In March of 1962 the Frankfurt Opera offered the world premiere of an opera by Thornton Wilder, *Die Alkestiade,* with music by Louise Talma, a professor of music at Hunter College. The production was a great success, with 50 curtain calls and a 20-minute ovation timed by a New York newspaperman who stood in the wings with a stopwatch. The opera is now under consideration by the Boston Opera Company.

Technical aspects of the three theaters are as follows:

Oper

Seating capacity: 1,387 seats.
Architect: Firma Apel, Letocha, Rohrer.
Theater Consultant: Adolf Linnebach.
Opened: December 23, 1951, with a performance of Wagner's *Die Meistersinger,* conducted by Georg Solti.
Proscenium size: 13 meters wide by 9 meters high.
Stage size: 40 meters by 40 meters.
Technical equipment: Very large revolving stage, 38 meters in diameter with a

smaller revolve inside having a diameter of 16 meters, tormentor platforms for follow spots, lighting console with control over 320 dimmer circuits.

Orchestra pit: 16 meters average width by 6 meters deep for 96 musicians.

Schauspiel

Seating capacity: 911 seats.

Architect: Firma Apel, Letocha, Rohrer.

Opened: December 14, 1963.

Proscenium size: Variable from 14 meters wide to 24 meters wide by 8 meters high.

Main stage size: 25 meters wide by 23.5 meters deep. Total depth, including the rear stage, is 40 meters. Total width, including the two side stages, is 63 meters.

Technical equipment: Side walls of the theater can be moved in or out to achieve the effect of either proscenium stage or thrust stage. The stage contains five lifts, two of which are double-decked, and a lift for drop storage between the main stage and the rear stage. The 44 overhead pipes are raised and lowered by hydraulic power. Wagon stages are employed, and the rear wagon carries a turntable 15.7 meters in diameter. The lighting console controls 220 dimmers, which are preset by a card system.

Orchestra pit: 15 meters average width by 5 meters deep for 80 musicians.

Kammerspiel

Located under the Schauspiel.

Seating capacity: 200 seats.

Opened: December 21, 1963.

Proscenium size: 8.5 meters wide by 4 meters high.

Stage size: 16 meters wide by 11.5 meters deep.

Technical equipment: Entire stage can be raked either up or down. Spot line fly system controlled by winches.

Several visitor subscription organizations support the Städtische Bühnen, among them the Kultur- und Theatergemeinde, the Rhein-Mainischer Besucherring, and the Volksbühne. The company tours to several towns and small cities in the area.

The head of the opera division of the Städtische Bühnen Frankfurt am Main is Michael Gielen. The spoken drama division, however, is headed by a triumvirate consisting of Dr. Karlheinz Braun, Peter Danzeisen, and Peter Palitzsch. Frankfurt was one of the first cities to try this type of management, the result of the post-1968 Mitbestimmung debate.

Personnel during 1976–77 numbered as follows:

Fig. 70. The old Opernhaus on Bockenheimer Anlage, about 1905. The motto over the main entrance dedicates the building and its operatic productions to the True, the Beautiful and the Good (Dem Wahren Schoenen Guten)

Fig. 71. The Theaterinsel in Frankfurt am Main. The Oper and the Schauspiel are connected by a single large lobby and refreshment room (Städtische Bühnen Frankfurt am Main)

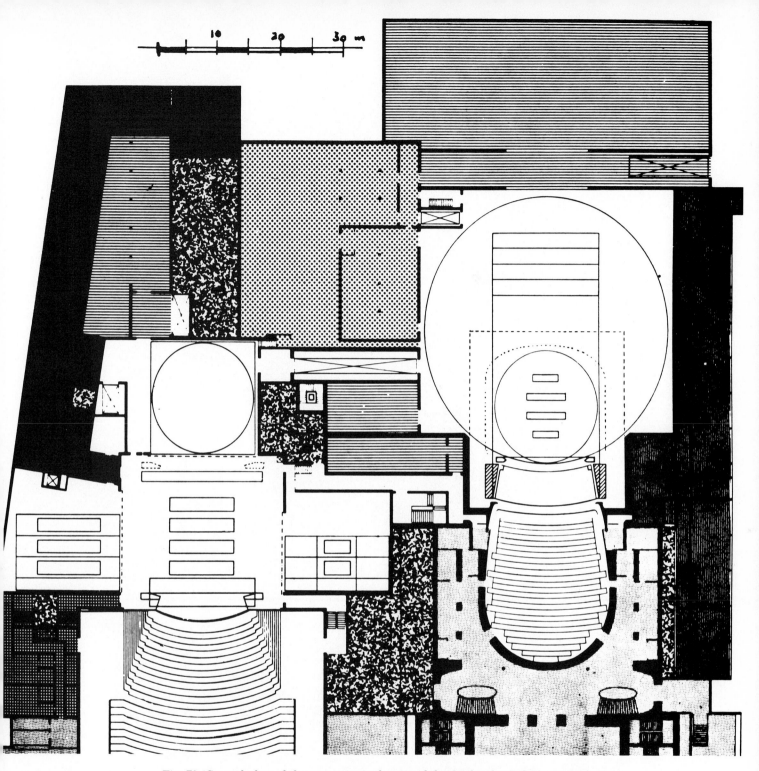

Fig. 72. Ground plan of the two principal units of the Städtische Bühnen Frankfurt am Main. The Schauspiel is to the left, the Oper to the right. Although the Schauspiel is equipped with side and rear stages and three full stage wagons for shifting scenery, the Oper had to be built within the walls of the old Schauspielhaus as an economy measure. There was thus no room for side or rear stages, and the level of the Main River nearby prevented double-decked lifts being employed. Professor Adolf Linnebach was called in to solve the problem, and he designed a huge turntable with built-in single deck lifts to shift scenery. A smaller turntable revolves within the perimeter of the large unit (Bühnen-technische Rundschau)

Fig. 73. Control gallery for the hydraulic-powered batten system in the Frankfurt Schauspiel. The position of the control handle determines the speed of the batten as it goes up or down. Any number of battens may be grouped together and moved in proportional relationships to one another. The operator watches the indicators instead of the battens (Maschinenfabrik Wiesbaden, A.G.)

V.   FRANKFURT AM MAIN, GERMANY • III

Fig. 74. Schematic diagram showing the operation of the hydraulic-powered batten system. The control valves are opened and closed by electromagnets, thus permitting remote electrical control from the fly gallery. The pipe travels six times the distance that the top of the plunger travels. Several battens can be grouped together, and since the pressure is the same on each plunger, the battens will move at exactly the same speed (Maschinenfabrik Wiesbaden, A.G.)

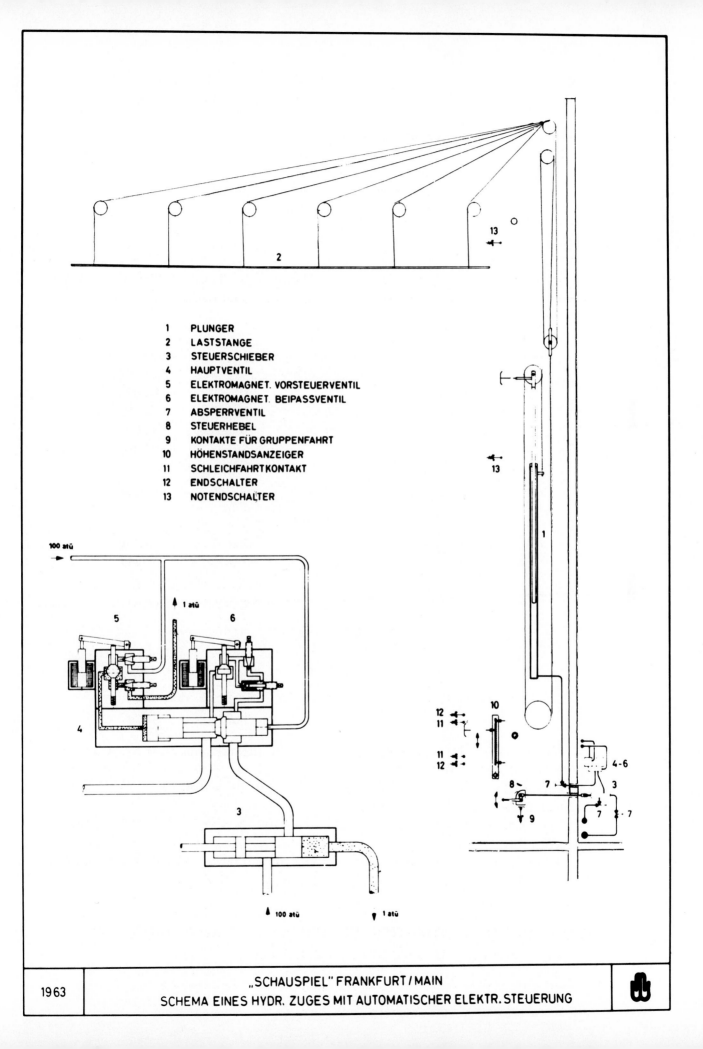

1 PLUNGER
2 LASTSTANGE
3 STEUERSCHIEBER
4 HAUPTVENTIL
5 ELEKTROMAGNET. VORSTEUERVENTIL
6 ELEKTROMAGNET. BEIPASSVENTIL
7 ABSPERRVENTIL
8 STEUERHEBEL
9 KONTAKTE FÜR GRUPPENFAHRT
10 HÖHENSTANDSANZEIGER
11 SCHLEICHFAHRTKONTAKT
12 ENDSCHALTER
13 NOTENDSCHALTER

100 atü

1 atü

100 atü   1 atü

1963

"SCHAUSPIEL" FRANKFURT / MAIN
SCHEMA EINES HYDR. ZUGES MIT AUTOMATISCHER ELEKTR. STEUERUNG

Artistic direction	68
Principal singers	32
Actors and actresses	37
Ballet dancers	32
Chorus singers	69
Orchestra musicians	104
Technical personnel	369
Administrative personnel	56
House personnel	<u>123</u>
Total	890

During the same season the Frankfurt companies offered the following numbers of performances of opera, operettas, musicals, plays, and ballets:

Oper

	PERFORMANCES	ATTENDANCE	PERCENT OF CAPACITY
Operas	188	219,500	84.2%
Ballets	45	53,597	85.9%
Operettas	14	18,569	95.6%
Musicals	8	<u>14,634</u>	<u>87.9%</u>
Guest companies	<u>4</u>	(included above)	
Totals	259	306,300	88.4%

Schauspiel

Adult plays	268	160,673	63.9%
Children's plays	36	<u>22,650</u>	<u>69.1%</u>
Guest companies	<u>8</u>	(included above)	
Totals	312	183,323	66.5%

Kammerspiel

Ballets	15	2,577	85.9%
Plays	186	<u>30,214</u>	<u>77.5%</u>
Guest companies	<u>9</u>	(included above)	
Totals	210	32,791	81.7%

The total attendance at the Frankfurt public theaters was thus 522,414, or 80.9 percent of the population of the city.

Figs. 75–78, pp. 115–119, show the repertory for the season 1978–79 and the subscription price lists.

Fig. 79, p. 120, shows a nine-year summary of the finances of the Städtische Bühnen Frankfurt am Main.

Scenes from recent productions of the drama, opera and ballet companies at Frankfurt are shown in Figs. 80–87, pp. 121–130.

Die Direktion der Oper Frankfurt bittet um Verständnis, daß für die Einhaltung aller folgenden Termine keine Garantie übernommen werden kann. Selbstverständlich waren wir bei der Planung der Spielzeit 1978/79 bestrebt, die Abonnements-Vorstellungen, die Sie – aufgeschlüsselt nach den verschiedenen Abonnements – auf den nachfolgenden Seiten finden, besonders abzusichern.

Al gran sole carico d'amore
(Unter der großen Sonne von Liebe beladen)
von Luigi Nono
(in Original-Sprachen)
20. 9. 1978
28. 9. 1978
28. 5. 1979
1. 6. 1979
28. 6. 1979

Der Barbier von Sevilla
(Il barbiere di Seviglia)
von Gioacchino Rossini
3. 9. 1978
16. 9. 1978
26. 10. 1978
29. 10. 1978
4. 7. 1979

Capriccio
von Richard Strauss
(Neuinszenierung)
24. 3. 1979
26. 3. 1979
30. 3. 1979
7. 4. 1979
10. 5. 1979
20. 5. 1979
10. 6. 1979
24. 6. 1979 (nachmittags)
1. 7. 1979

Carmen
von Georges Bizet
21. 10. 1978
25. 10. 1978
27. 10. 1978
1. 12. 1978
10. 12. 1978

Cavalleria rusticana*
(Sizilianische Bauernehre)
von Pietro Mascagni
Vier Vorstellungen
sind geplant.
Termine werden später
veröffentlicht.

Cosi fan tutte*
(So machen's alle)
von Wolfgang Amadeus Mozart
26. 5. 1979
2. 6. 1979
22. 6. 1979

Don Giovanni*
von Wolfgang Amadeus Mozart
21. 1. 1979
24. 1. 1979
28. 1. 1979
2. 2. 1979
16. 2. 1979
11. 3. 1979
2. 4. 1979
5. 5. 1979
31. 5. 1979
6. 6. 1979
18. 6. 1979

Elektra
von Richard Strauss
16. 10. 1978
22. 11. 1978

Fidelio
von Ludwig van Beethoven
6. 11. 1978
2. 12. 1978
7. 12. 1978
15. 12. 1978
5. 1. 1979
27. 1. 1979
30. 6. 1979

Die Fledermaus
von Johann Strauß
5. 10. 1978
22. 10. 1978
14. 3. 1979

Der fliegende Holländer
von Richard Wagner
(Neuinszenierung)
25. 2. 1979
28. 2. 1979
3. 3. 1979
15. 3. 1979
8. 4. 1979
22. 4. 1979 (nachmittags)
30. 4. 1979
4. 5. 1979
9. 5. 1979

Der Freischütz
von Carl Maria von Weber
3. 2. 1979
Weitere Vorstellungen werden später veröffentlicht.

Die Gezeichneten
von Franz Schreker
(Neuinszenierung)
17. 1. 1979
19. 1. 1979
26. 1. 1979
1. 2. 1979
11. 2. 1979 (nachmittags)
14. 2. 1979

Gianni Schicchi
von Giacomo Puccini
12. 10. 1978
17. 11. 1978
23. 11. 1978
21. 12. 1978

Hänsel und Gretel
von Engelbert Humperdinck
6. 12. 1978
11. 12. 1978
22. 12. 1978
26. 12. 1978 (nachmittags)
3. 1. 1979

Die Hochzeit des Figaro
(Le Nozze di Figaro)
von Wolfgang Amadeus Mozart
3. 11. 1978
11. 11. 1978
24. 11. 1978
3. 12. 1978
29. 12. 1978
4. 1. 1979
2. 3. 1979
4. 3. 1979
8. 3. 1979

Idomeneo*
von Wolfgang Amadeus Mozart
21. 9. 1978
30. 9. 1978
6. 10. 1978
11. 10. 1978
15. 10. 1978
28. 10. 1978

Giulio Cesare*
(Julius Caesar)
von Georg Friedrich Händel
Die nächsten Vorstellungen
sind in der Spielzeit 1979/80
vorgesehen.

Jenufa
von Leoš Janáček
(Neuinszenierung)
8. 7. 1979
11. 7. 1979
14. 7. 1979

Katja Kabanowa
von Leoš Janáček
27. 9. 1978
16. 11. 1978

My Fair Lady
von Frederick Loewe
24. 9. 1978
26. 11. 1978
16. 12. 1978
17. 3. 1979
5. 4. 1979
21. 4. 1979
9. 6. 1979

Lohengrin
von Richard Wagner
(Wiederaufnahme)
4. 2. 1979
10. 2. 1979
16. 4. 1979

Die Liebe zu den drei Orangen
von Sergej Prokofieff
In dieser Spielzeit sind keine
Vorstellungen geplant.

Die lustige Witwe
von Franz Lehár
3. 9. 1978 (nachmittags)
4. 9. 1978
15. 9. 1978
29. 10. 1978 (nachmittags)

Macbeth*
von Giuseppe Verdi
(Wiederaufnahme)
1. 11. 1978
4. 11. 1978
12. 11. 1978 (nachmittags)
15. 11. 1978
25. 11. 1978
9. 2. 1979

Der Mantel
(Il Tabarro)
von Giacomo Puccini
12. 10. 1978
17. 11. 1978
23. 11. 1978
21. 12. 1978

Die Meistersinger von Nürnberg
von Richard Wagner
15. 4. 1979

* in italienischer Sprache

Fig. 75. Repertory and performance dates for the Frankfurt Oper, 1978–79 . . . (Städtische Bühnen Frankfurt am Main)

Otello*
von Giuseppe Verdi
3. 6. 1979
8. 6. 1979
21. 6. 1979
25. 6. 1979
29. 6. 1979
9. 7. 1979

I Pagliacci*
(Der Bajazzo)
von Ruggiero Leoncavallo
Vier Vorstellungen
sind geplant.
Termine werden später
veröffentlicht.

Pariser Leben
(La Vie Parisienne)
von Jacques Offenbach
(Neuinszenierung)
1. 10. 1978
7. 10. 1978
14. 10. 1978
18. 10. 1978
5. 11. 1978
31. 12. 1978
7. 1. 1979(nachm. und abends)
5. 3. 1979
16. 3. 1979
18. 3. 1979
18. 4. 1979
12. 5. 1979
18. 5. 1979
23. 5. 1979
7. 6. 1979

Parsifal
von Richard Wagner
13. 4. 1979

Rigoletto*
von Giuseppe Verdi
18. 9. 1978
23. 9. 1978

Salome
von Richard Strauss
29. 3. 1979
20. 4. 1979
26. 4. 1979

Das schlaue Füchslein
(Příhody lišky bystroušky)
von Leoš Janáček
7. 3. 1979
18. 3. 1979 (nachmittags)
21. 3. 1979
31. 3. 1979
2. 5. 1979
17. 5. 1979
23. 6. 1979
6. 7. 1979
13. 7. 1979

Schwester Angelica
(Suor Angelica)
von Giacomo Puccini
(Wiederaufnahme)
12. 10. 1978
17. 11. 1978
23. 11. 1978
21. 12. 1978

Tannhäuser
von Richard Wagner
17. 9. 1978
8. 10. 1978
2. 11. 1978
25. 12. 1978
4. 4. 1979

Tosca*
von Giacomo Puccini
Vier Vorstellungen
sind geplant.
Termine werden später
veröffentlicht.

Tristan und Isolde
von Richard Wagner
1. 4. 1979
6. 5. 1979
30. 5. 1979
4. 6. 1979

Les Troyens
(Die Trojaner)
von Hector Berlioz
(Konzertante Aufführung in
französischer Sprache)
13. 5. 1979
16. 5. 1979
24. 5. 1979
27. 5. 1979

Il Trovatore*
(Der Troubadour)
von Giuseppe Verdi
29. 9. 1978
4. 10. 1978
19. 10. 1978
10. 11. 1978
30. 11. 1978
15. 2. 1979
17. 2. 1979
21. 2. 1979
24. 2. 1979
4. 3. 1979 (nachmittags)
22. 3. 1979
29. 4. 1979 (nachmittags)

Die verkaufte Braut
(Prodaná nevěsta)
von Friedrich Smetana
23. 12. 1978
8. 1. 1979
11. 1. 1979
13. 1. 1979
18. 2. 1979
20. 6. 1979

Wozzeck
von Alban Berg
(Wiederaufnahme)
9. 12. 1978
13. 12. 1978
20. 12. 1978
6. 1. 1979
20. 1. 1979

Die Zauberflöte
von Wolfgang Amadeus Mozart
14. 9. 1978
2. 10. 1978
19. 11. 1978

Ballett

Orpheus/Petruschka
Symphonies pour
instruments à vent
(Uraufführung)
Orpheus
Petruschka
(Neueinstudierung)
von Igor Strawinsky
18. 11. 1978
20. 11. 1978
3. 12. 1978 (nachmittags)
8. 12. 1978
17. 12. 1978
26. 12. 1978
18. 1. 1979
25. 1. 1979
12. 2. 1979
9. 3. 1979
28. 3. 1979
14. 4. 1979
29. 4. 1979

Prometheus
Die Geschöpfe des Prometheus
von Ludwig van Beethoven
Prométhée – Le poème du feu
von Alexander
Nikolajewitsch Skrjabin
(Uraufführung)
25. 4. 1979
27. 4. 1979
11. 5. 1979
19. 5. 1979
24. 6. 1979
27. 6. 1979
2. 7. 1979
5. 7. 1979
12. 7. 1979
15. 7. 1979

Golaud – Pelléas – Mélisande
Children's Corner
Trois Nocturnes
von Claude Debussy
Pelléas und Mélisande
von Arnold Schönberg
13. 10. 1978
9. 11. 1978
29. 11. 1978
10. 1. 1979
23. 2. 1979

Ballett im Schauspiel
»Ein Reigen«
Rondo
von Bruno Liberda
Fantasie
von Bruno Liberda
Sonate von Franz Schubert
(Sonate B-Dur op. posth.
DV 960)
21. 9. 1978
20. 10. 1978
Weitere Vorstellungen werden
später veröffentlicht.

Ballett im Kammerspiel
Drei Ballette zu Lorca
»Lied, Schrei, Yerma«
Lied
von
Roman Haubenstock-Ramati
Schrei
von George Crumb
Yerma
von Bruno Liberda
10. 9. 1978
23. 9. 1978
Weitere Vorstellungen werden
später veröffentlicht.

Sonderkonzerte

13. September 1978
Orchesterkonzert
Junge deutsche Philharmonie
Dirigent: Gary Bertini
Gustav Mahler: 7. Sinfonie

30. Oktober 1978
Liederabend
Barry McDaniel (Bariton)
Aribert Reimann (Klavier)

14. Mai 1979
Liederabend
Margaret Price (Sopran)
Geoffrey Parsons (Klavier)

Änderungen vorbehalten!

* in italienischer Sprache

Fig. 76. . . . continued . . . Also scheduled were a youth orchestra concert and two evenings
of Lieder. (Städtische Bühnen Frankfurt am Main)

Das Opern-Abonnement

Im Abonnement gibt es kein »Ausverkauft«.

30 % Ermäßigung
Also: Jeder 3. Theaterbesuch ist gratis

Vorkaufsrecht für alle Vorstellungen, Gastspiele und Sonderveranstaltungen.

Tausch von Stück und Tag, ohne Aufschlag, ohne Probleme.

Das sind die Vorzüge des OPERN-ABONNE-MENTS.
★ Ausverkauft gibt es für Sie nicht mehr. Bei den Vorstellungen der von Ihnen gewählten Abonnementsreihe haben Sie »Ihren festen Platz«. Darüber hinaus gewähren wir Ihnen ein Vorkaufsrecht für alle Vorstellungen, Gastspiele und Sonderveranstaltungen. Das heißt: Sie können mit Ihrem Abonnementsausweis schon einen Tag vor dem offiziellen Vorverkaufsbeginn Ihre Eintrittskarte lösen.
★ Kein zeitraubendes Warten und lästiges

Schlangestehen, keine unnötigen Telefonate. Und außerdem:
★ Ca. 30 % Ermäßigung gegenüber dem Normalpreis für alle regulären Vorstellungen, auch für Vorstellungen außerhalb Ihrer Abonnementsreihe (ausgenommen sind lediglich Premieren, Gastspiele, Sonderveranstaltungen zu erhöhten Preisen).
★ Das OPERN-ABONNEMENT kennt keine Zwänge: Wenn Ihnen Tag oder Stück nicht passen — tauschen Sie einfach um: Einen anderen Tag, ein anderes Stück. Das geht ohne Aufschlag und ohne Probleme.

Abonnementsmöglichkeiten

Nr.	Abonnementsart	Preisgruppen						
		I Parkett Reihe 1-8 1. Rang Reihe 1	II Parkett Reihe 9-11 1. Rang Mitte Reihe 2-5	III Parkett Reihe 12-17 1. Rang Mitte Reihe 6 Seite Reihe 2-4 2. Rang Mitte Reihe 1	IV Parkett Reihe 18-22 2. Rang Mitte Reihe 2-4 2. Rang Seite Reihe 1	V 2. Rang Mitte Reihe 5 2. Rang Seite Reihe 2-4 3. Rang Mitte Reihe 1 3. Rang prosz. Plätze	VI 3. Rang Mitte Reihe 2-7 3. Rang Seite Reihe 1	VII 3. Rang Halbmitte Reihe 2-5
		DM	DM	DM	DM	DM	DM	DM
	Musiktheater-Abonnements							
1	6 Aufführungen in der Oper an einem selbstgewählten Wochentag (außer dienstags)	144,— (statt 198,—)	114,— (statt 162,—)	96,— (statt 132,—)	78,— (statt 108,—)	60,— (statt 84,—)	42,— (statt 60,—)	33,— (statt 42,—)
2	6 Aufführungen in der Oper an einem Sonntagnachmittag	114,— (statt 156,—)	90,— (statt 126,—)	72,— (statt 102,—)	60,— (statt 84,—)	48,— (statt 66,—)	36,— (statt 48,—)	27,— (statt 36,—)
3	8 Aufführungen in der Oper donnerstags oder sonntags	192,— (statt 264,—)	152,— (statt 216,—)	128,— (statt 176,—)	104,— (statt 144,—)	80,— (statt 112,—)	56,— (statt 80,—)	44,— (statt 56,—)
4	7 Premieren in der Oper an wechselnden Wochentagen (ausgebucht — keine Neuanmeldungen möglich)	322,—	252,—	203,—	161,—	126,—	91,—	63,—
5	7 B-Premieren in der Oper Die B-Premiere folgt der Premiere in gleicher Besetzung mit wenigen Tagen Abstand	231,—	189,—	154,—	126,—	98,—	70,—	49,—
6	Sonderabonnements Reihe A, B, C je 5 Sondergastspiele (je 4 zu Premierenpreisen und je 1 zu doppelten Normalpreisen)	250,—	195,—	160,—	125,—	100,—	70,—	50,—
7	Extra-Abonnement Wagner-Reihe 1979 6 Vorstellungen (s. S. 7)	144,— (statt 198,-)	114,— (statt 162,-)	96,— (statt 132,-)	78,— (statt 108,-)	60,— (statt 84,-)	42,— (statt 60,-)	33,– (statt 42,-)
	Die Halb-Halb-Abonnements							
8	12 Aufführungen: 6 in der Oper 6 im Schauspiel an einem selbstgewählten Wochentag (außer dienstags)	255,— (statt 351,—)	201,— (statt 285,—)	165,— (statt 231,—)	129,— (statt 183,—)	99,— (statt 135,—)	63,— (statt 87,—)	54,— (statt 69,—)
9	12 Aufführungen sonntagnachmittags: 6 in der Oper 6 im Schauspiel	201,— (statt 279,—)	159,— (statt 225,—)	123,— (statt 177,—)	99,— (statt 141,—)	75,— (statt 105,—)	51,— (statt 69,—)	42,— (statt 57,—)

Fig. 77. Subscription plans available in Frankfurt at a 30 percent saving. Plans available are six opera performances, six Sunday afternoon operas, eight opera performances, seven premieres, seven second-night premieres (which take place a few nights later), special subscriptions to guest company performances, and a Wagner series. There are also two half-and-half subscriptions, one for six operas and six plays and another for six operas and six plays on Sunday afternoons (Städtische Bühnen Frankfurt am Main)

Fig. 78. Subscription plans in the Schauspiel and Kammerspiel. Available are six plays, six Sunday matinees, seven plays, eight plays (four in the Schauspiel, four in the Kammerspiel), and seven premieres (Städtische Bühnen Frankfurt am Main)

Spielplan 1978/79

Schauspiel

Baumeister Solness von Henrik Ibsen

Die Antigone des Sophokles in der Übertragung von Friedrich Hölderlin

Othello von William Shakespeare

Märchen von einem, der auszog, das Fürchten zu lernen. Kinderstück zur Weihnachtszeit nach den Brüdern Grimm

Bürger Schippel von Carl Sternheim

Germania Tod in Berlin von Heiner Müller

König Ödipus und Ödipus auf Kolonos von Sophokles

Torquato Tasso von Johann Wolfgang von Goethe

Beitrag zur Experimenta 1978

Das siebte Kreuz von Anna Seghers

Kammerspiel

Zufälliger Tod eines Anarchisten von Dario Fo

Der erste Tag des Friedens von Horst Laube

Michael Kramer von Gerhart Hauptmann

Die Rassen von Ferdinand Bruckner

König Ubu von Alfred Jarry

Kiebich und Dutz von Friedrich Karl Waechter

Kammerspiel-Extra

In diesem Programm finden Veranstaltungen und Aufführungen zur Ergänzung des Spielplans statt.

Wiederaufnahmen Schauspiel

Die Möwe von Anton Tchechov

Warten auf Godot von Samuel Beckett

Im Weißen Rößl von Ralph Benatzky

Wiederaufnahmen Kammerspiel

Der Hausmeister von Harold Pinter

Späte Liebe von Aleksander N. Ostrovskij

Zwangsvorstellungen von Karl Valentin

Das Bacchusfest von Arthur Schnitzler

Schauspiel-Abo

	Preisgruppe:	I	II	III	IV	V	VI
	Platzwahl:	Reihe 1—5	Reihe 6—10	Reihe 11—13	Reihe 14—18	Reihe 19—21	Reihe 22
1	6 Vorstellungen – an einem selbstgewählten Wochentag außer Dienstag	111,— (153,—)	87,— (123,—)	60,— (99,—)	51,— (75,—)	30,— (51,—)	21,— (27,—)
2	– am Sonntagnachmittag	87,— (123,—)	60,— (99,—)	51,— (75,—)	30,— (57,—)	27,— (39,—)	15,— (21,—)
3 4	7 Vorstellungen – montags, donnerstags, sonntags – an wechselnden Wochenendtagen (Freitag, Samstag, Sonntag)	129,50 (178,50)	101,50 (143,50)	80,50 (115,50)	59,50 (87,50)	45,50 (59,50)	24,50 (31,50)
5 6	8 Vorstellungen (4 Schauspiel, 4 Kammerspiel) – montags – Spätabonnement an wechselnden Wochenendtagen (Freitag, Samstag, Sonntag 20.30 Uhr)	116,— (164,—)	100,— (144,—)	76,— (108,—)	64,— (92,—)	42,— (56,—)	
7	Premieren-Abonnement 7 Vorstellungen	234,50	185,50	150,50	115,50	87,50	59,50

YEAR	1969	1970	1971	1972	1973	1974	1975	1976	1977
VALUE OF DEUTSCHE MARK	28¢	29¢	30¢	34¢	40¢	42¢	44¢	48¢	50¢
EXPENSES									
Artists' salaries	DM 9,401,000	DM 9,444,000	DM 11,770,000	DM 14,058,000	DM 15,214,000	DM 17,917,000	DM 18,765,000	DM 20,208,000	DM 20,939,000
Technical salaries	6,581,000	7,223,000	8,635,000	9,806,000	11,091,000	12,252,000	13,798,000	14,962,000	16,171,000
Administration	1,065,000	1,963,000	1,293,000	1,387,000	1,542,000	1,782,000	2,040,000	2,195,000	2,214,000
Other personnel	802,000	1,652,000	1,885,000	227,000	241,000	410,000	779,000	1,136,000	630,000
Pension funds	803,000	979,000	1,378,000	1,296,000	1,408,000	1,556,000	1,566,000	548,000	1,668,000
Production costs	3,448,000	3,761,000	3,952,000	4,418,000	5,209,000	5,534,000	5,603,000	7,353,000	7,030,000
Loan payments	3,069,000	2,995,000	2,942,000	2,900,000	2,859,000	2,817,000	6,528,000	5,528,000	5,980,000
Building maintenance	90,000	1,268,000	2,939,000	---	---	54,000	161,000	355,000	---
TOTAL	DM 25,259,000	DM 29,285,000	DM 34,794,000	DM 34,092,000	DM 37,564,000	DM 42,322,000	DM 49,240,000	DM 52,285,000	DM 54,632,000
INCOME									
Single tickets	DM 1,597,000	DM 1,534,000	DM 1,860,000	DM 1,878,000	DM 1,819,000	DM 3,239,000	DM 4,667,000	DM 2,123,000	DM 2,507,000
Subscriptions	1,681,000	1,548,000	957,000	967,000	1,395,000	3,085,000	3,340,000	2,360,000	2,236,000
Children's theater subscriptions	109,000	104,000	161,000	162,000	157,000	161,000	---	---	66,000
Visitor groups	809,000	790,000	660,000	669,000	648,000	1,100,000	---	1,085,000	1,136,000
Cloakroom charges	224,000	208,000	187,000	182,000	169,000	162,000	158,000	147,000	153,000
Radio and TV fees	40,000	3,000	3,000	95,000	48,000	300,000	100,000	96,000	---
Touring	428,000	230,000	117,000	110,000	187,000	273,000	217,000	512,000	198,000
Guest performances by other companies	---	318,000	375,000	359,000	345,000	321,000	479,000	380,000	244,000
Program sales	184,000	173,000	150,000	166,000	195,000	200,000	215,000	249,000	284,000
Other income	1,204,000	2,551,000	4,175,000	1,288,000	565,000	518,000	419,000	355,000	360,000
TOTAL	DM 6,276,000	DM 7,459,000	DM 8,645,000	DM 5,876,000	DM 5,528,000	DM 9,359,000	DM 9,595,000	DM 7,307,000	DM 7,184,000
TAX SUBSIDY	DM 18,983,000	DM 21,826,000	DM 26,149,000	DM 28,216,000	DM 32,036,000	DM 32,963,000	DM 39,645,000	DM 44,978,000	DM 47,448,000
SUBSIDY PERCENTAGE	75.0%	74.5%	75.1%	82.7%	85.4%	77.9%	80.6%	86.0%	86.9%

Fig. 79. Expenses and income for the Städtische Bühnen Frankfurt am Main, 1969–77
(Deutscher Bühnenverein, Köln)

Fig. 80. Harold Pinter's *Der Hausmeister*, directed by Peter Palitzsch and designed by A. Christian Steiof. From left, Albert Hoerrmann as Davis, Michael Altman as Aston, and Klaus Wennemann as Mick (Städtische Bühnen Frankfurt am Main/Mara Eggert)

Fig. 81. *Penthesilea*, tragedy by Heinrich von Kleist in the Kammerspiel as directed by Frank-Patrick Steckel. Christian Redl as Achilles and Marlen Diekhoff as Penthesilea (Städtische Bühnen Frankfurt am Main/Mara Eggert)

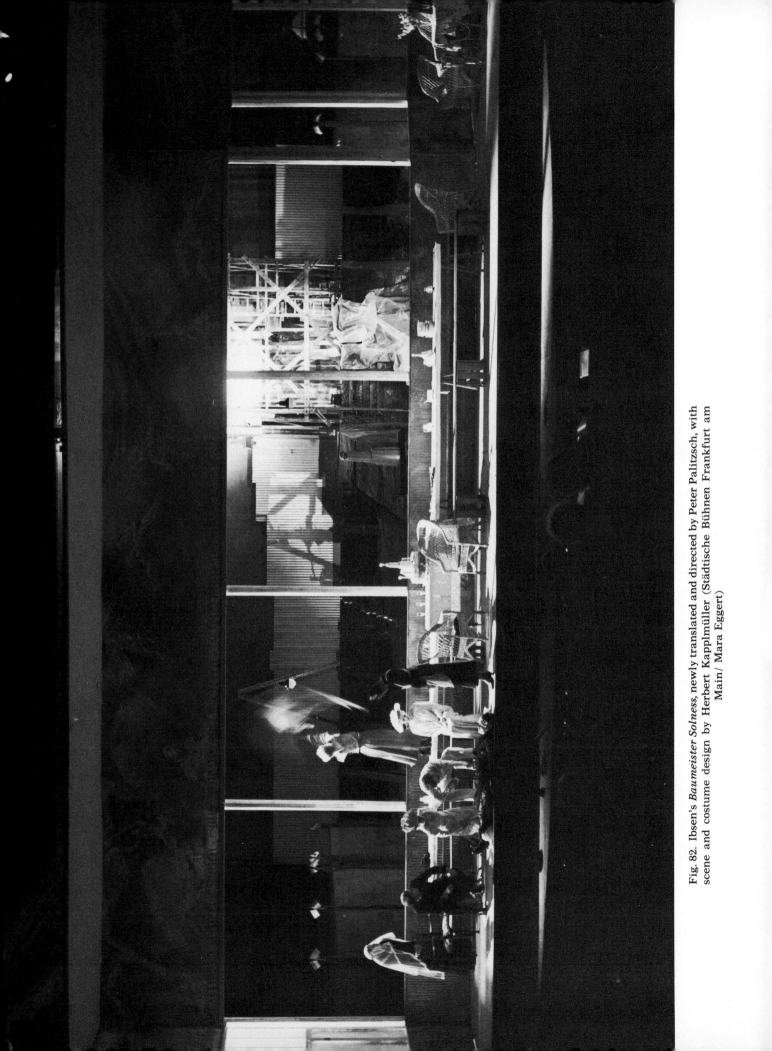

Fig. 82. Ibsen's *Baumeister Solness*, newly translated and directed by Peter Palitzsch, with scene and costume design by Herbert Kapplmüller (Städtische Bühnen Frankfurt am Main / Mara Eggert)

Fig. 83. The Italian playwright Dario Fo's *Zufälliger Tod eines Anarchisten,* directed and designed by Arturo Corso. From left, Gerhard Retschy as the Polizeipräsident, Peter Siegenthaler as Kommissar Sportsmann, Ernst-Ludwig Grau as the second Wachtmeister, Klara Höfels as a Journalistin, Wilfried Elste as Kommissar Bertozzo, and Peter Danzeisen as the Verrückter (Städtische Bühnen Frankfurt am Main/Mara Eggert)

Fig. 84. Janáček's *Das schlaue Füchslein* in a new German translation by Hans Hartleb, directed by Jonathan Miller, designed by Patrick Robertson, and costumed by Rosemary Vercoe. Gabriele Fuchs as Füchslein Schlaukopf and Matti Juhani as Fuchs (Städtische Bühnen Frankfurt am Main/Mara Eggert)

Fig. 85. The first German production of Luigi Nono's *Al gran sole carico d'amore,* the experiences of woman in the ages of revolution. Nono is a member of the Central Committee of the Italian Communist party, and his aim is to spread the gospel of Marxism through the musical drama. In this respect his work recalls Brecht, who made valuable use of songs in his many Marxist plays. This production was conducted by Michael Gielen, directed by Jürgen Flimm, designed by Karl-Ernst Herrmann, and costumed by Nina Ritter. Center, Sona Cervena as the woman (Städtische Bühnen Frankfurt am Main/Mara Eggert)

Fig. 86. Offenbach's musical comedy *Pariser Leben,* directed by Jérôme Savary (Städtische Bühnen Frankfurt am Main/Mara Eggert)

Fig. 87. The scenic cantata *Johanna auf dem Scheiterhaufen* by Paul Claudel, as set to music by Arthur Honegger. Orchestral direction by Robert Satanowski, direction by Friedrich Petzold, and scenery by Heinz Heckroth (Städtische Bühnen Frankfurt am Main/ Günter Englert)

VI. COLOGNE, GERMANY

Bühnen der Stadt Köln

Cologne is one of northern Europe's oldest cities, having been founded in 38 B.C. by Marcus Vispanius Agrippa, a son-in-law of the Emperor Augustus, under the name "oppidum Ubiorum" or city of the Ubii, a German tribe friendly to the Romans. An altar dedicated to the Emperor, the "ara Ubiorum," enabled the settlement to grow into the spiritual center of the new Roman province of Germania. In 48 A.D. the Emperor Claudius married Julia Agrippina, daughter of General Germanicus who had been born and raised in Cologne. With the title "Augusta," she became coregent of the Roman Empire, and to demonstrate her majesty and power to the world she presented her birthplace with the rights of a Roman city in 50 A.D. Henceforth, Cologne bore the name Colonia Claudia Ara Agrippinensis, that is, Claudian Colony of the family of Agrippa, site of an imperial altar.

Soon afterward the building of the city wall was begun, a structure about a thousand meters square, and today one can still see remarkably well-preserved sections of it. At the corner of Zeughausstrasse and St. Apernstrasse the entire tower of the northwest corner of the Roman city wall is completely preserved. Many more remnants of the Roman period of Cologne's history are preserved in the Römisch-Germanisches Museum near the Cologne Cathedral.

The foundation stone of the great Cathedral, one of the most impressive buildings in the world, was laid in 1248, and the structure was completed after prolonged delays in 1880, exactly as it had been designed 600 years earlier. The Elector-archbishops moved out of the city in the 13th century, and in 1475 Cologne was declared a free imperial city by the Emperor Frederick III, with the right to collect tolls on the Rhine, mint its own coins, and raise its own army for self-defense. Its location was propitious for trade and profit, and the fine and performing arts were supported by the citizenry. The old Opernhaus, built in 1902, was destroyed during World War II, but a new one was built, together with a Schauspielhaus, on Offenbachplatz in the heart of the city. Today the Cologne public theaters are among the finest in Germany.

Cologne is situated on the Rhine River in the state of North Rhine-Westphalia;

it had a population of 981,021 in 1976. The two principal theaters of the Bühnen der Stadt Köln are the Opernhaus, used for operas, operettas, and ballets, and the Schauspielhaus, used for adult and children's plays. There is also a small experimental theater located at 45 Ubierring, used for plays, chamber operas, and modern dance programs.

Technical aspects of the theaters are as follows:

Opernhaus

Seating capacity: 1,346 seats.
Architect: Wilhelm Riphan.
Theater Consultant: Walther Unruh.
Opened: May 18, 1957, with a production of Carl Maria von Weber's *Oberon* directed by Herbert Maisch.
Proscenium size: 13 meters wide by 7.8 meters high.
Main stage size: 25.5 meters wide by 22 meters deep.
Side stages: 18.2 meters wide by 22 meters deep.
Rear stage: 18 meters wide by 17.5 meters deep.
Technical equipment: Rundhorizont; three stage wagons, two of which contain turntables; six stage lifts, three of which are double-decked; large scene projection layout.
Orchestra pit: Average width 16 meters by 6 meters deep on two lifts for 100 musicians.

Schauspielhaus

Seating capacity: 920 seats.
Architect: Wilhelm Riphan.
Opened: September 8, 1962.
Proscenium size: 16 meters wide by 6 meters high.
Stage size: 23 meters wide by 26 meters deep.
Technical equipment: Adjustable tormentors, 44 overhead pipes for scene shifting, and standard lighting layout for small theater.
Orchestra pit: 15 meters wide by 2.5 meters deep for 35 musicians.

The theater companies tour in the region around Cologne. Visitor organizations with specially priced subscriptions number about 25,000 persons.

The Bühnen der Stadt Köln are under two managements, one for the Opernhaus and one for the Schauspielhaus. Dr. Michael Hampe is Intendant for the former, and John Pritchard is principal conductor. The ballet company is headed by Jochen Ulrich. Intendant of the Schauspielhaus is Hansgünther Heyme.

Personnel of the two companies in 1976–77 numbered as follows:

Artistic direction	70
Principal singers	30

Fig. 88. The Bühnen der Stadt Köln, facing Offenbachplatz in downtown Cologne. The twin office towers, recalling the twin spires of the Cologne Cathedral a short distance to the east of the theater, are designed so that staff employees and technical stage personnel can enjoy balconies and sunlight while hard at work. The Opernhaus is to the right and the Schauspielhaus to the left (Bühnen der Stadt Köln)

Fig. 89. The spacious lobby area of the Opernhaus. The doors toward the back of the photograph lead to the refreshment rooms (Bühnen der Stadt Köln)

Fig. 90. Auditorium of the Opernhaus, showing the main floor and 16 of the 22 flying galleries that take the place of the balconies of more traditional theaters (Bühnen der Stadt Köln)

Fig. 91. The modernistic interior of the Schauspielhaus, looking toward the functional proscenium arch. Lighting beams are situated overhead (Bühnen der Stadt Köln)

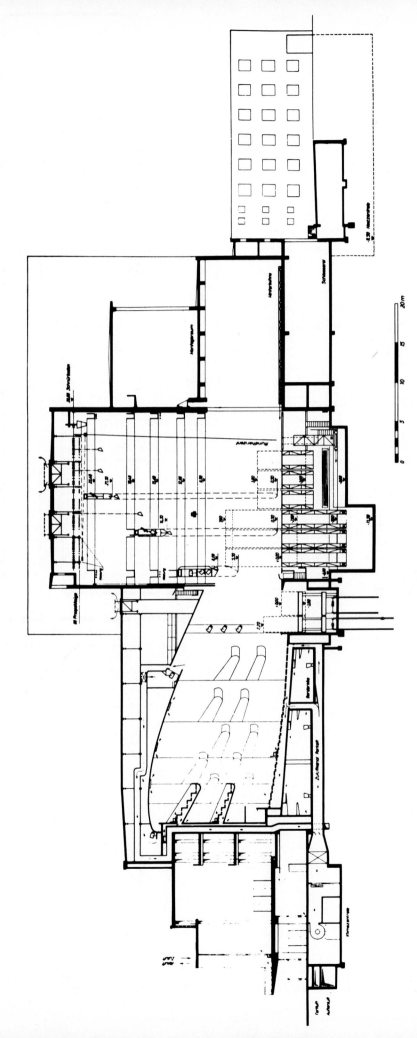

Fig. 92. Longitudinal section through the Opernhaus. To the left are the lobbies, below which is the heating and air conditioning equipment. There are various lighting slots in the ceiling of the auditorium used to mount large ellipsoidal-reflector spotlights that light the stage. The six stage lifts and the backdrop storage lifts are shown to the right of the orchestra pit lifts. The six main stage lifts are each 16 meters wide and 2.5 meters deep. The first three are double-decked and can be raised and lowered from 2 meters below to 9 meters above the stage. Scenery set up on the two decks can be shifted by simply moving the lifts up and down. The upstage lifts are single-decked and can move from 3 meters above stage to 3 meters below. Drops can be stored on racks below stage and are retrieved when needed with the help of the drop storage lifts. Over the stage are the three main lighting bridges. The scene shop is below the rear stage, and the paint shop is above it (Bühnen der Stadt Köln)

139

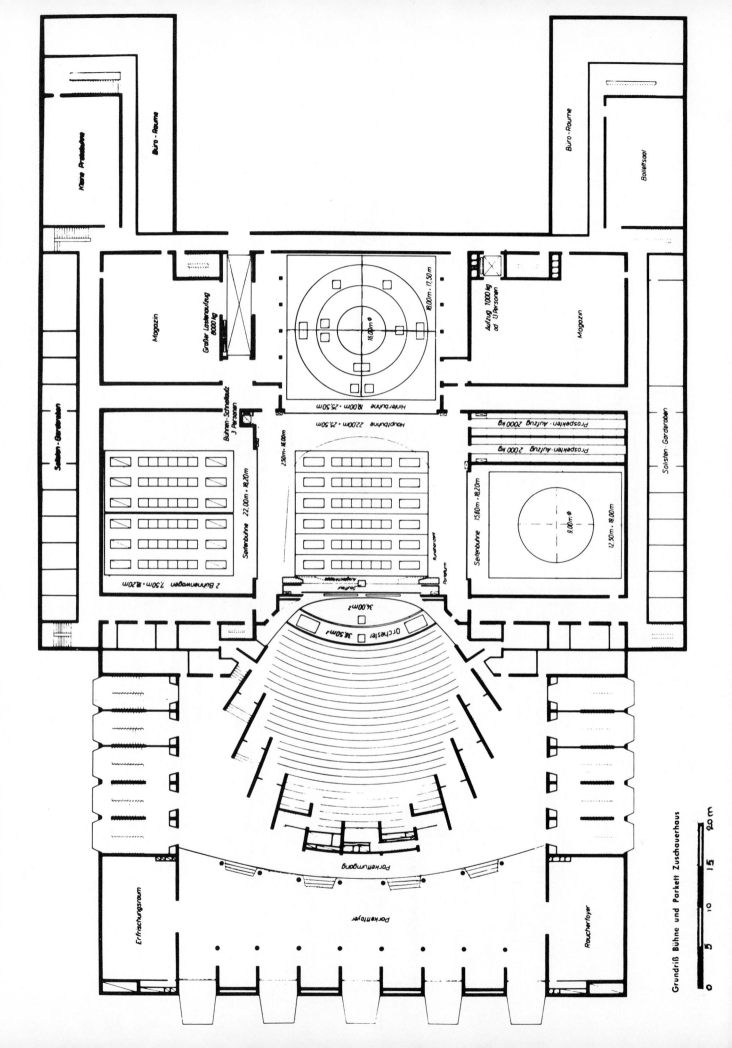

Grundriß Bühne und Parkett Zuschauerhaus

Fig. 93. Ground plan of the Opernhaus at stage level. To the left are the lobby and the foyers for smoking and refreshments. The auditorium, with its typically continental seating, is to the right of the lobby. The two orchestra pit lifts hold over 100 musicians. The lifts are lowered to reduce the sound of large-orchestra operas and raised to increase the volume of smaller ensembles. The main stage is surrounded by two side stages and a rear stage. The rear stage wagon carries three concentric turntables with a maximum diameter of 16 meters. The stage left wagon also carries a turntable, which is 9 meters in diameter. The stage right wagon can be handled in two sections or locked together as one unit. In the up right work area is a large freight elevator. Loaded trucks can drive onto this elevator from street level and be raised to any floor desired for unloading. The elevator in the up left work area is an express unit for 13 persons; it runs from below stage to the gridiron. Dressing rooms surround the stage area on three sides. Rehearsal rooms and offices are on both sides of an open space at rear (Bühnen der Stadt Köln)

Actors and actresses	52
Ballet dancers	29
Chorus singers	69
Orchestra musicians	114
Technical personnel	356
Administrative personnel	62
House personnel	76
Total	858

During the same season the two companies offered the following numbers of performances of opera, drama, and ballet:

Opernhaus

	PERFORMANCES	ATTENDANCE	PERCENT OF CAPACITY
Operas	167	215,399	95.8%
Ballets	24	30,694	91.8%
Operettas	20	26,711	99.2%
Musicals	15	20,190	100.0%
Plays	1	771	57.3%
Guest companies	17	(included above)	
Totals	244	293,765	88.8%

Schauspielhaus

Ballets	12	8,674	58.8%
Adult plays	189	132,835	72.8%
Children's plays	26	16,393	68.4%
Guest companies	13	(included above)	
Totals	240	157,902	66.7%

Kammerspiele

Adult plays	168	40,055	69.2%
Children's plays	28	6,654	72.2%
Guest companies	8	(included above)	
Totals	204	46,799	70.7%

The total attendance during 1976–77 was thus 498,466, or about 50.8 percent of the population of the city.

For the Spielzeit 1978–79, the following productions were staged:

Opernhaus

Operas

New Productions Schönberg: *Moses und Aron*

Verdi: *Die Macht des Schicksals*

Rossini: *Aschenbrödel*

Strauss, R.: *Ariadne auf Naxos*

Matthus, Siegfried: *Omphale*

de Falla: *Nächte in Spanischen Gärten* (ballet)

Wagner: *Die Meistersinger von Nürnberg*

Puccini: *Turandot*

Revivals Bartók: *Herzog Blaubarts Burg*

Cimarosa: *Der verzweifelte Ehemann*

Donizetti: *Don Pasquale*

          Der Liebestrank

Gluck: *Orfeo ed Euridice*

Humperdinck: *Hänsel und Gretel*

Kagel: *Kagels Musiktheater*

    Kontra/Danse

    Recitativarie

    Camera Obscura

    Kantrimiusik

Mozart: *Idomeneo*

    Die Entführung aus dem Serail

    Le Nozze di Figaro

    Don Giovanni

    Così fan tutte

    Titus

    Die Zauberflöte

Puccini: *Tosca*

    Madame Butterfly

Rossini: *Der Barbier von Sevilla*

Strauss, R.: *Salome*

    Arabella

    Die schweigsame Frau

Strawinski: *Oedipus Rex*

Tschaikowsky: *Pique Dame*

Verdi: *Rigoletto*

    Der Troubadour

    La traviata

    Don Carlos

    Aida

Wagner: *Der fliegende Holländer*

    Tannhäuser

Lohengrin
Tristan und Isolde
Das Rheingold
Die Walküre
Siegfried
Götterdämmerung

Porter: *Kiss Me, Kate!*

Strauss, J.: *Der Zigeunerbaron*

Ballets	Joplin/Veredon: *The Ragtime Dance Company*
	Vivaldi/Ulrich: *Die vier Jahreszeiten*
	Cohen/Joos: *Der grüne Tisch*
	Beethoven/van Manen: *Grosse Fuge*
	Poulenc/Horváth: *Le Bal Masqué*
	Zimmermann/Ulrich: *Caprichos*
	Schumann/Ulrich: *Sinfonische Etüden*
	Ravel/Joos: *Pavane auf den Tod einer Infantin*
	Lanner/Joos: *Ein Ball in Alt-Wien*
	Micus/Gray/Veredon: *Koan*
	Strawinsky/van Manen: *Tilt*
	Downs/Bruce: *Wings*
	Mahler/Ulrich: *Des Knaben Wunderhorn*
	Schwertsik/Ulrich: *Walzerträume*
	Serocki/Ulrich: *Sinfonietta*
	Foss/Tetley: *Der wandelbare Garten*
	Berio/Morrice: *That Is the Show*
	Bredemeyer/Ulrich: *Die Musse*
	Achim Freyer: *Re-Aktion*
	Schnebel/Ulrich/Freyer: *Drei Klang*
	Pheloung/Hoffmann: *Chimäre*
	Copland/Ulrich: *Pierrot-Pierrot*
	Fritsch/Ulrich: *Ein Requiem*
	Schönberg/Veredon: *Pelléas und Mélisande*
	Ravel/Ulrich: *Für Maurice Ravel*
	Britten/Ulrich: *In dieser Nacht*
	Les Illuminations
	Schostakowitsch/Veredon: *Der Tod geht ein und aus*
	Dvořák/Ulrich: *Serenade*

Schauspielhaus

New Productions	Offenbach: *Der Dr. Ox*
	O'Neill: *Alle Reichtümer der Welt*
	Gombrowicz: *Operette*

	Von Lohenstein: *Agrippina*
	Shakespeare: *Hamlet*
	Feuchtwanger: *Die Petroleuminseln*
	de Castro: *Der Cid*
Ballet	Limon/Ulrich/Veredon: *Aus dem Südamerikanischen Reise-buch*

Kammerspiel

New Productions	Euripides: *Der Zyklop*
	Wenzel: *Weit weg von Hagedingen*
	Michelsen: *Alltag*
	Zuckmayer: *Der Hauptmann von Köpenick*
	Lessing: *Der junge Gelehrte*
	Schneider: *Die Wiedergutmachung*
	Dario Fo: *Misterio buffo*
	Hamsun: *An des Reiches Pforten*
	Schnitzler: *Liebelei*
	Nestroy: *Der Häuptling Abendwind* oder *Das greuliche Fest-mahl*

In addition to direct box office sales, tickets are sold by the Bühnen der Stadt Köln through the following subscription plans. Prices are those for the 1978–79 season.

Opernhaus

1. Evening subscriptions; seven performances of musical works in the Opernhaus; Wednesdays, Thursdays, Fridays, or Saturdays; 30 percent price reduction; price ranges: DM 177, DM 144, DM 120, DM 99, DM 78, DM 63, DM 48.

2. Youth subscriptions; seven performances of musical works in the Opernhaus; 60 percent price reduction; arranged through the schools.

3. Afternoon subscriptions; seven performances of musical works in the Opernhaus; Saturday and Sunday afternoons; 60 percent price reduction; price ranges: DM 90, DM 75, DM 63, DM 54, DM 42, DM 36, DM 27.

4. Premiere subscriptions; seven opening-night performances of musical works in the Opernhaus; price ranges: DM 382, DM 336, DM 290, DM 244, DM 205.

5. Choice subscriptions; eight coupons exchangeable for a ticket any time in the Opernhaus; price ranges: DM 226, DM 202, DM 176, DM 120.

Schauspielhaus

1. Evening subscriptions; seven performances in the Schauspielhaus; Wednesdays, Thursdays, Fridays, or Saturdays; 30 percent price reduction; price ranges: DM 126, DM 84, DM 75, DM 63, DM 54, DM 42.

2. Youth subscriptions; seven evenings in the Schauspielhaus; 60 percent price reduction; arranged through the schools.

3. Afternoon subscriptions; seven performances in the Schauspielhaus; Saturday afternoons; 60 percent price reduction; price ranges: DM 66, DM 45, DM 42, DM 33, DM 30, DM 24.

4. Premiere subscriptions; eight opening-night performances in the Schauspielhaus; price ranges: DM 330, DM 242, DM 198, DM 163, DM 119, DM 93.

Choice subscriptions; eight coupons exchangeable for a ticket anytime in the Schauspielhaus; price ranges: DM 150, DM 110, DM 94, DM 78.

Kammerspiele

1. Choice subscriptions; six coupons exchangeable for a ticket anytime in the Kammerspiele; price ranges: DM 84, DM 72, DM 66, DM 60, DM 48, DM 42.

2. Choice subscriptions mixed; four coupons exchangeable for a ticket anytime in the Schauspielhaus and four coupons exchangeable for a ticket anytime in the Kammerspiele; price ranges: DM 130, DM 102, DM 90, DM 78.

Fig. 94, p. 147, shows a nine-year summary of the financing of the Bühnen der Stadt Köln.

Scenes from recent productions of the Bühnen der Stadt Köln are shown in Figs. 95–104, pp. 148–165.

YEAR	1969	1970	1971	1972	1973	1974	1975	1976	1977
VALUE OF DEUTSCHE MARK	28¢	29¢	30¢	34¢	40¢	42¢	44¢	48¢	50¢
EXPENSES									
Artists' salaries	DM 10,770,000	DM 12,249,000	DM 14,085,000	DM 13,980,000	DM 15,865,000	DM 15,937,000	DM 16,894,000	DM 17,611,000	DM 20,371,000
Technical salaries	6,613,000	7,608,000	8,806,000	9,678,000	10,751,000	12,728,000	13,850,000	14,879,000	14,675,000
Administration	1,418,000	1,683,000	1,919,000	2,035,000	2,329,000	2,783,000	4,674,000	5,536,000	5,239,000
Other personnel	185,000	252,000	246,000	282,000	268,000	518,000	1,021,000	584,000	875,000
Pension funds	238,000	275,000	283,000	318,000	107,000	318,000	318,000	309,000	358,000
Production costs	5,126,000	5,097,000	5,391,000	6,214,000	6,971,000	7,368,000	8,737,000	8,223,000	8,666,000
Loan payments	589,000	558,000	676,000	703,000	127,000	5,529,000	110,000	127,000	467,000
Building maintenance	151,000	287,000	88,000	122,000	424,000	1,085,000	506,000	10,000	161,000
TOTAL	DM 25,090,000	DM 28,009,000	DM 31,494,000	DM 33,332,000	DM 36,842,000	DM 46,266,000	DM 46,110,000	DM 47,279,000	DM 50,812,000
INCOME									
Single tickets	DM 1,006,000	DM 912,000	DM 917,000	DM 1,366,000	DM 1,045,000	DM 786,000	DM 1,393,000	DM 1,580,000	DM 1,423,000
Subscriptions	1,459,000	1,273,000	1,216,000	1,424,000	1,898,000	1,666,000	1,600,000	1,714,000	1,860,000
Children's theater subscriptions	215,000	208,000	200,000	174,000	252,000	299,000	---	---	---
Visitor groups	762,000	947,000	876,000	849,000	876,000	932,000	883,000	1,067,000	1,241,000
Cloakroom charges	---	---	---	---	---	---	---	---	---
Radio and TV fees	300,000	24,000	1,000	180,000	129,000	270,000	12,000	---	1,000
Touring	453,000	94,000	354,000	664,000	702,000	251,000	218,000	312,000	252,000
Guest performances by other companies	---	310,000	309,000	388,000	378,000	498,000	586,000	691,000	789,000
Program sales	239,000	154,000	169,000	156,000	150,000	139,000	176,000	184,000	190,000
Other income	1,008,000	704,000	954,000	1,643,000	737,000	5,811,000	463,000	385,000	692,000
TOTAL	DM 5,442,000	DM 4,626,000	DM 4,996,000	DM 6,844,000	DM 6,167,000	DM 10,652,000	DM 5,331,000	DM 5,933,000	DM 6,448,000
TAX SUBSIDY	DM 19,648,000	DM 23,383,000	DM 26,498,000	DM 26,488,000	DM 30,675,000	DM 35,614,000	DM 40,779,000	DM 41,346,000	DM 44,364,000
SUBSIDY PERCENTAGE	78.6%	83.5%	84.1%	79.5%	83.4%	76.9%	88.4%	87.4%	87.3%

Fig. 94. Expenses and income for the Bühnen der Stadt Köln, 1967–1976 (Deutscher Büh-nenverein, Köln)

Fig. 95. Puccini's *Tosca*, Act III, with Janis Martin as Tosca and Robert Ilosfalvy as Cavaradossi, in a production directed by Michael Hampe and designed by Ezio Frigerio (Oper der Stadt Köln/Stefan Odry)

Fig. 96. Debussy's opera *Pelléas et Mélisande* in a sensual and somewhat controversial production by Hans Neugebauer with striking scenery and costumes by Achim Freyer. From left, Eliane Manchet as Mélisande, Francisco Vergara as the Doctor, Eva Tamassay as Geneviève, and James Johnson as Arkel (Oper der Stadt Köln/Stefan Odry)

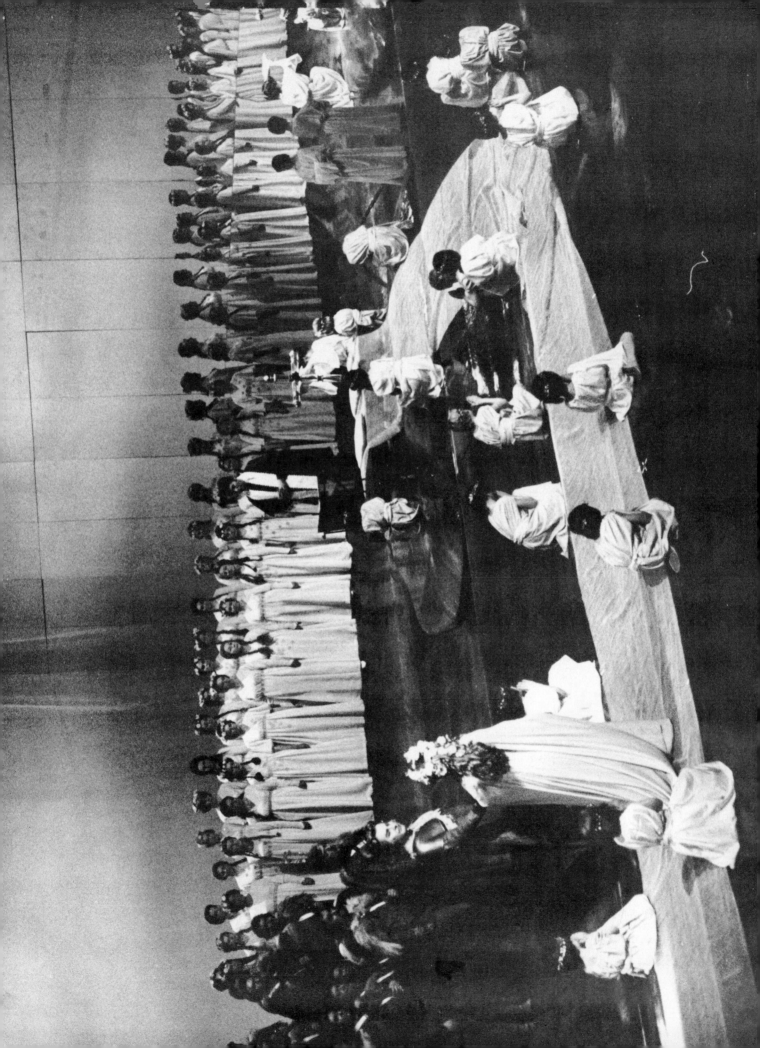

Fig. 97. Wagner's *Lohengrin*, Act III, the bridal procession. Robert Ilosfalvy as Lohengrin leads Gerlinde Lorenz as Elsa toward the altar, in a production directed by Hans Neugebauer (Oper der Stadt Köln/Stefan Odry)

Fig. 98. The Hans Neugebauer/Achim Freyer "white" *Wozzeck* at the Cologne Opernhaus. The opera was set in a white corridor with a white wall on the left side and on the right, another white wall with many doors, behind which one imagines the enlisted men of the army, all dressed in white. Gisela Schröter as Marie approaches her child by Wozzeck (Oper der Stadt Köln/Stefan Odry)

Fig. 99. The Tanz-Forum of the Oper der Stadt Köln performs for the people of the city in front of the Dom (Schauspiel der Stadt Köln/Stefan Odry)

Fig. 100. Athol Fugard's play *Buschmann und Lena* in its first German production at the Cologne Kammerspiele, directed by Nicolas Brieger, with scenery and costumes by Franz Koppendorfer. Rotraut de Neve as Lena and Bernt Hahn as Buschmann (Schauspiel der Stadt Köln/Stefan Odry)

Fig. 101. Ludwig Holberg's comedy *Jeppe vom Berge*, with music by Werner Haetnjes, directed by Volker Feissler, and designed by Wolf Münzer (Schauspiel der Stadt Köln/Stefan Odry)

Fig. 102. Ibsen's *Die Frau vom Meer* at the Schauspielhaus, Cologne, in a production directed by Angelika Hurwicz and designed by Frank Schultes. From left, Barbara Nüsse, Wolfgang Robert, Angelike Zielke, Christiane Müller, and Lothar Ostermann (Schauspiel der Stadt Köln/Stefan Odry)

Fig. 103. Eugène Labiche's *Ein Florentinerhut*, directed by Roberto Ciulli and designed by Helmut Stürmer. The musicians are rendering the popular air "Floh de Cologne" (Schauspiel der Stadt Köln/Stefan Odry)

Fig. 104. Pirandello's *Sechs Personen suchen einen Autor,* directed by Roberto Ciulli. Peter Eschberg as the Father and Veronika Bayer as the Stepdaughter (Schauspiel der Stadt Köln/Stefan Odry)

VII. MUNICH, GERMANY

Bayerische Staatsoper—Nationaltheater

Like Düsseldorf, Munich developed in the vicinity of a monastic settlement, "Munichen" (with the monks), which was established in 746 A.D. on the Isar River. The city's coat of arms, in fact, depicts a monk, the "Münchner Kindl" as a significant part of its design. In 1158, the date of the official founding of the city, Duke Henry the Lion destroyed a toll bridge over the Isar that belonged to the Bishop of Freising and built his own bridge on which to collect tolls some miles upstream near the village of München. The settlement was fortified and received civic rights in 1294. Thus, the lion also became a symbol of Munich and appears in various forms about the city—from the two stone lions that guard the Odeonsplatz to the labels on the popular Löwenbräu beer bottles.

In the 16th century the influence of Duke Albrecht enabled the city to develop into an important center of commerce and art. The basis of the modern State Library of Bavaria dates from this period, and eventually, in 1806, when the last Elector of Bavaria became its first king, the city entered on a period of growth that led to its present eminence as one of the three largest cities of West Germany.

The theater began to develop in Munich during the 16th century with the establishment of the Jesuit college in 1559. The Jesuits were in the habit of writing and producing morality plays in Latin, which were intended to instruct the audience in the Catholic scheme of salvation. These plays were performed all over Europe in the 16th and 17th centuries and had considerable influence on the development of subsequent dramatic literatures.

At Munich, it was the custom to offer a play on the occasion of the annual prizegiving, and in the early years of the 17th century the scholar and author in charge of providing a suitable piece was Jacob Bidermann. One of the most successful of his nine plays, all written in Latin, was *Cenodoxus, sive Doctor Parisiensis,* which was performed before a distinguished assemblage of citizens, ecclesiastics, and nobles of the court in 1609, following an earlier production at the Jesuit college in Augsburg in 1602. The Munich audience was deeply impressed with this play on a Faustian theme, which depicts the struggle between freedom of thought and divine faith. Bidermann made use of comic scenes, placed both Heaven and Hell on the stage, and called for nearly every stage device known at the time. It was performed later in Ingolstadt (1617), Paris (1636), and Vienna (1637) and was translated into Old Bavarian dialect in 1635. For the celebration of the 800th anniversary of Munich in 1958, a new production of this remarkable play was staged by Werner Düggelin, and further performances took place at the Salzburg festivals as a counterpart to the annual Hofmannsthal version of *Jedermann*.

The Jesuit plays were accompanied by instrumental dances, songs, odes, and choral pieces, and over the years, as more music was added to these productions, they gradually turned into Singspiele—plays with music. The earliest German opera whose music has been preserved, *Seelewig* by Sigmund Staden, is a morality piece on the subject of the struggle between the soul and the villain Trügewalt involving such characters as Art, the Senses, Wisdom, and Conscience. This development, along with the interest in northern countries in the new Italian opera, explains why the first court theater in Munich was an opera house, built between the years 1654 and 1657 on the Salvatorplatz. A little earlier, in 1653, the first Italian opera to be performed in Munich, *L'arpa festante* by Giovanni Battista Maccioni, was staged in the Herkulessaal of the Residenz. Over the years, the Opernhaus am Salvatorplatz served very well for the needs of the French and Italian opera companies that soon established residence in the city.

During the reign of the Elector Maximilian III Joseph, the court architect François Cuvilliés designed a new Residenztheater to be used for both play and opera production. It was finished in 1753 and, together with the Markgräfliches Opernhaus in Bayreuth, which dates from 1748, serves as one of two baroque theaters still in use in Germany today. Mozart's *Idomeneo* received its first performance in the Cuvilliéstheater in 1781. When war broke out in Europe in 1939, the inner decorations of the theater were stored in a safe place, and after 1945 the theater was restored on a site near the original.

Technical aspects of this famous theater are as follows:

Seating capacity: 525 seats for plays, 462 for opera productions.
Architect: François Cuvilliés.
Opened: October 12, 1753, with Giovanni Ferrandini's bel canto opera *Catone in Utica,* on a text by Metastasio. Damaged during World War II, restored, and reopened June 12, 1958, with Mozart's *Die Hochzeit des Figaro* as part of the celebration of Munich's 800th anniversary.
Proscenium opening: 10 meters wide by 7 meters high.
Stage size: 20 meters wide by 15 meters deep.
Technical equipment: In 1883 it was the first German theater to be equipped with electric lighting; shortly afterward, in 1896, Carl Lautenschläger designed the first revolving stage to be installed in a German theater.
Orchestra pit: 10 meters wide by 4.5 meters deep for 45 musicians.

At the beginning of the 19th century, Munich entered a period of rapid expansion

Fig. 105. Proscenium arch decorations in the Cuvilliéstheater, Munich. The coat of arms is that of the Elector Maximilian III Joseph (Bayer. Verwaltung der staatl. Schlösser, Gärten u. Seen)

Fig. 106. The Electoral box in the Cuvilliéstheater. Atlas figures hold up the various boxes
and entrance ways (Bayer. Verwaltung der staatl. Schlösser, Gärten u. Seen)

Fig. 107. Satyr figure, carved out of linden wood and covered with stone chalk decorates the interior of the theater (Bayer. Verwaltung der staatl. Schlösser, Gärten u. Seen)

and growth. The Elector Maximilian IV Joseph became King Maximilian I Joseph in 1806 at the pleasure of Napoleon, and German opera began to mature. Weber's *Der Freischütz* was seen for the first time in the city in 1822, the work of Meyerbeer and Beethoven became known, and the operas of Mozart were finally recognized for the masterpieces they were. A new theater, the Hof- und Nationaltheater, was built on the Marstallplatz and opened in 1818. It burned down in 1823 but was rapidly rebuilt and improved; it opened once again in 1825 with help from a special beer tax paid by thirsty Münchener.

The new theater, with its classical facade, gained international fame during the reign of King Ludwig II (1864–86) for its hospitality to the theatrical and musical genius Richard Wagner. The King's patronage of Wagner enabled his new Hofkapellmeister, Hans von Bülow, to conduct the world premieres of *Tristan und Isolde* on June 10, 1865, and *Die Meistersinger* on June 21, 1868. Later, Franz Wüllner conducted the first performances of *Das Rheingold* (September 22, 1869) and *Die Walküre* (June 26, 1870).

The city was by now a cultural rival to Berlin and Vienna, and it continues even today to exert an international influence out of all proportion to its population of 1,315,000. Still another opera house, the Prinzregententheater, designed by Max Littman in the Bayreuth Festspielhaus style, was opened in 1901 and became the center of an annual festival of music, opera, and drama that currently rivals those of Bayreuth and Salzburg. This theater is undergoing renovation but is expected to be back in use in a few years. Meanwhile, in July and August the Munich Festival draws visitors from all corners of the world to see exemplary performances of the operas of Wagner, Mozart, Verdi, Strauss, Berg, and Orff in the Nationaltheater and the Cuvilliéstheater and to hear orchestra concerts and Liederabende in the Herkulessaal and the Brunnenhof of the Residenz.

Technical aspects of the two opera houses are as follows:

Nationaltheater

Seating capacity: 2,100 seats.
Architect: Karl von Fischer.
Opened: October 12, 1818, with the festival play *Die Weihe* by Ferdinand Fränzl.
    Burned to the ground in 1823, rebuilt by Karl von Klenze, and reopened in
    1825. Destroyed by fire bombs in 1943, rebuilt by Gerhard Graubner and
    Karl von Fischer, and opened again on November 21, 1963, with *Die Frau
    ohne Schatten* by Richard Strauss and on November 23, 1963, with Wagner's
    Die Meistersinger.
Proscenium size: Up to 16 meters wide by up to 13.5 meters high.
Stage size: 30 meters wide by 26 meters deep.
Fore and rear side stage: 20 meters wide by 42 meters deep.
Rear stage: 30 meters wide by 24 meters deep.
Technical equipment: Three main stage lifts each 20 meters wide by 6 meters
    deep, seven stage wagons each 6 meters by 20 meters, and a very large lighting

installation: 272 spotlight groups, 144 large cyc lighting units, and 20 Xenon scene projectors. The lighting console controls 320 magnetic amplifier dimmers.

Orchestra pit: 15 meters wide by 8 meters deep for 120 musicians.

Prinzregententheater

Seating capacity: 1,122 seats.

Architects: Heilmann and Littman.

Opened: August 28, 1901, under the management of Ernst von Possart with Wagner's *Die Meistersinger.*

Proscenium size: 11.4 meters wide by 8.4 meters high.

Stage size: 29 meters wide by 23 meters deep.

Orchestra pit: Covered, as at Bayreuth. Space for 90 musicians.

The principal Besucherorganizationen are the Theatergemeinde e.V., the Volksbühne München e.V., and the Freie Volksbühne, with about 60,000 members.

The Staatsintendant of the Nationaltheater is August Everding. Personnel of the company numbered, during the Spielzeit 1976–77, as follows:

Artistic direction	40
Principal singers	31
Ballet dancers	59
Chorus singers	100
Orchestra musicians	139
Technical personnel	409
Administrative personnel	33
House personnel	148
Total	959

During the same season the Nationaltheater offered the following numbers of performances of opera, operetta, and ballet:

	PERFORMANCES	ATTENDANCE	PERCENT OF CAPACITY
Operas	262	457,861	92.3%
Ballets	53	108,766	92.4%
Operettas	11	21,384	92.5%
Guest companies	5	(included above)	
Totals	331	588,011	92.4%

During the season 1977–78 the Nationaltheater staged the following productions:

Fig. 108. The Nationaltheater in Munich, about 1865. The archway passage enabled the shy King Ludwig II to go from his Residenz to his private box in the theater without encountering the masses in the lobby (Bayerische Staatstheater)

Fig. 109. Interior of the Nationaltheater showing the auditorium, the chandelier, boxes and balconies. TV, lighting, and sound control rooms are at the rear of the main floor (Bayerische Staatstheater)

Fig. 110. Auditorium of the Prinzregententheater, strongly reminiscent of Wagner's Festspielhaus at Bayreuth with its steep rake in the seating bank, the boxes at rear but not
at the sides, and the fan shape of the auditorium (Bayerische Staatsoper)

Operas	Mozart: *Die Hochzeit des Figaro*
	Don Giovanni
	Così fan tutte
	Die Entführung aus dem Serail
	Tschaikowsky: *Eugen Onegin*
	Beethoven: *Fidelio*
	Puccini: *La Bohème*
	Tosca
	Madame Butterfly
	Strauss, R.: *Der Rosenkavalier*
	Capriccio
	Ariadne auf Naxos
	Elektra
	Daphne
	Die Frau ohne Schatten
	Salome
	Arabella
	Wagner: *Das Rheingold*
	Die Walküre
	Siegfried
	Götterdämmerung
	Tannhäuser
	Der fliegende Holländer
	Parsifal
	Verdi: *Don Carlos*
	Othello
	Der Troubadour
	Ein Maskenball
	Rigoletto
	Janáček: *Jenufa*
	Moussorgsky: *Boris Goudonov*
	Rossini: *Der Barbier von Sevilla*
	Smetana: *Die verkaufte Braut*
	Massenet: *Werther*
	Humperdinck: *Hänsel und Gretel*
	Reimann: *Lear* (world premiere)
Operetta	Strauss, J.: *Die Fledermaus*

Ballets	
New Productions	Janáček/Seymour: *Intime Briefe*
	Schtschedrin/Kura: *Leidenschaft*
Revivals	Adam/Wright: *Giselle*

Beethoven/van Manen: *Grosse Fuge*
Bizet/Balanchine: *Sinfonie in C*
Czerny/Lander: *Etudes*
Dutilleux/Butler: *Les Doubles*
Hart/Marcus: *Vergänglichkeit*
Haupt/Gackstetter: *Moira*
Haupt/Gackstetter: *Rilke*
Haupt/Gackstetter: *Zofen*
Korngold/Gackstetter: *Illusion*
Liszt/Hill: *Eulogy*
Martin/Gackstetter: *Das Lächeln am Fusse der Leiter*
Prokofieff/Cranko: *Romeo und Julia*
Rachmaninoff/Vámos: *Rhapsodie*
Scarlatti/Stolze/Cranko: *Der Widerspenstigen Zähmung*
Strawinsky/Balanchine: *Apollon Musagète*
Strawinsky/Tetley: *Le Sacre du Printemps*
Tschaikowsky/Wright: *Dornröschen*
Tschaikowsky/Cranko: *Onegin*
Tschaikowsky/Cranko: *Schwanensee*

There follows a subscription price list, based on seven performances per year, for the Nationaltheater during the season 1978–79 (Fig. 111, p. 178).

Prices are raised for the annual Munich Festival. Price ranges and seating plans for the Nationaltheater and the Cuvilliéstheater are shown in Figs. 112 and 113, pp. 180–181.

Fig. 114, p. 182, shows a nine-year financial summary for the Nationaltheater.

Scenes from recent productions at the Nationaltheater are shown in Figs. 115–129, pp. 183–199.

Staatstheater am Gärtnerplatz

The Staatstheater am Gärtnerplatz, like the Volksoper in Vienna and the Deutsche Oper Berlin, began as a private theater and was later taken over by a government agency and supported with tax revenues. Also like the Volksoper, it is dedicated to the art of the operetta and the musical comedy in a city that has a very heavily endowed state opera company. Both the Vienna Volksoper and the Munich Gärtnerplatztheater produce some operas each year, but the emphasis is specifically on operetta, musical comedy, and musical plays.

The lack of such a theater in New York has long puzzled observers of the American theater scene. Broadway is always interested in new musicals, and now and then a musical is revived for a short run in a Broadway or off-Broadway house. In fact, the Broadway theater has made distinguished contributions to a theatrical form that was first developed by Jacques Offenbach in Paris and then grew in stature and interest through the work of Johann Strauss, Franz Lehár, Robert Stolz, Emerich Kálmán, Karl Millöcker, and others in Vienna as well as in London through the works of Gilbert

BAYERISCHE STAATSOPER
Platzmiete-Preise ab Spielzeit 1978/79

Plätze		Jahrespreis für 7 Vorstellungen einschl. Heftgebühr DM
Parkett	1. und 2. Reihe	289,—
	3. mit 13. Reihe	247,—
	14. mit 18. Reihe	205,—
	19. Reihe Nr. 776 mit 788	205,—
	20. Reihe Nr. 803 mit 808	205,—
	19. Reihe Nr. 760 mit 775	163,—
	20. Reihe Nr. 789 mit 802	163,—
	21. und 22. Reihe	163,—
Balkon	1. Reihe	289,—
	2. Reihe Nr. 1 mit 25	247,—
	2. Reihe Nr. 26 mit 41	205,—
	2. Reihe Nr. 42 mit 49	163,—
	3. Reihe Nr. 1 mit 26	247,—
	3. Reihe Nr. 27 mit 38	163,—
	3. Reihe Nr. 39 mit 46	121,—
	4. Reihe Nr. 1 mit 23	205,—
	4. Reihe Nr. 24 mit 31	163,—
	4. Reihe Nr. 32 mit 39	121,—
	5. Reihe Nr. 1 mit 16	205,—
	Sessel	205,—
1. Rang	1. Reihe Nr. 1 mit 28	247,—
	1. Reihe Nr. 29 mit 36	205,—
	2. Reihe Nr. 1 mit 20	205,—
	2. Reihe Nr. 21 mit 32	163,—
	2. Reihe Nr. 33 mit 36	121,—
	3. Reihe Nr. 1 mit 20	163,—
	3. Reihe Nr. 21 mit 32	121,—
	3. Reihe Nr. 33 mit 36	86,—
	4. Reihe Nr. 1 mit 16	163,—
	Sessel	163,—
2. Rang	1. Reihe Nr. 1 mit 28	205,—
	1. Reihe Nr. 29 mit 32	163,—
	2. Reihe Nr. 1 mit 20	163,—
	2. Reihe Nr. 21 mit 29	121,—
	3. Reihe Nr. 1 mit 20	121,—
	3. Reihe Nr. 21 mit 30	86,—
	Sessel	121,—
3. Rang	1. Reihe Nr. 1 mit 29	163,—
	1. Reihe Nr. 30 mit 41	121,—
	1. Reihe Nr. 42 mit 45	86,—
	2. Reihe Nr. 1 mit 30	121,—
	3. Reihe Nr. 1 mit 31	86,—
	Sessel	86,—
Galerie	1. Reihe Nr. 1 mit 32	121,—

Fig. 111. Subscription prices, 1978–79, for seven performances in the Nationaltheater, program included.

Eintrittspreise Nationaltheater

Platzgruppe I	Preise	S	F	FP
		62,50	100,50	116,—
Parkett	1. und 2. Reihe			
Balkon	1. Reihe			
Platzgruppe II		53,—	85,—	97,50
Parkett	3. mit 13. Reihe			
Balkon	2. und 3. Reihe Mitte			
1. Rang	1. Reihe Mitte			
Platzgruppe III		43,—	69,—	79,50
Parkett	14. mit 18. Reihe			
	19. und 20. Reihe Mitte			
Balkon	2. Reihe Seite			
Balkon	4. und 5. Reihe Mitte			
Balkon	Sessel			
1. Rang	1. Reihe Seite			
1. Rang	2. Reihe Mitte			
2. Rang	1. Reihe Mitte			
Platzgruppe IV		33,50	53,—	61,50
Parkett	19. mit 22. Reihe Seite			
Balkon	2. mit 4. Reihe Seite			
1. Rang	1. und 2. Reihe Seite			
1. Rang	3. und 4. Reihe Mitte			
1. Rang	Sessel			
2. Rang	1. Reihe Seite			
2. Rang	2. Reihe Mitte			
3. Rang	1. Reihe Mitte			

Platzgruppe V	Preise	S	F	FP
		23,50	37,50	43,—
Balkon	2. mit 4. Reihe Seite			
1. Rang	1. mit 3. Reihe Seite			
2. Rang	1. und 2. Reihe Seite			
2. Rang	3. Reihe Mitte			
2. Rang	Sessel			
3. Rang	1. Reihe Seite			
3. Rang	2. Reihe Mitte			
Galerie	1. Reihe Mitte			
Platzgruppe VI		15,50	24,50	28,—
Balkon	3. und 4. Reihe Seite			
1. Rang	2. und 3. Reihe Seite			
2. Rang	1. mit 3. Reihe Seite			
3. Rang	1. Reihe Seite			
3. Rang	3. Reihe Mitte			
3. Rang	Sessel			
Galerie	1. Reihe Seite			
Galerie	2. Reihe Mitte			
Platzgruppe VII		10,—	15,—	17,—
Balkon	3. Reihe Seite			
1. Rang	2. Reihe Seite			
2. Rang	3. Reihe Seite			
3. Rang	1. Reihe Seite			
Galerie	Sessel			
	Stehplatz Mitte			
Platzgruppe VIII		5,50	7,50	9,—
	Stehplatz Seite			

Sitzplan Nationaltheater

Fig. 112. Seating plan and price scale in the Nationaltheater for the 1976 Munich Festival (Bayerische Staatsoper)

Eintrittspreise Altes Residenztheater (Cuvilliés-Theater)

Für »Titus« (10. Juli) nur beschränkter Kartenverkauf

Sitzplan Cuvilliés-Theater

Platzgruppe I — DM 85,–
Parkett Reihe 1 mit 6
Parterre-Logen Vorderplätze Loge 1 mit 6
1. Rang-Logen Vorderplätze Loge 1 mit 6

Platzgruppe II — DM 75,–
Parkett Reihe 7 mit 12
Parterre-Logen Vorderplätze Loge 7
Rückplätze Loge 1 und 2
1. Rang-Logen Vorderplätze Loge 7
Rückplätze Loge 1 und 2

Platzgruppe III — DM 66,–
2. Rang-Logen Vorderplätze Loge 1 mit 5

Platzgruppe IV — DM 56.50
Parterre-Logen Rückplätze Loge 3 mit 5
2. Rang-Logen Vorderplätze Loge 6 und 7
Rückplätze Loge 1 und 2
3. Rang-Logen Vorderplätze Loge 1 und 2

Platzgruppe V — DM 47,–
3. Rang-Logen Vorderplätze Loge 3 mit 5
Rückplätze Loge 1

Platzgruppe VI — DM 37.50
Parterre-Logen Rückplätze Loge 6
3. Rang-Logen Vorderplätze Loge 6

Platzgruppe VII — DM 27.50
1. Rang-Logen Rückplätze Loge 3 mit 6
2. Rang-Logen Rückplätze Loge 3
3. Rang-Logen Vorderplätze Loge 7
Rückplätze Loge 2

Platzgruppe VIII — DM 15,–
Parterre-Logen Rückplätze Loge 7
1. Rang-Logen Rückplätze Loge 7
2. Rang-Logen Rückplätze Loge 4 mit 7
3. Rang-Logen Rückplätze Loge 3 mit 7

Serenaden im Brunnenhof der Residenz: 1. bis 10. Reihe 15.– DM / 11. bis 16. Reihe 11.50 DM / 17. bis 20. Reihe 8.– DM / 21. bis 23. Reihe 6.– DM / 24. bis 29. Reihe 5.– DM.

Die Plätze der Kategorie A werden bei ungünstiger Witterung entsprechend auf das Cuvilliés-Theater verteilt (siehe Rückseite der Eintrittskarte). Plätze der Kategorie B werden nur am Tage der Aufführung bei günstiger Witterung ausgegeben.

Bei »Titus« und »The Rake's Progress« stehen im Parkett nur 10 Reihen zur Verfügung.

Die ersten sechs Reihen: DM 85,–
Die letzten vier Reihen: DM 75,–

Liedermatinée und Liederabend im Alten Residenztheater (Cuvilliés-Theater) DM 5.50 bis DM 17.50

Liederabende im Herkulessaal der Residenz DM 6.– bis DM 25.–

Fig. 113. Seating plan and price scale in the Cuvilliéstheater for the 1976 Munich Festival.

YEAR	1969	1970	1971	1972	1973	1974	1975	1976	1977
VALUE OF DEUTSCHE MARK	28¢	29¢	30¢	34¢	40¢	42¢	44¢	48¢	50¢
EXPENSES									
Artists' salaries	DM 14,538,000	DM 15,809,000	DM 18,160,000	DM 19,549,000	DM 21,941,000	DM 25,194,000	DM 26,664,000	DM 27,604,000	DM 29,018,000
Technical salaries	5,703,000	6,688,000	8,017,000	9,030,000	10,274,000	11,580,000	12,760,000	13,444,000	14,215,000
Administration	1,973,000	2,297,000	2,911,000	3,166,000	3,511,000	3,864,000	4,481,000	4,713,000	4,952,000
Other personnel	15,000	95,000	125,000	132,000	148,000	117,000	114,000	125,000	121,000
Pension funds	---	---	---	---	---	---	---	---	---
Production costs	4,684,000	5,170,000	6,308,000	7,725,000	6,588,000	7,707,000	6,954,000	7,803,000	8,710,000
Loan payments	---	---	---	---	---	---	69,000	75,000	98,000
Building maintenance	7,000	49,000	---	128,000	---	---	128,000	151,000	196,000
TOTAL	DM 26,920,000	DM 30,108,000	DM 35,521,000	DM 39,730,000	DM 42,462,000	DM 48,462,000	DM 51,170,000	DM 53,915,000	DM 57,310,000
INCOME									
Single tickets	DM 3,856,000	DM 4,194,000	DM 4,081,000	DM 5,559,000	DM 5,589,000	DM 6,274,000	DM 7,466,000	DM 7,584,000	DM 8,520,000
Subscriptions	1,747,000	1,900,000	1,703,000	2,021,000	2,197,000	1,890,000	2,230,000	2,325,000	2,743,000
Children's theater subscriptions	368,000	426,000	440,000	269,000	285,000	243,000	24,000	---	---
Visitor groups	1,706,000	1,618,000	1,549,000	1,529,000	1,743,000	1,637,000	1,887,000	2,071,000	2,337,000
Cloakroom charges	163,000	151,000	140,000	182,000	280,000	268,000	266,000	264,000	301,000
Radio and TV fees	372,000	286,000	454,000	195,000	578,000	317,000	210,000	419,000	139,000
Touring	264,000	59,000	372,000	136,000	33,000	934,000	203,000	137,000	328,000
Guest performances by other companies	---	107,000	---	16,000	15,000	---	---	56,000	59,000
Program sales	293,000	286,000	278,000	308,000	354,000	352,000	466,000	470,000	513,000
Other income	205,000	235,000	232,000	372,000	226,000	361,000	335,000	362,000	359,000
TOTAL	DM 8,974,000	DM 9,262,000	DM 9,249,000	DM 10,587,000	DM 11,300,000	DM 12,276,000	DM 13,087,000	DM 13,688,000	DM 15,299,000
TAX SUBSIDY	DM 17,946,000	DM 20,846,000	DM 26,272,000	DM 29,143,000	DM 31,162,000	DM 36,186,000	DM 38,083,000	DM 40,227,000	DM 42,011,000
SUBSIDY PERCENTAGE	65.0%	69.2%	73.9%	73.4%	73.4%	74.7%	74.4%	74.6%	73.3%

Fig. 114. Expenses and income for the Nationaltheater, 1969–77 (Deutscher Bühnenverein, Köln)

Fig. 115. A new production of Mozart's *Die Zauberflöte*, directed by August Everding, conducted by Wolfgang Sawallisch, and designed by Jürgen Rose. Sarastro (Siegfried Vogel) questions Tamino (Francisco Araiza) (Bayerische Staatsoper/Anne Kirchbach)

Fig. 116. A new production of Verdi's *Aida*, directed by Franco Enriquez, conducted by Riccardo Muti, and designed by Beni Montresor. Brigette Fassbaender as Amneris and Placido Domingo as Radames (Bayerische Staatsoper/Anne Kirchbach)

Fig. 117. Two scenes from a recent production of Mascagni's *Cavalleria rusticana,* directed by Giancarlo del Monaco, conducted by Nello Santi, designed by Gunther Schneider-Siemssen, and costumed by Silvia Strahammer. Santuzza (Leonie Rysanek) tells Alfio (Benito di Bella) that his wife has been unfaithful with Turiddu . . . (Bayerische Staatsoper/ Anne Kirchbach)

Fig. 118. . . . and in Scene 2, Turiddu (Placido Domingo) faces Alfio before the townsfolk
(Bayerische Staatsoper/Sabine Toepffer)

Fig. 119. Leoncavallo's *Pagliacci*, by the same production team. Peppe (Norberth Orth) and Tonio (Benito di Bella) prevent Canio (Placido Domingo) from strangling Nedda (Teresa Stratas) . . . (Bayerische Staatsoper/Anne Kirchbach)

Fig. 120. . . . Canio continues to press Nedda for the name of her lover . . . (Bayerische Staatsoper/Sabine Toepffer)

Fig. 121. . . . "La commedia è finita!" (Bayerische Staatsoper/Sabine Toepffer)

Fig. 122. Scenes from the impressive Munich production of Bernd Alois Zimmermann's *Die Soldaten*, directed by Vaclav Kaslik, designed by Josef Svoboda, and conducted by Michael Gielen. Simultaneous scenic action is an essential aspect of this landmark work in modern opera. The stage lifts were employed to set scenes above other scenes so that four separate activities could go on simultaneously. The projection screens also received both still photographs and motion picture footage. Here, the world of the soldiers is contrasted with the world of middle class respectability . . . (Bayerische Staatsoper/Sabine Toepffer)

Fig. 123. . . . A closer view of the same sequence, showing the officers drinking, philoso-phizing and flirting . . . (Bayerische Staatsoper/Sabine Toepffer)

Fig. 124. . . . On the many projection screens are thrown scenes of empty streets against lighted buildings at night . . . (Bayerische Staatsoper/Sabine Toepffer)

Fig. 125. . . . and the booted feet of marching armies (Bayerische Staatsoper/Sabine Toepffer)

Fig. 126. Two scenes from Aribert Reimann's new interpretation of Shakespeare's tragedy *Lear,* set to an adaptation by Claus H. Henneberg. Commissioned by the Nationaltheater, it was directed and designed by Jean-Pierre Ponnelle. Edmund (Werner Götz) watches as Lear (Dietrich Fischer-Dieskau) comforts Cordelia (Julia Varady) . . . (Bayerische Staatsoper/Anne Kirchbach)

Fig. 127. . . . Lear on the heath (Bayerische Staatsoper/Sabine Toepffer)

Fig. 128. John Cranko's ballet *Der Widerspenstigen Zähmung*, as designed by Jürgen Rose. Katherine (Konstanze Vernon) turns desperately away from her admirer Petrucchio (Peter Breuer) (Bayerische Staatsoper/Sabine Toepffer)

Fig. 129. In honor of the 100th anniversary of the death of the choreographer August Bournonville, the Nationaltheater ballet revived his *La Sylphide* in 1979. The music is by Herman S. Løvenskiold. Grislinde Skroblin as the Sylph and Peter Breuer as James (Bayerische Staatsoper/Sabine Toepffer)

and Sullivan. It is to be hoped that in the not too distant future such cities as New York, Chicago, and Los Angeles may have theaters which, with the help of tax subsidies, perform on a repertory basis the works of such eminent American operetta and musical comedy composers as Victor Herbert, Sigmund Romberg, Rudolf Friml, Jerome Kern, George Gershwin, Cole Porter, Irving Berlin, Richard Rodgers, Frederick Loewe, and Leonard Bernstein.

Legend has it that the origin of the Theater am Gärtnerplatz lies in an ad lib remark delivered by a popular Munich comedian, Ferdinand Lang, who was playing in Nestroy's farce *Eulenspiegel* for the first time in the august Nationaltheater. He expressed the desire for a Volkstheater in Munich in which he could have more fun playing comedy than he could in the stately Nationaltheater. The audience applauded vigorously and, although the authorities were not amused (he spent two days in jail for his impudence), talk continued among theatergoers and in the newspapers about a Volkstheater where one could go and relax a bit during the show. Finally, a group of businessmen formed a consortium, bought a piece of ground in the vicinity of the Viktualienmarkt, and in 1863 hired the architect J. M. Reifenstuel to design their new people's theater. In 1865 the project was completed and the Munich Volkstheater opened with *Was wir wollen,* a festival piece in one act with songs, dances, and vivid scenes by Herman Schmid.

The work of Nestroy and Offenbach dominated the early seasons, along with that of Johann Strauss and Franz Lehár later on. The theater had many financial ups and downs and, in fact, had to declare bankruptcy in April of 1870. An appeal was made to King Ludwig II, whose interest in dramatic and musical art had already manifested itself in his support of Richard Wagner; and in October of 1870 the theater reopened under his patronage. The activity surrounding preparations for the first production under the new management, Ferdinand Raimund's *Der Barometermacher auf der Zauberinsel,* attracted far more attention from the people of Munich than the daily bulletins in the newspapers reporting the progress of the Franco-Prussian War.

The theater was damaged by various bombing attacks during World War II but was repaired and reopened in 1948 with a Strauss operetta, *Eine Nacht in Venedig.* Gustaf Gründgens directed a memorable production of Offenbach's *Die Banditen* in 1949, and in 1953 the ballet company under the direction of the choreographer Heinz Rosen staged the world premiere of a new ballet by Jean Cocteau, *Die Dame und das Einhorn.* American operettas have found a secure place in the repertory, and on July 4, 1976, the company gave a stirring performance of *Hallo Dolly!* for the Americans in town.

Technical aspects of the theater are as follows:

Seating capacity: 932 seats.
Architect: J. M. Reifenstuel.
Opened: November 4, 1865, with *Was wir wollen* by Herman Schmid. Closed and
    reopened several times. After a two-year period of remodeling, its most recent

reopening was on September 10, 1969, with a production of *Die Hochzeit der Platäa* by Rameau under the direction of Kurt Pscherer.

Proscenium size: 9.5 meters wide by 7 meters high.

Stage size: 20 meters wide by 20 meters deep.

Technical equipment: Rundhorizont, revolving stage, and wagon stages. Large lighting layout with scene projectors.

Orchestra pit: 12 meters wide by 6 meters deep for 75 musicians.

The Staatsintendant of the Theater am Gärtnerplatz is Kurt Pscherer. Personnel of the company numbered, during 1976–77, as follows:

Artistic direction	25
Principal singers	31
Ballet dancers	31
Choral singers	43
Orchestra musicians	72
Technical personnel	149
Administrative personnel	27
House personnel	64
Total	442

During the same season, the Staatstheater am Gärtnerplatz offered the following numbers of performances of opera, ballet, operettas, and musicals:

	PERFORMANCES	ATTENDANCE	PERCENT OF CAPACITY
Operas	204	159,614	83.5%
Ballets	35	25,481	78.1%
Operettas	58	49,627	91.8%
Musicals	16	13,002	87.2%
Guest company	1	(included above)	
Totals	314	247,724	85.2%

The following productions were staged during the Spielzeit 1977–78:

New Productions	Händel: *Alcina*
	Puccini: *Madame Butterfly*
	Rossini: *Die Italienerin in Algier*
	Henze: *Undine* (ballet)
	Strauss, J.: *Wiener Blut*
	Loewe: *Gigi*
Restudied Productions	Strauss, R.: *Der Zigeunerbaron*
	Offenbach: *Orpheus in der Unterwelt*

Fig. 130. Sketch of the Bayerisches Staatstheater am Gärtnerplatz made about 1865 by
K. Gunkel (Staatstheater am Gärtnerplatz)

Fig. 131. The elegant interior of the Gärtnerplatztheater with its classical balconies and chandelier. Stage lighting ports are concealed where the ceiling meets the top of the balcony structure (Staatstheater am Gärtnerplats)

Repertory Productions	Purcell: *Die Feenkönigin*
	Rameau: *Die Hochzeit der Platäa*
	Mozart: *Die Entführung aus dem Serail*
	Die Hochzeit des Figaro
	Die Zauberflöte
	Weber: *Der Freischütz*
	Rossini: *Der Barbier von Sevilla*
	Donizetti: *Lucia von Lammermoor*
	Auber: *Fra Diavolo*
	Lortzing: *Zar und Zimmermann*
	Nicolai: *Die lustigen Weiber von Windsor*
	Bizet: *Carmen*
	Verdi: *La traviata*
	Offenbach: *Hoffmanns Erzählungen*
	Pariser Leben
	Massenet: *Manon*
	Smetana: *Die verkaufte Braut*
	Suppé: *Die schöne Galathee*
	Strauss, J.: *Die Fledermaus*
	Eine Nacht in Venedig
	Zeller: *Der Vogelhändler*
	Mascagni: *Cavalleria rusticana*
	Leoncavallo: *Der Bajazzo*
	d'Albert: *Tiefland*
	Humperdinck: *Hänsel und Gretel*
	Giordano: *André Chénier*
	Lehár: *Die lustige Witwe*
	Schostakowitsch: *Die Nase*
	Strauss, R.: *Intermezzo*
	Orff: *Die Bernauerin*
	Walton: *Der Bär*
	Kirchner: *Die Trauung*
	Porter: *Kiss Me, Kate!*
	Herman: *Hallo, Dolly!*
Ballets	Delibes: *Coppelia*
	Prokofieff: *Cinderella*
	Brecht/Weill: *Die sieben Todsünden der Kleinburger*
	Stranz: *Diversono*
	Veerhoff: *Dualis für Schlagzeug und Tänzer*

Fig. 133, p. 206, shows a nine-year summary of the finances of the Staatstheater am Gärtnerplatz.

Scenes from some recent productions of the Staatstheater am Gärtnerplatz are shown in Figs. 134–139, pp. 207–212.

STAATSTHEATER AM GÄRTNERPLATZ

ORCHESTER

Eintrittspreise
ab 1. 9. 1977

	H-Preise DM	S-Preise DM	G-Preise DM	A-Preise DM	Abo-Preise DM ab
Parkett:					
1. und 2. Reihe	34,—	30,—	27,—	24,—	21,—
3. bis 7. Reihe	31,—	27,—	24,—	21,—	19,—
8. bis 12. Reihe	28,—	24,—	20,—	18,—	16,50
13. bis 16. Reihe	24,—	19,—	16,—	14,—	13,—
17. Reihe	20,—	16,—	13,—	11,—	10,—
Balkon:					
1. Reihe Mitte	34,—	30,—	27,—	24,—	21,—
1. Reihe Seite	31,—	27,—	24,—	21,—	19,—
2. Reihe Mitte	28,—	24,—	20,—	18,—	16,50
2. Reihe Seite	16,—	12,—	10,—	9,—	7,50
3. Reihe Mitte	28,—	24,—	20,—	18,—	16,50
3. Reihe Seite	16,—	12,—	10,—	9,—	7,50
I. Rang:					
1. Reihe Mitte	31,—	27,—	24,—	21,—	19,—
1. Reihe halbe Mitte	28,—	24,—	20,—	18,—	16,50
1. Reihe Seite	24,—	19,—	16,—	14,—	13,—
2. Reihe Mitte	24,—	19,—	16,—	14,—	13,—
2. Reihe Seite	16,—	12,—	10,—	9,—	7,50
II. Rang					
1. Reihe Mitte	24,—	19,—	16,—	14,—	13,—
1. Reihe Seite	20,—	16,—	13,—	11,—	10,—
2. und 3. Reihe Mitte	20,—	16,—	13,—	11,—	10,—
2. Reihe Seite	16,—	12,—	10,—	9,—	7,50
III. Rang:					
1. Reihe Mitte	20,—	16,—	13,—	11,—	10,—
1. Reihe Seite	16,—	12,—	10,—	9,—	7,50
2. Reihe	16,—	12,—	10,—	9,—	7,50
Mittelloge:	34,—	30,—	27,—	24,—	21,—
Balkonlogen:	20,—	16,—	13,—	11,—	10,—
I. Ranglogen:	16,—	16,—	13,—	11,—	10,—
Stehplätze:	7,—	5,50	5,50	5,50	—

Ermäßigungen jeglicher Art werden nur aus vollen DM-Beträgen (ohne Sonderabgaben) auf Eintrittskarten ab DM 10,— gewährt.
In den obenstehenden Preisen sind die Sonderabgaben mit DM 1,20 enthalten.

Fig. 132. Ticket prices and seating plan for the Staatstheater am Gätnerplatz (Staatstheater am Gätnerplatz)

YEAR	1969	1970	1971	1972	1973	1974	1975	1976	1977
VALUE OF DEUTSCHE MARK	28¢	29¢	30¢	34¢	40¢	42¢	44¢	48¢	50¢
EXPENSES									
Artists' salaries	DM 4,189,000	DM 4,978,000	DM 5,589,000	DM 6,567,000	DM 7,275,000	DM 7,729,000	DM 8,547,000	DM 9,090,000	DM 9,828,000
Technical salaries	2,137,000	2,759,000	3,423,000	3,875,000	4,389,000	4,616,000	5,228,000	5,503,000	6,372,000
Administration	780,000	919,000	986,000	1,057,000	1,325,000	1,638,000	1,857,000	2,087,000	1,648,000
Other personnel	8,000	29,000	32,000	41,000	46,000	39,000	45,000	42,000	42,000
Pension funds	---	---	---	---	---	---	---	---	---
Production costs	1,378,000	1,555,000	1,500,000	1,945,000	1,747,000	2,023,000	2,435,000	2,257,000	2,756,000
Loan payments	---	---	---	---	---	210,000	61,000	98,000	70,000
Building maintenance	2,700,000	---	---	---	---	---	---	---	1,840,000
TOTAL	DM 11,192,000	DM 10,240,000	DM 11,530,000	DM 13,485,000	DM 14,782,000	DM 16,255,000	DM 18,173,000	DM 19,077,000	DM 22,556,000
INCOME									
Single tickets	DM 391,000	DM 648,000	DM 854,000	DM 1,143,000	DM 1,189,000	DM 1,182,000	DM 1,719,000	DM 2,045,000	DM 2,400,000
Subscriptions	104,000	163,000	133,000	198,000	237,000	165,000	275,000	296,000	295,000
Children's theater subscriptions	115,000	372,000	241,000	259,000	287,000	318,000	---	---	---
Visitor groups	240,000	430,000	396,000	323,000	433,000	346,000	571,000	631,000	690,000
Cloakroom charges	27,000	65,000	60,000	75,000	125,000	109,000	124,000	123,000	134,000
Radio and TV fees	4,000	214,000	9,000	312,000	3,000	4,000	22,000	---	244,000
Touring	151,000	154,000	46,000	7,000	38,000	224,000	296,000	129,000	422,000
Guest performances by other companies	---	40,000	---	---	---	---	---	---	---
Program sales	47,000	45,000	46,000	86,000	66,000	51,000	67,000	119,000	116,000
Other income	30,000	70,000	48,000	43,000	77,000	47,000	63,000	79,000	92,000
TOTAL	DM 1,109,000	DM 2,201,000	DM 1,833,000	DM 2,446,000	DM 2,455,000	DM 2,446,000	DM 3,137,000	DM 3,422,000	DM 4,393,000
TAX SUBSIDY	DM 10,083,000	DM 8,039,000	DM 9,697,000	DM 11,039,000	DM 12,327,000	DM 13,809,000	DM 15,036,000	DM 15,655,000	DM 18,163,000
SUBSIDY PERCENTAGE	90.1%	78.5%	84.1%	81.9%	83.4%	85.0%	82.7%	82.1%	80.5%

Fig. 133. Expenses and income for the Staatstheater am Gärtnerplatz, 1969–77 (Deutscher Bühnenverein, Köln)

Fig. 134. The comedian Ferdinand Lang as "Menschenfresser," the spiritual father of the Staatstheater am Gärtnerplatz. He played many roles in classical comedy and was much admired for his work in such pieces as Nestroy's *Zwei ewige Juden für Einen, oder Der fliegende Holländer zu Fuss* (Staatstheater am Gärtnerplatz)

Fig. 135. Two modern musical comedy performers at the theater, the twins Alice and Ellen Kessler who sang and danced . . . (Staatstheater am Gärtnerplatz)

Fig. 136. . . . Anna I and Anna II in the Brecht/Weill dance satire *Die sieben Todsünden der Kleinbürger,* which was directed and choreographed by William Milié, designed by Hans Ulrich Schmückle, and costumed by Sylta Busse (Staatstheater am Gärtnerplatz/ Hildegard Steinmetz)

Fig. 137. Tamara Lund shows the colors in *Hallo Dolly!* by Michael Stewart and Jerry Herman, directed by Kurt Pscherer, designed by Werner Juhrke, and choreographed by William Milié (Hildegard Steinmetz)

Fig. 138. Anny Schlemm watches Olive Moorefield perform for the trappers in a production of the Brecht/Weill operetta *Aufstieg und Fall der Stadt Mahagonny*, directed by Harry Buckwitz (Hildegard Steinmetz)

Fig. 139. Cole Porter's *Kiss Me, Kate!* directed by Kurt Pscherer, designed by Wolfram Skalicki, and costumed by Ronny Reiter. Tamara Lund as Kate and Barry Hanner as Petruchio (Hildegard Steinmetz)

Bayerisches Staatsschauspiel

The modern inheritor of the traditions established in the 18th century by the Cuvilliéstheater, or Altes Residenztheater as it is now often called, is the Bayerisches Staatsschauspiel, or Neues Residenztheater, which has been built on the site once occupied by the older building. When it was determined that a new theater for spoken drama was needed, the Cuvilliéstheater was rebuilt and restored with the original decorations (which had been preserved during the bombing raids of World War II) on a site about 30 meters to the north; and the Neues Residenztheater was built on the site next to the Nationaltheater. Today both the opera company and the spoken drama company use the Cuvilliéstheater for various kinds of productions, such as plays by Molière or Goldoni and operas by Paisiello or Mozart.

The Staatsschauspiel also uses another small theater, the free-form Theater im Marstall, which is located nearby in quarters formerly assigned to the King's horses and carriages. The seating varies depending on the relationship desired between audience and actors. These relationships can be altered from complete arena staging to many kinds of thrust staging. Capacity is 170 seats.

Technical aspects of the Bayerisches Staatsschauspiel are as follows:

Seating capacity: 1,039 seats.
Architect: Karl Hocheder.
Theater consultant: Adolf Linnebach.
Opened: January 28, 1951, with Ferdinand Raimund's *Der Verschwender*.
Proscenium size: 8 meters to 13 meters wide by 4.5 meters to 8 meters high.
Stage size: 18 meters wide by 20 meters deep.
Technical equipment: Two Rundhorizonte, a 16-meter turntable, and platform tormentors with scene projection apparatus and follow spot equipment.
Orchestra pit: 16 meters wide by 3 meters deep for 50 musicians.

The Staatsintendant of the Bayerisches Staatsschauspiel is Kurt Meisel. During 1976–77 the company numbered as follows:

Artistic direction	18
Actors and actresses	48
Technical personnel	201
Administrative personnel	19
House personnel	49
Total	335

During the same season the company offered the following numbers of performances of adult plays in its three theaters:

	PERFORMANCES	ATTENDANCE	PERCENT OF CAPACITY
Residenztheater	288	265,010	88.6%
Cuviliéstheater	94	42,087	85.6%
Marstalltheater	56	8,303	88.3%
Totals	438	315,400	87.5%

During 1977–78 the company offered the following productions:

Ayckbourn: *Normans Eroberungen*
Strindberg: *Traumspiel*
Sternheim: *Tabula Rasa*
Goethe: *Faust I*
Brecht: *Mann ist Mann*
Labiche: *Herr Perrichon auf Reisen*
Aischylos: *Agamemnon*
Schnitzler: *Liebelei*
Horváth: *Geschichten aus dem Wienerwald*
Shakespeare: *Richard II*
Valentin: *Das Leben ist wie eine Lawine—einmal rauf und einmal runter*
Tschechow: *Drei Schwestern*

Figs. 140 and 141, pp. 215–216, show ticket prices for 1978–79 and a financial summary for 1969–77.

Scenes from recent productions at the Staatsschauspiel are shown in Figs. 142–152, pp. 217–231.

Münchner Kammerspiele

One of the best-known theaters in Germany devoted to productions of the spoken drama, to experiment, to new ideas and new theater techniques is the Munich Kammerspiele, a few blocks down Maximilianstrasse from the Nationaltheater and the Staatsschauspiel on Max-Joseph-Platz. In 1922 the theater's Intendanz invited the promising young Augsburger Bertolt Brecht to join the staff as a Dramaturg and soon produced two of his earliest plays, *Trommeln in der Nacht* (September 30, 1922) under the direction of Otto Falckenberg, and *Leben Edwards des Zweiten von England* (March 18, 1924) with Brecht himself directing and scenery by Casper Neher.

Over the years since then, the theater has mounted the work of many new playwrights, directed and designed by well-established artists of the German theater. Two plays of Friedrich Dürrenmatt were first performed at the Munich Kammerspiele—*Die Ehe des Herrn Mississippi* in 1952 and *Ein Engel kommt nach Babylon* in 1953. Other world premieres staged in this theater have been Martin Walser's *Der Abstecher* (1961), Heiner Kipphardt's *Der Hund des Generals* (1962) and his *Joel Brand* (1965), Ödön von Horváth's *Geschichten aus dem Wienerwald* (1966), Martin Sperr's *Landshuter Erzählungen* (1967), Walser's *Die Zimmerschlacht* (1967), the first German

Platz kategorien	Eintritts-preis (S)	Eintritts-preis (H)	Eintritts-preis (G)	Eintritts-preis (A)	Abonne-ments-preis	8 Vorstellungen einschließlich Heftgebühr 2,– DM	8 Premieren einschließlich Heftgebühr 2,– DM
Parkett							
Reihe 1 bis 7	34,—	30,—	26,—	23,—	18,50	150,—	210,—
Reihe 8 bis 13	30,—	26,—	23,—	20,—	16,—	130,—	186,—
Reihe 14 bis 18	26,—	22,—	20,—	17,—	13,50	110,—	162,—
Reihe 19 bis 21	22,—	19,—	17,—	14,—	11,50	94.—	138,—
Balkon							
Reihe 1	30,—	26,—	23,—	20,—	16,—	130,—	186,—
Reihe 2 und 3	26,—	22,—	20,—	17,—	13,50	110,—	162,—
Reihe 4 und 5	22,—	19,—	17,—	14,—	11,50	94,—	138,—
Rang							
Reihe 1 und 2	19,—	16,—	14,—	12,—	9,50	78,—	114,—
Reihe 3 und 4	16,—	14,—	12,—	10,—	7,50	62,—	98,—

Bei allen Fragen zum Abonnement wenden Sie sich bitte an den Abonnement-Schalter des Bayerischen Staatsschau-spiels, Schalter 4, Residenztheater, Max-Joseph-Platz. Unsere Mitarbeiter sind gern bereit, Sie zu beraten: montags bis freitags von 10 bis 13 Uhr und von 16 bis 18 Uhr. Telefon 2 18 54 16.
Wenn Ihre Einzahlung auf unser Konto nicht rechtzeitig erfolgen konnte, bitten wir Sie, Ihre Abonnementhefte gegen Barzahlung abzuholen.

Serie rot:	2. Mai – 11. Mai
Serie grün:	14. Mai – 23. Mai
Serie gelb:	25. Mai – 6. Juni
Serie blau:	7. Juni – 19. Juni
Premierenabonnement:	2. Mai – 19. Juni

In den oben angeführten Preisen sind 1,20 DM Sonderabgaben enthalten. Nach dem Beschluß des Bayerischen Landtags wird auf jede Karte eine Abgabe von 1,— DM für die nichtstaat-lichen Theater Bayerns erhoben. Altersversorgungsabgabe für Bühnenschaffende 0,20 DM.

Fig. 140. Ticket prices at the Bayerisches Staatsschauspiel during the 1978–79 season. Subscriptions are for eight regular performances or eight premieres (Bayerisches Staats-schauspiel)

YEAR	1969	1970	1971	1972	1973	1974	1975	1976	1977
VALUE OF DEUTSCHE MARK	28¢	29¢	30¢	34¢	40¢	42¢	44¢	48¢	50¢
EXPENSES									
Artists' salaries	DM 2,691,000	DM 2,783,000	DM 3,120,000	DM 4,381,000	DM 4,113,000	DM 4,805,000	DM 5,099,000	DM 5,791,000	DM 6,898,000
Technical salaries	2,634,000	3,458,000	4,144,000	4,792,000	5,770,000	6,516,000	7,073,000	7,615,000	7,688,000
Administration	885,000	1,084,000	1,257,000	1,453,000	1,621,000	1,833,000	2,086,000	1,894,000	2,164,000
Other personnel	94,000	58,000	85,000	106,000	89,000	53,000	85,000	56,000	46,000
Pension funds	---	---	---	---	---	31,000	---	28,000	35,000
Production costs	1,652,000	1,583,000	2,071,000	2,113,000	2,299,000	2,580,000	2,989,000	3,186,000	3,681,000
Loan payments	---	---	---	---	---	---	22,000	---	---
Building maintenance	---	---	---	---	---	---	---	---	---
TOTAL	DM 7,956,000	DM 8,966,000	DM 10,677,000	DM 12,845,000	DM 13,892,000	DM 15,818,000	DM 17,354,000	DM 18,570,000	DM 20,512,000
INCOME									
Single tickets	DM 620,000	DM 568,000	DM 642,000	DM 904,000	DM 893,000	DM 1,101,000	DM 1,691,000	DM 1,808,000	DM 2,164,000
Subscriptions	435,000	501,000	404,000	364,000	524,000	504,000	592,000	540,000	700,000
Children's theater subscriptions	191,000	180,000	180,000	213,000	141,000	153,000	---	---	---
Visitor groups	335,000	338,000	359,000	353,000	404,000	428,000	525,000	547,000	605,000
Cloakroom charges	80,000	83,000	73,000	88,000	127,000	124,000	142,000	155,000	169,000
Radio and TV fees	17,000	---	134,000	---	149,000	384,000	274,000	312,000	485,000
Touring	511,000	67,000	177,000	392,000	332,000	464,000	439,000	582,000	633,000
Guest performances by other companies	---	18,000	---	40,000	131,000	---	3,000	53,000	18,000
Program sales	79,000	81,000	75,000	84,000	101,000	124,000	133,000	158,000	173,000
Other income	49,000	46,000	56,000	100,000	59,000	49,000	82,000	90,000	136,000
TOTAL	DM 2,317,000	DM 1,882,000	DM 2,100,000	DM 2,538,000	DM 2,861,000	DM 3,331,000	DM 3,881,000	DM 4,245,000	DM 5,083,000
TAX SUBSIDY	DM 5,639,000	DM 7,084,000	DM 8,577,000	DM 10,307,000	DM 11,031,000	DM 12,487,000	DM 13,473,000	DM 14,325,000	DM 15,429,000
SUBSIDY PERCENTAGE	70.9%	79.0%	80.3%	80.2%	79.4%	78.9%	77.6%	77.1%	75.2%

Fig. 141. Expenses and income for the Bayerisches Staatsschauspiel, 1969–77 (Deutscher Bühnenverein, Köln)

Fig. 142. Three scenes from Alan Ayckbourn's comedy *Normans Eroberungen.* Reg (Hans Jürgen Diedrich) works on his new game while Ruth (Kathrin Ackermann) and her sister Annie (Rita Russek) talk about Norman . . . (Bayerisches Staatsschauspiel/Jean-Marie Bottequin)

Fig. 143. . . . Norman (Peter Fricke) comes in from the kitchen for an embrace with
Annie . . . (Bayerisches Staatsschauspiel/Jean-Marie Bottequin)

Fig. 144. . . . Tom (Hans Stetter) tries to understand something Annie is explaining to him (Bayerisches Staatsschauspiel/Jean-Marie Bottequin)

Fig. 145. Marianne (Anne-Marie Kuster) accuses Alfred (Hans Brenner) of insincerity in Ödön von Horváth's image of Viennese life in the 1930's *Geschichten aus dem Wienerwald* (Bayerisches Staatsschauspiel/Jean-Marie Bottequin)

Fig. 146. Anouilh's bittersweet *Das Orchester,* directed by Hans Lietzau and designed by Jürgen Rose, with music for the orchestra composed by Mark Lothar. The orchestra assembled for the photographers . . . (Bayerisches Staatsschauspiel/Rudolf Betz)

Fig. 147. . . . Pamela Suchard (Carla Hagen), first violin and principal singer . . . (Bayerisches Staatsschauspiel/Rudolf Betz)

Fig. 148. . . . Léona Dellaud (Barbara Nüsse), clarinet . . . (Bayerisches Staatsschauspiel/ Rudolf Betz)

VII. MUNICH, GERMANY • 223

Fig. 149. . . . Madame Hortense (Marianne Hoppe), conductor and double bass . . . (Bayerisches Staatsschauspiel/Rudolf Betz)

Fig. 150. . . . Monsieur Léon (Herbert Mensching), pianoforte . . . (Bayerisches Staats-schauspiel/Rudolf Betz)

Fig. 151. . . . Ermeline Marivelle (Gaby Dohm), viola . . . (Bayerisches Staatsschauspiel/ Rudolf Betz)

Fig. 152. . . . and Susanne Délicias (Gustl Halenke), violoncello (Bayerisches Staatsschauspiel/Rudolf Betz)

VII. MUNICH, GERMANY • 231

production of Edward Bond's *Gerettet,* directed by Peter Stein (1967), Heiner Mueller's *Halbdeutsch* (1970), Franz Xaver Kroetz's *Heimarbeit* (1971), and Rolf Hochhuth's *Die Hebamme* (1972).

Technical aspects of the theater building are as follows:

Seating capacity: 730 seats.

Opened: April 19, 1901, with Sudermann's *Johannes,* under the management of Stollberg-Schmederer.

Architect: Richard Riemerschmid. Remodeled in 1970 in Jugendstil.

Proscenium opening: 8.4 meters wide by 5 meters high.

Stage size: 16 meters wide by 12 meters deep.

Technical equipment: Rundhorizont, wagon stages, and decked tormentors with scene projection apparatus.

Orchestra pit: Large enough for 18 musicians.

The company also operates a Werkraumtheater on Herrnstrasse and a Theater der Jugend on Reitmorstrasse.

The principal Besucherorganisationen that support the Kammerspiele are the Freie Volksbühne with 1,000 members, the Theatergemeinde with 50,000 members, and the Volksbühne with 20,000 members. The company tours to Bregenz, Erlangen, Freising, Garmisch-Partenkirchen, Kempten, Landshut, Lindau, Schweinfurt, and elsewhere.

The Intendant of the Münchner Kammerspiele is Hans-Reinhard Müller. During the Spielzeit 1976–77 the company numbered as follows:

Artistic direction	33
Actors and actresses	52
Technical personnel	143
Administrative personnel	27
House personnel	50
Total	305

During the same season, the company offered performances of adult and children's plays as follows:

	PERFORMANCES	ATTENDANCE	PERCENT OF CAPACITY
Kammerspiele	321	198,537	84.7%
Werkraumtheater	104	13,686	44.0%
Theater der Jugend	55	13,083	47.5%
Totals	480	225,306	58.7%

The total attendance at the four public theaters in Munich during 1976–77 was thus 1,376,441, or 104.7 percent of the city's population.

During 1977–78 the following works were performed by the Münchner Kammerspiele:

Schauspielhaus

Fleisser: *Fegefeuer in Ingolstadt*
Hochhuth: *Tod eines Jägers*
Wedekind: *Erdgeist*
             Die Büchse der Pandora
Sophokles/Müller: *Ödipus*
Hacks: *Ein Gespräch im Haus Stein über den abwesenden Herrn von Goethe*
Tschechow: *Die Möwe*
Müller: *Germania Tod in Berlin* (world premiere)
Coburn: *Gin-Romme* (first German production)

Werkraumtheater

Widmer: *Nepal*
Ionesco: *Der Mann mit den Koffern* (first German production)
             Es geht alles vorüber
             Schlager und Dokumente aus den Goldenen
             Vierzigern. Beiprogramm zu *Germania Tod in Berlin*
Brasch: *Lovely Rita*
             Kabarett im Werkraum

Ticket prices and the main theater's seating plan are shown in Fig. 153, p. 234.
Fig. 154, p. 235, shows a nine-year financial summary for the theater follows:
Scenes from recent productions at the Kammerspiele are shown in Figs. 155–167, pp. 236–248.

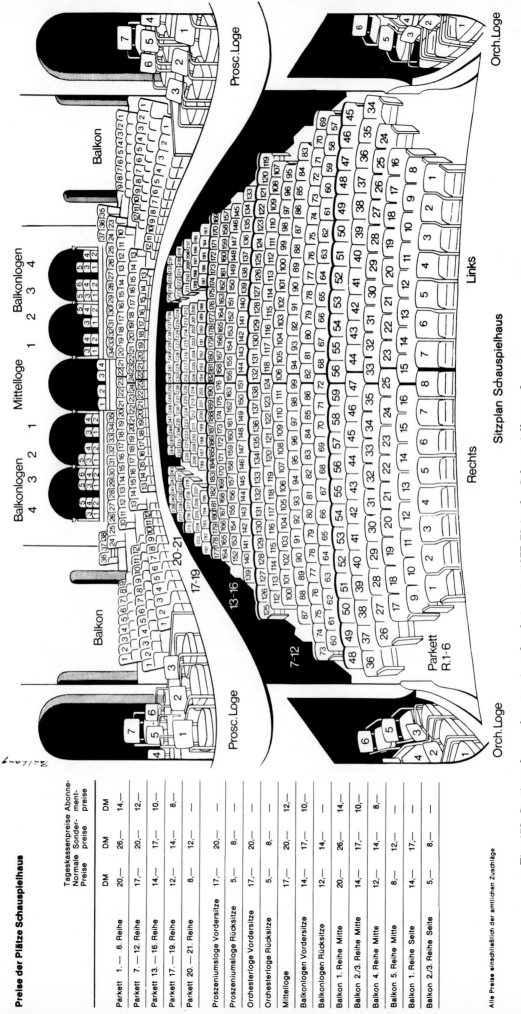

Preise der Plätze Schauspielhaus

	Tageskassenpreise		Abonne- ment- preise
	Normale Preise	Sonder- preise	
	DM	DM	DM
Parkett 1.— 6. Reihe	20,—	26,—	14,—
Parkett 7.—12. Reihe	17,—	20,—	12,—
Parkett 13.—16. Reihe	14,—	17,—	10,—
Parkett 17.—19. Reihe	12,—	14,—	8,—
Parkett 20.—21. Reihe	8,—	12,—	—
Proszeniumsloge Vordersitze	17,—	20,—	—
Proszeniumsloge Rücksitze	5,—	8,—	—
Orchesterloge Vordersitze	17,—	20,—	—
Orchesterloge Rücksitze	5,—	8,—	—
Mittelloge	17,—	20,—	12,—
Balkonlogen Vordersitze	14,—	17,—	10,—
Balkonlogen Rücksitze	12,—	14,—	—
Balkon 1. Reihe Mitte	20,—	26,—	14,—
Balkon 2./3. Reihe Mitte	14,—	17,—	10,—
Balkon 4. Reihe Mitte	12,—	14,—	8,—
Balkon 5. Reihe Mitte	8,—	12,—	—
Balkon 1. Reihe Seite	14,—	17,—	—
Balkon 2./3. Reihe Seite	5,—	8,—	—

Alle Preise einschließlich der amtlichen Zuschläge

Fig. 153. Seating plan and seat prices for the season 1977–78 in the Schauspielhaus of the Münchner Kammerspiel (Münchner Kammerspiel)

YEAR	1969	1970	1971	1972	1973	1974	1975	1976	1977
VALUE OF DEUTSCHE MARK	28¢	29¢	30¢	34¢	40¢	42¢	44¢	48¢	50¢
EXPENSES									
Artists' salaries	DM 2,719,000	DM 2,668,000	DM 2,949,000	DM 3,467,000	DM 4,052,000	DM 4,614,000	DM 4,861,000	DM 5,323,000	DM 5,818,000
Technical salaries	2,086,000	2,328,000	2,639,000	3,230,000	4,866,000	3,787,000	4,110,000	4,595,000	4,319,000
Administration	695,000	880,000	1,000,000	1,110,000	54,000	1,804,000	2,083,000	1,831,000	2,690,000
Other personnel	59,000	65,000	63,000	79,000	34,000	39,000	42,000	46,000	51,000
Pension funds	215,000	573,000	392,000	349,000	385,000	413,000	492,000	657,000	586,000
Production costs	1,385,000	1,393,000	1,477,000	2,130,000	1,850,000	2,099,000	2,386,000	2,426,000	3,286,000
Loan payments	218,000	362,000	110,000	112,000	111,000	63,000	2,188,000	1,022,000	92,000
Building maintenance	108,000	12,000	1,865,000	1,323,000	587,000	---	700,000	188,000	(+)168,000
TOTAL	DM 7,485,000	DM 8,281,000	DM 10,495,000	DM 11,800,000	DM 11,939,000	DM 12,819,000	DM 16,862,000	DM 16,088,000	DM 16,674,000
INCOME									
Single tickets	DM 932,000	DM 692,000	DM 541,000	DM 865,000	DM 745,000	DM 960,000	DM 1,094,000	DM 1,173,000	DM 1,256,000
Subscriptions	384,000	231,000	160,000	280,000	364,000	307,000	335,000	335,000	313,000
Children's theater subscriptions	85,000	68,000	75,000	156,000	156,000	165,000	---	---	---
Visitor groups	259,000	165,000	112,000	217,000	250,000	229,000	281,000	364,000	362,000
Cloakroom charges	79,000	60,000	45,000	62,000	68,000	65,000	61,000	99,000	89,000
Radio and TV fees	150,000	31,000	261,000	17,000	185,000	1,000	157,000	2,000	220,000
Touring	142,000	56,000	142,000	77,000	21,000	107,000	176,000	173,000	128,000
Guest performances by other companies	---	---	---	---	---	---	---	---	---
Program sales	60,000	43,000	33,000	55,000	64,000	60,000	59,000	67,000	91,000
Other income	195,000	214,000	144,000	160,000	127,000	131,000	138,000	180,000	165,000
TOTAL	DM 2,286,000	DM 1,560,000	DM 1,513,000	DM 1,889,000	DM 1,980,000	DM 2,021,000	DM 2,301,000	DM 2,391,000	DM 2,624,000
TAX SUBSIDY	DM 5,199,000	DM 6,721,000	DM 8,982,000	DM 9,911,000	DM 9,959,000	DM 10,798,000	DM 14,561,000	DM 13,697,000	DM 14,050,000
SUBSIDY PERCENTAGE	69.5%	81.2%	85.6%	84.0%	83.4%	84.2%	86.4%	85.1%	84.3%

Fig. 154. Expenses and income for the Münchner Kammerspiel, 1969–77 (Deutscher Bühnenverein, Köln)

Fig. 155. Clifford Odets' prizefight play *Golden Boy,* in a revival directed by Harald Clemen and designed by Jörg Zimmermann. Joe Bonaparte (Manfred Zapatka) prepares for a fight while his trainer (Wolfried Lier) and his manager, Tom Moody (Bruno Dallansky), give him advice . . . (Hildegard Steinmetz)

Fig. 156. . . . Joe talks to his manager's girlfriend, Lorna (Barbara Petritsch), about his love for fast cars (Hildegard Steinmetz)

Fig. 157. An unconventional conception of Shakespeare's *Ein Mittsommernachtstraum* in a new translation by Michael Wachsmann and Dieter Dorn, directed by Dorn and designed and costumed by Jürgen Rose. Accompanied by the elves of the forest, Titania (Elisabeth Schwarz) trifles with Oberon (Claus Eberth) (Hildegard Steinmetz)

Fig. 158. Lessing's *Minna von Barnhelm,* directed by Dieter Dorn and designed by Jürgen Rose. Minna (Cornelia Froboess) thinks over the predicament of Major von Tellheim (Helmut Griem) (Hildegard Steinmetz)

Fig. 159. Scenes from Genet's *Der Balkon,* directed by Ernst Wendt with scenery and costumes by Johannes Schütz, a production that aroused the ire of the Catholic establishment in Munich. The Judge (Rudolf Wessely) confronts Carmen (Regina Lemnitz) in the bordello . . . (Hildegard Steinmetz)

Fig. 160. . . . Madam Irma (Agnes Fink) and her girls engage the Chief of Police (Romuald Pekny) in a nocturnal ceremony . . . (Hildegard Steinmetz)

Fig. 161. . . . The Bishop (Lambert Hamel), the Queen—Madam Irma—the General (Helmut Stange), and the Chief of Police step out onto the grand balcony to face the people . . . (Hildegard Steinmetz)

Fig. 162. . . . The Judge, the General, and the Bishop contemplate the effects of the revolution (Hildegard Steinmetz)

Fig. 163. Scenes from *Frühlings Erwachen* by Frank Wedekind, whose work has long been associated with the Münchner Kammerspiele. Frau Bergmann (Grete Wurm) is unable to tell her daughter Wendla (Lisi Mangold) the facts of life . . . (Hildegard Steinmetz)

Fig. 164. . . . Melchior Gabor (Bernd Herberger) meets Wendla in an abstract hayloft
. . . (Hildegard Steinmetz)

Fig. 165. . . . Moritz Stiefel (Felix von Manteuffel) thinks over his situation at the Realgym-
nasium . . . (Hildegard Steinmetz)

Fig. 166. . . . Moritz offers Melchior his head in the graveyard scene . . . (Hildegard Steinmetz)

VII. MUNICH, GERMANY • 247

Fig. 167. . . . but a masked man (Romuald Pekny) convinces Melchior that life is better than death. The production was directed by Ernst Wendt and designed by Hans Kleber (Hildegard Steinmetz)

VIII. VIENNA, AUSTRIA

Burgtheater

The village of Vindobona on the Danube was settled by Celtic and Veneto-Illyrian fishermen before the birth of Christ. At the end of the 1st century A.D. the Romans established a fort near the village, which they maintained until the end of the 5th century when they were forced to abandon the outer reaches of their empire. The Babenberg family established its residence in what had become known as Vienna in 1141, and the oldest municipal deed extant dates from 1221. Eventually, Vienna became the Imperial Residence of the Hapsburgs, the hub of a huge empire. During the Baroque era particularly, it flourished—materially, artistically, and intellectually.

In 1741 the Empress Maria Theresa founded a court theater called the Theater nächst der Burg, or Burgtheater, for short. It was situated on the present-day Michaelerplatz, just north of the Hofburg, the collection of government buildings from which the Hapsburgs ruled the Holy Roman Empire of the German Nation. The theater was used at first exclusively for court entertainments, but in 1776, under the influence of ideas published by Lessing in his *Hamburgische Dramaturgie,* the Emperor Joseph II reorganized it into a national theater with a tax subsidy, which made available to the citizenry productions in all three performance media—drama, opera, and ballet. Three of Mozart's operas received their first performances at the Burgtheater, and for a time it housed both a German and an Italian singing ensemble. Later, in 1810, opera and ballet productions were moved to the Kärntnertortheater.

The older building was torn down in the middle of the 19th century to make way for some additions to the Hofburg, and a new structure was erected between 1884 and 1888 on Dr. Karl Lueger-Ring, across from the new Rathaus. In 1922 the Burgtheater acquired a second theater for its productions, the Akademietheater, on Lisztstrasse.

The policy of the Burgtheater has always included at least three objectives. The first, based on Lessing's vision, is to offer a very broad repertory of plays from all languages and literatures and from all periods of the history of the theater. There are busts of nine famous playwrights on the upper facade of the building: Calderon, Shakespeare, Molière, Lessing, Goethe, Schiller, Hebbel, Grillparzer, and Friedrich Halms, a group symbolic of the international character of the theater's repertory.

The second goal of the theater was enunciated by the Emperor himself: the company was established for the "propagation of good taste and the refinement of good manners." The status of the acting profession was vastly improved, and the theater became known throughout the Empire for setting standards of excellence in the speaking of German.

Finally, the ideals of ensemble acting were established and firmly adhered to no matter how luminous a star performer might have become. No role is too small to be accepted and played well, even by leading actors, and the custom of the curtain call, which can lead to claques and personal rivalries among the performers, has always been forbidden.

Technical aspects of the Burgtheater and the Akademietheater are as follows:

Burgtheater

Seating capacity: 1,310 seats and room for 210 standees.
Architect: Karl Freiherr von Hasenauer, who developed a design by Gottfried Semper.
Opened: October 14, 1888, with a "Scenic Prologue" by Josef Weilen, *Esther* by Franz Grillparzer, and Schiller's *Wallensteins Lager.*
Reopened after World War II: October 15, 1955, with Grillparzer's *König Ottokars Glück und Ende,* under the direction of Adolf Rott.
Proscenium size: 12 meters wide by 14 meters high.
Stage size: 30.5 meters wide by 25 meters deep.
Rear stage size: 12 meters wide by 9 meters deep.
Technical equipment: Large revolving stage with four stage lifts inside on which scenery can be raised and lowered. This Drehzylinderbühne is 21 meters in diameter and 14.4 meters high. There is also a set of wagon stages that fit the revolve lifts, multidecked lighting bridge, large projection machines, and a Rundhorizont 25 meters high and 60 meters long. The lighting console controls 192 dimmers (Siemens).
Orchestra pit: 12 meters wide by 4 meters deep for 45 musicians.

Akademietheater

Seating capacity: 486 seats and space for 26 standees.
Architects: Fellner and Hellmer, and Ludwig Baumann.
Opened: September 8, 1922, with Goethe's *Iphigenie auf Tauris* under the direction of Max Paulsen.
Reopened after World War II: May 19, 1945, with Ibsen's *Hedda Gabler,* directed by Raoul Aslan.
Proscenium size: 11.4 meters wide by 6.7 meters high, maximum. Proscenium height is adjustable.
Stage size: 15 meters wide by 9.6 meters deep.
Orchestra pit: 12 meters wide by 3 meters deep for 36 musicians.

Fig. 168. The Wiener Burgtheater after it was reopened in 1955. At the top of the facade
is the figure of Apollo between the Muse of Tragedy (Melpomene) and the Muse of Comedy
(Thalia) (Waagner-Biró, A. G., Vienna)

Fig. 169. The auditorium of the Burgtheater. Lighting ports can be seen toward the rear of the ceiling (Waagner-Biró, A. G., Vienna)

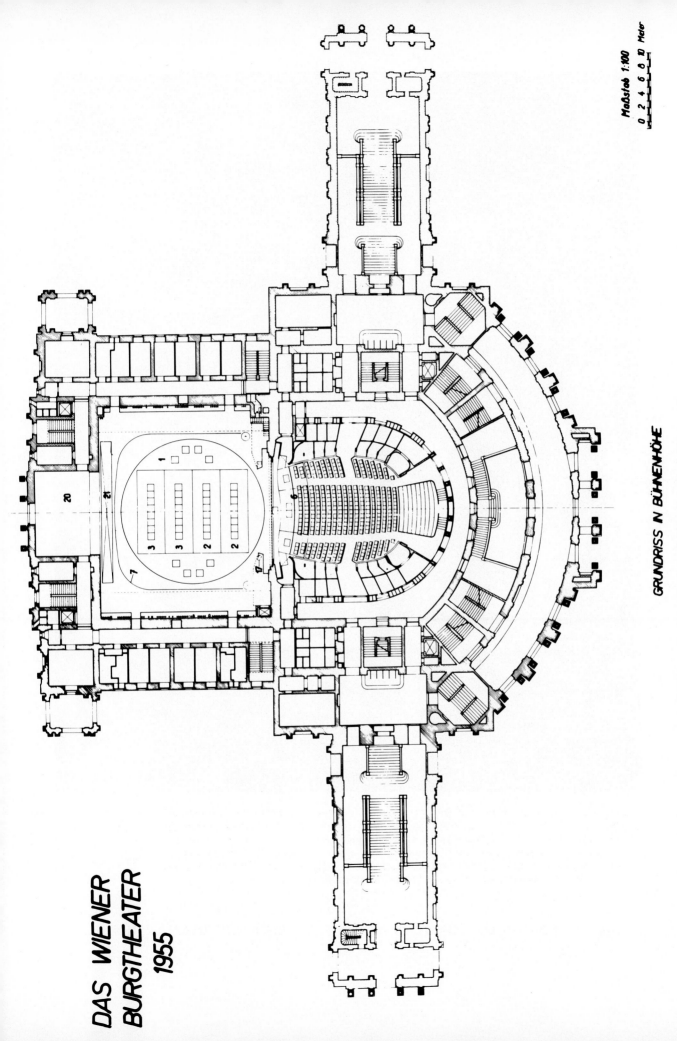

DAS WIENER
BURGTHEATER
1955

GRUNDRISS IN BÜHNENHÖHE

Maßstab 1:100
0 2 4 6 8 10 Meter

Fig. 170. Ground plan of the Burgtheater showing the front lobby, the side lobbies and
staircases, the auditorium, and the stage area (Waagner-Biró, A. G., Vienna)

Fig. 171. The Drehzylinderbühne (model) installed in the main stage of the Burgtheater. The unit consists of four stage lifts that move up and down within a huge revolving unit. Since there is little offstage space at stage level, scenery can be shifted by means of wagons below stage. The main control room is at the bottom of the unit as shown, but there is also a signal repeater station on the main stage level from which cues can be relayed to the operators below (Waagner-Biró, A. G., Vienna)

Fig. 172. The main lighting bridge over the stage of the Burgtheater. Large fluorescent units and a cloud machine center are used to light the cyclorama. Platforms built into the movable tormentors are used by operators of hand follow spots. The lighting layout and the Drehzylinderbühne were planned by the theater's technical director, Sepp Nordegg (Waagner-Biró, A. G., Vienna)

Fig. 173. The interior of the Akademietheater. The gardens at Schönbrunn are painted
on the Eiserner Vorhang (Bundestheaterverband, Vienna)

Staatsoper Wien

The inadequacies of the Kärntnertortheater prompted the Emperor Franz Joseph to agree to the building of a new opera house in the 1850's. It was to be one of the leading buildings on a series of streets forming a ring that started at the Danube Canal to the west, ran to the Schottenring, then turned south and east, past Kärntner Strasse to the Schubertring, then north past the Stadtpark to the Canal again. The new house would occupy a site approximately in the center of these Ring streets, on Opernring.

The theater soon became world famous as one of the great opera houses of Europe. Bizet's *Carmen* achieved the success here that was denied it by the Parisian critics, and under the direction of Gustav Mahler the ensemble presented exemplary productions of the major operas of Wagner, Mozart, Beethoven, Verdi, Weber, and Puccini. During World War II the theater was badly damaged in a bombing raid, and it took ten years, from 1945 to 1955, to rebuild it. The scenery, costume, and property shops had been in the basement under the stage and the auditorium; by moving all scene construction and painting operations to a central Dekorationswerkstatt near the Armory, valuable space was made available for rehearsal rooms, a company cafeteria, and even air-conditioning equipment. Costume storage was moved to a building across the street and a tunnel dug under the street to connect it with the backstage areas. Technical aspects of the rebuilt Staatsoper are as follows:

Seating capacity: 1,642 seats and space for 567 standees.

Architects: Eduard van der Nüll and August Siccard von Siccardsburg.

Opened: May 25, 1869, with Mozart's *Don Giovanni.*

Reopened after World War II: November 5, 1955, with Beethoven's *Fidelio,* conducted by Karl Böhm.

Proscenium size: 13 meters wide by 12 meters high.

Stage size: 27.5 meters wide by 22.5 meters deep.

Rear stage size: 19.5 meters wide by 21 meters deep.

Side stage: 20 meters by 10.5 meters.

Technical equipment: Rundhorizont, large portable turntable that can be flown when not needed, wagon stages, multideck bridge and tormentors with lighting platforms, 10 KW projection machines, and a lighting console with control over 270 dimmers (Siemens-Bordoni).

Orchestra pit: 16 meters average width by 7 meters deep for 105 musicians.

Fig. 174. The Staatsoper Wien on the Opernring. Beyond, the Stephansdom (Maschinenfabrik Wiesbaden, G.m.b.H.)

Fig. 175. The auditorium of the rebuilt Staatsoper. The motif of Orpheus and Euridice was painted on the Eiserner Vorhang by Rudi Eisenmenger (Bundestheaterverband, Vienna)

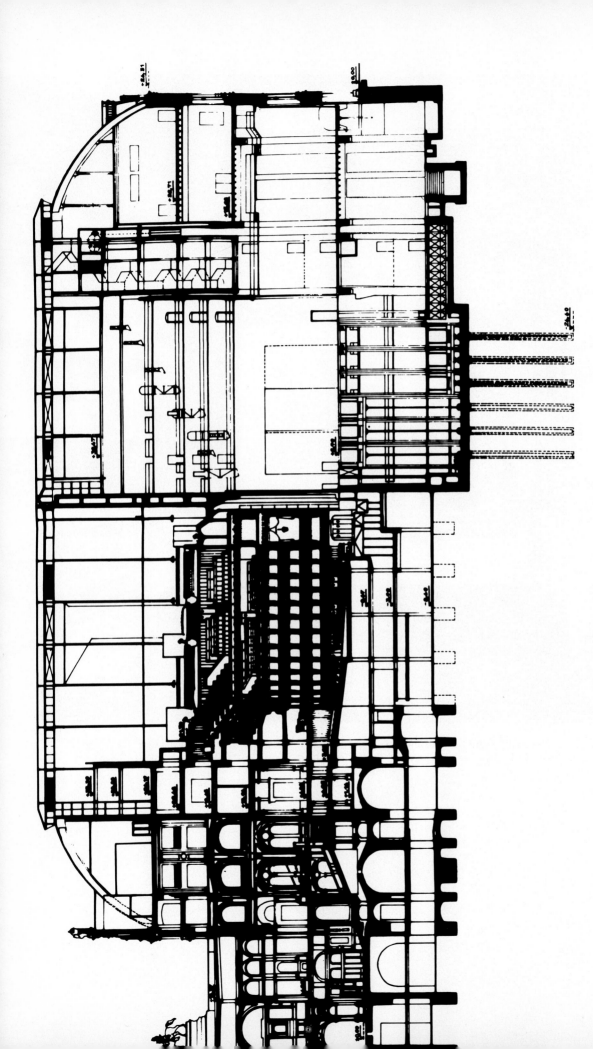

Fig. 176. Cross section through the Staatsoper Wien. The six stage lifts can be raised 2.5 meters above stage level and sunk to 11.13 meters below. They are used to alter elevations on stage and to shift scenery (Maschinenfabrik Wiesbaden, G.m.b.H.)

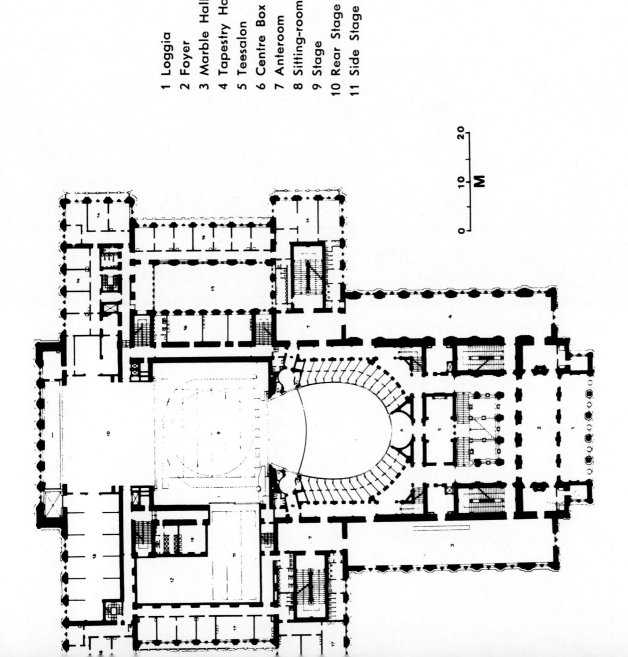

1 Loggia
2 Foyer
3 Marble Hall
4 Tapestry Hall
5 Teesalon
6 Centre Box
7 Anteroom
8 Sitting-room
9 Stage
10 Rear Stage
11 Side Stage

12 Workshops
13 Scenery storage
14 Directors' and stage inspec-
tors' offices
15 Courtyard
16 Chorus dressing rooms (men)
17 Chorus dressing rooms
(women)
18 Building administration
19 Juvenile ballet dressing rooms

Fig. 177. Plan at stage level of the Staatsoper Wien. A full stage wagon can slide from the rear stage to the main stage. The turntable can be flown out when not in use. The six stage lifts are 3 meters by 18 meters each (Maschinenfabrik Wiesbaden, G.m.b.H.)

Fig. 178. The turntable in position for use on the stage. It is 17.6 meters in diameter and weighs 40 metric tons (Maschinenfabrik Wiesbaden, G.m.b.H.)

Fig. 179. The turntable being lifted up into the stage house for storage (Maschinenfabrik Wiesbaden, G.m.b.H.)

Volksoper Wien

The Volksoper, or "People's Opera," was established in Vienna in 1898 by private subscription and was called originally the Kaiser Jubiläums Stadttheater in honor of 50 years of rule by the Emperor Franz Joseph. It was designed by Franz Freiherr von Kraus and Alexander Graf and opened on December 14, 1898, with a patriotic play by Heinrich von Kleist, *Die Hermannsschlacht.* Today the theater seats 1,472 with room for 114 standees.

The theater was intended from the beginning as a place where the people could see plays and operas at modest prices. It was built on a site that made it easily accessible from the suburbs, on Währinger Strasse where it intersects the Gürtel. There Felix Weingartner directed operas and operettas for many years, and one of the principal play directors was Otto Preminger. Maria Jeritza got her start at this theater, as did the Vienna career of the sensational opera *Salome* by Richard Strauss, a piece considered too decadent for the Hofoper.

By 1928 the theater had got into financial difficulties as it had no tax subsidy to help support its operations. It closed and opened again several times, and it was reduced to running cabaret shows when the federal government took it over in 1938 and provided a satisfactory subsidy. It was renamed the Volksoper and after 1946 became part of the Bundestheaterverband, the Federal Theater Association. Today it offers operas that are not generally done at the Staatsoper, together with a large variety of operettas, musical comedies, and musical plays. American musicals are especially popular in translations by Marcel Prawy, a durable hit being Leonard Bernstein's *West Side Story.*

In addition to the four theaters, the Österreichischer Bundestheaterverband occupies an administration building in Goethegasse just across from the Staatsoper, and also administers the Zentrale Dekorationswerkstätten near the Armory, across Prinz Eugen-Strasse from the South Railway Station. These scene shops are used to build and paint all scenery and properties for the four theaters. There is also space to store scenery and props for dozens of opera and drama productions that may be kept in the repertories of the theaters for years. The truck parking and maintenance areas are also located here.

The two-story administration building houses a large number of offices as well as a central ticket bureau where tickets for performances at all four theaters are placed on sale ten days in advance. There is also a subscription office, press and advertising offices, quarters for the artistic and administrative leadership, business and statistics offices, the departments of transportation and building maintenance, a ballet school, and other units of an organization with over 2,500 employees and an annual budget in excess of $85 million.

Of special interest to the theater historian is the large theater museum, opened in 1975, which offers displays of programs, photographs, paintings, scene and costume sketches, and other memorabilia drawn from the huge theater collection of the Austrian National Library. There is even a scale model of the old Burgtheater, with its 18th-century stage machinery in good working order.

Fig. 180. The Volksoper, at the intersection of Währinger Strasse and the Gürtel (Bundestheaterverband, Vienna)

The Direktors of the Burgtheater, the Staatsoper, and the Volksoper are, respectively, Achim Benning, Egon Seefehlner, and Karl Dönch. The Generalsekretär of the Bundestheaterverband is Robert Jungbluth. During the 1976–77 season, the total company numbered as follows:

	STAATS-OPER	BURG-THEATER	VOLKS-OPER	BUNDES-THEATER-VERBAND
Artistic direction	75	51	50	63
Principal singers	58		42	
Actors and actresses		84	2	
Chorus singers	105		72	
Orchestra musicians	149		94	40
Ballet dancers	86		41	
Technical personnel	265	237	137	871
Administration and house personnel	___	___	___	101
Totals	738	372	438	1,075

The total number of employees of the Bundestheaterverband and its four Viennese theaters comes to 2,623 persons, the highest such figure in the German-speaking area of Europe. The Munich complex has the second-highest employment rate, with 2,041 persons on the payroll. The 71 national theaters in West Germany and the seven in Austria employ altogether about 30,000 persons.

There follow performance statistics, attendance figures, percentages of capacity, and royalty costs for the four Viennese national theaters during 1976–77. Total attendance was 1,548,944 persons. Since the population of Vienna was about 1,635,000 at the time, the attendance at Vienna's national theaters came to about 95 percent of the population of the city (Figs. 181–184, pp. 268–271).

Seat price ranges for the four theaters follow. In addition to pricing different seat locations differently within the house, the German theaters also frequently establish separate price ranges for different productions. The least expensive repertory works are priced at A, B, or C levels. But a new production of *Fidelio* conducted by Leonard Bernstein or a new *Don Carlos* with Herbert von Karajan in the pit would have to be priced at the F level in order to cover the enormous extra expenses. These price levels are marked on the posters outside the theaters that list the week's repertory. The Austrian schilling was valued at about 7¢ during 1977 and 1978 (Figs. 185–188, pp. 272–275).

Figs. 189–191, pp. 276–278, show a nine-year summary of the finances of the Bundestheaterverband and a more detailed listing of the expenses and income at the four national theaters for the years 1976 and 1977.

Scenes from recent productions by the Viennese national theaters are shown in Figs. 192–205, pp. 279–293.

Aufgeführte Werke Saison 1976/77 (in Klammern Zahl der Aufführungen dieser Inszenierung seit der Premiere)	Anzahl der Vor-stellungen	Besucherzahl	Haus-ausnützung in %	Einnahmen in Schilling	Ausbezahlte Tantiemen in Schilling
Burgtheater					
Bunbury (N)	47	58.842	82,64	6,076.438,40	281.316,55
Faust, I. Teil (32)	17	21.863	84,89	2,077.664,70	153.901,06
Die Juden / Biedermann und die Brand-stifter (siehe auch Akademietheater)	10	12.458	69,03	1,048.116,70	126.162,53
Juno und der Pfau (N)	6	5.760	63,37	628.443,—	75.645,91
König Ottokars Glück und Ende (34)	15	15.523	68,31	1,617.439,70	104.834,03
Mandragola (N)	29	29.657	67,50	2,118.156,30	—
Maria Tudor (N)	29	30.064	68,43	2,451.220,40	1.699,40
Die Orestie: Agamemnon (32)	10	9.625	63,53	778.500,40	—
Choëphoren/Eumeniden (17)	9	7.511	55,09	624.685,—	—
Der Raub der Sabinerinnen (s. auch Aka.)	5	6.155	81,25	424.703,40	23.594,62
Der Ruf des Lebens (N)	23	25.836	74,15	2,543.476,30	306.159,14
Umsonst (N)	36	40.958	75,10	4,095.365,—	303.360,32
Der Verschwender (N)	55	71.593	85,92	7,208.491,20	100.017,88
Die verzauberten Brüder (N)	50	59.815	78,96	3,116.207,30	375.098,97
GASTSPIELE					
Kroatisches Nationaltheater: Kiklop/Hasanaginica	2	2.200	72,61	72.414,—	—
Akademietheater					
Audienz (U) / Vernissage (U) / Polizei (N)	26	12.074	87,29	1,056.961,—	125.479,40
Drei Schwestern (34)	31	16.087	97,54	2,260.580,—	230.244,19
Eines langen Tages Reise in die Nacht (37)	7	3.329	89,39	387.740,—	46.672,39
Ein Gespräch im Hause Stein über den abwesenden Herrn von Goethe (ÖE)	15	6.705	84,02	439,832,—	52.934,28
Die Heimkehr (N)	25	12.039	90,52	1,436.040,—	172.856,63
Impromptu v. Versailles/George Dandin (32)	8	3.503	82,31	245.174,—	22.701,27
Die Juden / Biedermann und die Brand-stifter (N, siehe auch Burgtheater)	4	2.091	98,26	314.600,—	37.868,51
Kabale und Liebe (51)	5	2.370	89,10	213.664,—	14.229,09
Kleinbürger (N)	30	15.028	94,16	1,669.397,—	200.945,88
Liebesgeschichten u. Heiratssachen (47)	23	11.288	92,25	1,715.316,—	15.488,20
Magnetküsse (18)	7	3.006	80,72	221.250,—	66.728,08
Mich hätten Sie sehen sollen! (ÖE)	29	14.314	92,78	2,797.044,—	400.641,87
Nestroy-Abend (N, Premiere der Bundes-länder-Tournee)	1	528	99,25	37.737,—	524,12
Der Raub der Sabinerinnen (siehe auch Burgtheater, insgesamt 10 A + 56 B)	1	434	81,58	44.000,—	2.444,44
Der Sturmgeselle Sokrates (ÖE)	11	4.766	81,44	471.490,—	56.753,41
Totentanz (N)	31	12.743	77,27	1,119.305,—	100.716,86
Travesties (DE)	26	12.788	92,45	1,782.326,—	214.298,45
Der zerbrochene Krug (31)	20	9.751	91,64	1,075.927,—	—
MATINEEN					
In memoriam Carl Zuckmayer	1	496	93,23	22.660,—	—
1848 und die Folgen (Sudermann)	1	466	87,59	1.280,--	—
GASTSPIELE					
Ensembletheater: Turandot	3	1.483	92,92	117.841,—	7.092,23

N = Neuinszenierung   U = Uraufführung   ÖE = österreichische Erstaufführung   DE = deutschsprachige Erstaufführung

Fig. 181. Performance statistics, Burgtheater, 1976–77 (Bundestheaterverband)

Aufgeführte Werke Saison 1976/77 (in Klammern Zahl der Aufführungen dieser Inszenierung seit der Premiere)	Anzahl der Vor- stellungen	Besucherzahl	Haus- ausnützung in %	Einnahmen in Schilling	Ausbezahlte Tantiemen in Schilling
Opern:					
Aïda (32)	1	2.209	100,00	346.705,—	—
Arabella (WA)	9	17.099	86,01	2,856.859,—	343.881,15
Ariadne auf Naxos (N)	7	14.690	95,00	2,706.681,—	325.804,18
Der Bajazzo* (132)	4	8.282	93,73	1,874.575,—	121.500,21
Der Barbier von Sevilla (79)	13	25.447	88,61	4,137.383,50	—
La Bohème+ (142)	8	16.664	94,30	4,159.442,—	500.673,54
Boris Godunow (17)	8	15.885	89,89	3,650.623,—	—
Carmen (67)	4	8.836	100,00	1,792.330,—	107.871,69
Cavalleria rusticana* (127)	4	8.282	93,73	1,874.575,—	86.785,86
Così fan tutte (11)	4	7.364	83,34	1,117.498,—	—
Don Carlos (51)	8	15.590	88,22	3,109.515,—	—
Don Giovanni (51)	5	10.656	96,48	2,003.004,—	—
Don Pasquale (N, Inszenierung für die Bundesländertournee)	2	3.734	84,52	431.148,—	31.938,88
Elektra (38)	4	6.891	77,99	1,124.536,—	135.360,79
Die Entführung aus dem Serail (98)	10	18.146	82,15	2,852.644,50	—
Fidelio (67)	8	16.672	94,34	3,348.170,—	—
Der fliegende Holländer (35)	5	10.304	93,29	1,689.990,—	—
Die Frau ohne Schatten (NE)	3	6.621	99,91	1,654.993,—	199.212,11
Der Freischütz (32)	2	4.317	97,71	936.830,—	—
Götterdämmerung (27)	2	4.184	94,70	803.750,—	—
Die Hochzeit des Figaro (121)	5	9.445	85,51	1,772.343,—	—
Die Hochzeit des Figaro (N)+	3	6.602	99,62	2,199.090,—	—
Hoffmanns Erzählungen (86)	6	11.959	90,23	1,860.821,—	86.149,09
Kabale und Liebe (U)	6	8.966	67,65	1,356.883,—	162.328,49
Lohengrin (14)	2	4.111	93,05	738.550,—	—
Die Macht des Schicksals (23)	4	7.820	88,50	1,824.054,—	—
Madame Butterfly (199)	6	10.980	82,84	1,875.268,—	225.726,68
Das Mädchen aus dem goldenen Westen (10)	4	7.066	79,97	1,060.348,—	127.634,47
Margarethe (54)	3	5.391	81,35	999.850,—	—
Ein Maskenball (121)	6	11.623	87,69	2,263.095,—	—
Die Meistersinger von Nürnberg (13)	2	3.641	82,41	626.315,—	—
Moses und Aron (14)	3	5.020	75,75	630.645,—	75.910,96
Norma (N)	9	16.457	82,78	3,847.214,—	—
Othello (90)	1	2.151	97,37	394.612,—	—
Parsifal (43)	2	3.647	82,55	559.606,—	—
Das Rheingold (40)	2	4.182	94,66	742.910,—	—
Rigoletto (118)	5	10.701	96,89	1,714.385,—	—
Der Rosenkavalier (101)	14	25.598	82,77	5,107.565,—	614.799,45
Salome (38)	6	12.136	91,56	2,031.874,50	244.577,46
Siegfried (33)	2	4.033	91,29	690.633,—	—
Tosca (216)	15	30.092	90,82	5,295.279,50	637.394,70
La Traviata (46)	7	14.796	95,69	2,723.609,—	—
Tristan und Isolde (24)	3	5.980	90,24	1,224.587,—	—
Die Trojaner (ÖE)	7	13.334	86,26	2,654.415,—	159.756,43
Der Troubadour (93)	3	6.104	92,11	1,225.795,—	—
Der Troubadour (N)+	3	6.627	100,00	2,299.655,—	—

Fig. 182. Opera performances, Staatsoper, 1976–77 (Bundestheaterverband)

STAATSOPER – Fortsetzung Aufgeführte Werke	Anzahl der Vorstellungen	Besucherzahl	Hausausnützung in %	Einnahmen in Schilling	Ausbezahlte Tantiemen in Schilling
Opern (Fortsetzung):					
Die Walküre (94)	5	9.383	84,95	1,487.639,—	—
Die Zauberflöte (39)	12	25.151	94,88	4,270.769,—	—
Operetten:					
Die Fledermaus (67)	5	9.414	85,23	2,437.030,—	33.847,59
Ballette:					
Apollo* (NE, insges. 30)	10	17.785	80,51	2,616.590,—	134.038,39
Cry* (EA)	3	6.333	95,56	1,013.340,—	—
Désir* (EA)	3	6.333	95,56	1,013.340,—	—
Duo Concertant* (EA)	2	3.510	79,45	526.961,—	14.637,80
Estri* (17)	3	5.134	77,47	740.410,—	10.283,47
Grand Pas aus La Bayadère* (EA)	4	7.857	88,92	1,238.330,—	—
Josephs Legende* (N)	7	12.278	79,40	2,021.942,—	157.333,46
Liebeslieder Walzer* (EA, insges. 8**)	4	6.654	75,31	1.084,015,—	10.800,—
Nomos Alpha* (4)	1	1.524	68,99	224.990,—	8.332,96
Der Nußknacker (29)	6	12.623	95,24	2,186.393,—	—
Pas de deux aus Don Quixote*	3	6.333	95,56	1,013.340,—	—
Pelleas und Melisande* (EA)	7	12.278	79,40	2,021.942,—	100.958,41
Romeo und Julia (24)	8	15.003	84,90	2,498.310,—	300.722,49
Balkonszene aus Romeo und Julia*	4	7.857	88,92	1,238.330,—	17.199,02
Serenade* (NE, insges. 28)	4	6.654	75,31	1,084.015,—	2.580,—
Sylvia (11)	6	10.919	82,38	1,915.247,—	—
Symphonie in C* (26)	9	16.129	81,13	2,369.614,—	10.350,—
Der wunderbare Mandarin* (20)	5	8.074	73,10	1,131.284,—	50.846,06
Twilight* (insges. 6**)	3	5.025	75,83	744.590,—	—

* = nicht abendfüllend   WA = Wiederaufnahme   N = Neuinszenierung   NE = Neueinstudierung   U = Uraufführung   ÖE = österreichische Erstaufführung   EA = Erstaufführung
+3 dieser Aufführungen wurden von Herbert von Karajan dirigiert.
** Liebeslieder Walzer davon 4 im Theater an der Wien, Twilight: davon 3 im Theater an der Wien

AUFFÜHRUNGEN UNTER HERBERT VON KARAJAN

La Bohème	3	6.627	100,00	2,307.450,—	277.748,60
Die Hochzeit des Figaro (N)	3	6.602	99,62	2,199.090,—	—
Der Troubadour (N)	3	6.627	100,00	2,299.655,—	—

Fig. 183. Operetta and ballet performances, Staatsoper, 1976–77 (Bundestheaterverband)

Aufgeführte Werke Saison 1976/77 (in Klammern Zahl der Aufführungen dieser Inszenierung seit der Premiere)	Anzahl der Vor- stellungen	Besucherzahl	Haus- ausnützung in %	Einnahmen in Schilling	Ausbezahlte Tantiemen in Schilling
Opern:					
Albert Herring (15)	10	11.874	74,73	675.342,—	81.291,14
Carmen (34)	4	5.564	87,54	421.290,—	50.710,82
Die Entführung aus dem Serail (23)	8	10.613	83,49	672.692,60	24.914,51
Der Evangelimann (55)	2	2.928	92,13	133.806,—	13.008,91
Hänsel und Gretel (64)	6	7.864	82,48	381.937,80	45.973,98
Die Hochzeit des Figaro (56)	9	12.955	90,59	966.648,90	—
Hoffmanns Erzählungen (N)	14	19.825	89,12	2,178.639,—	262.243,54
Mignon (N)	10	13.545	85,24	1,064.656,10	59.147,55
Notre Dame (17)	5	5.959	75,00	430.560,20	51.826,69
Die Regimentstochter (43)	2	2.966	93,33	206.582,80	21.997,21
Das schlaue Mädchen (N)	6	7.632	80,05	440.577,60	36.714,78
Tiefland (62)	5	6.326	79,62	415.371,50	49.998,35
Die verkaufte Braut (74)	19	27.383	90,70	1,740.599,70	112.816,59
Die Zauberflöte (194)	7	10.414	93,62	623.391,10	—
Operetten:					
Der Bettelstudent (360)	18	26.118	91,31	2,000.871,—	138.949,22
Boccaccio (N)	4	4.345	68,36	601.194,—	—
Die Csardasfürstin (125)	12	16.829	88,25	1,916.111,80	230.643,02
Die Fledermaus (442)	17	24.715	91,49	3,057.897,—	184.040,04
Gräfin Mariza (240)	10	13.890	87,41	1,592.990,60	176.998,82
Der Graf von Luxemburg (NE)	11	13.939	79,75	1,919.048,20	230.996,52
Das Land des Lächelns (294)	2	3.079	96,88	302.585,40	37.823,31
Die lustige Witwe (55)	6	8.155	85,54	901.602,—	112.700,17
Madame Pompadour (NE, insges. 102)	19	24.332	80,59	2,420.997,80	319.171,57
Eine Nacht in Venedig (38)	18	25.478	89,08	2,759.601,50	166.087,08
Der Vogelhändler (55)	10	13.104	82,47	1,634.036,—	98.344,73
Ein Walzertraum (55)	6	7.795	81,76	848.686,—	110.014,82
Im weißen Rössl (50)	30	43.827	91,94	5,245.387,20	736.985,67
Wiener Blut (129)	10	14.971	94,22	1,766.681,40	218.219,02
Zwei Herzen im Dreivierteltakt (50)	14	17.782	79,93	1,970.225,30	237.136,72
Ballett:					
Etüden* (WA)	14	17.293	77,73	1,129.923,80	—
Ein Faschingsschwank aus Wien* (U)	2	1.796	56,51	121.368,—	—
Pas de deux aus Le Corsaire*	3	4.767	99,87	420.076,—	7.779,18
Pas de Duke* (EE)	3	4.767	99,87	420.076,—	—
Souvenirs* (N)	14	17.293	77,73	1,129.923,80	62.480,13
The Still Point* (EA)	14	17.293	77,73	1,129.923,80	47.080,13
Titus Feuerfuchs* (N)	2	1.796	56,51	121.368,—	3.933,22
Symphony in C*	2	1.796	56,51	121.368,—	2.300,—
GASTSPIELE					
Slowakisches Nationaltheater Bratislava: Margarethe	1	1.236	77,78	89.223,—	10.739,80

* = nicht abendfüllend   N = Neuinszenierung   NE = Neueinstudierung   U = Uraufführung   WA = Wiederaufnahme   EA = Erstaufführung   EE = europäische Erstaufführung

Fig. 184. Performance statistics, Volksoper, 1976/77 (Bundestheaterverband)

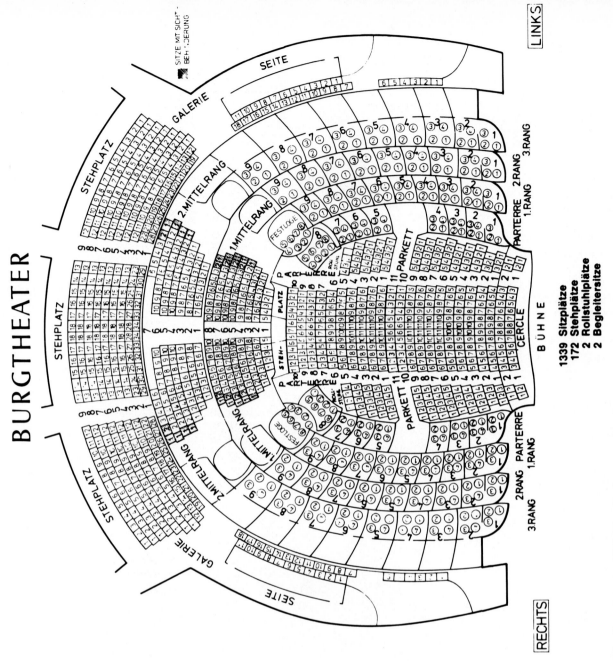

BURGTHEATER

Fig. 185. Seating plan and price list for the Burgtheater, 1978 (Bundestheaterverband)

BURGTHEATER

Preise der Plätze ab 1. Jänner 1978

(einschl. Garderobegebühr)

Preise in Schilling

	A	B	C	D	E	F
Cercle 1 und 2 Reihe	200	250	300	350	400	500
Parkett 1 bis 5 Reihe	200	250	300	350	400	500
Parkett 6 bis 11 Reihe	150	190	230	260	300	380
Parterre 1 bis 3 Reihe	150	190	230	260	300	380
Parterre 4 bis 10 Reihe	120	150	180	210	240	300
Parterre Logen 1 bis 4 1 Reihe	120	150	180	210	240	300
Parterre Logen 1 bis 4 2 Reihe*	60	80	90	110	120	150
Parterre Logen 5 bis 8 1 Reihe	200	250	300	350	400	500
Parterre Logen 5 bis 8 2 Reihe	100	130	150	180	200	250
I. Rang Logen 1 bis 5. 1 Reihe	120	150	180	210	240	300
I. Rang Logen 1 bis 5. 2 Reihe*	60	80	90	110	120	150
I. Rang Logen 6 bis 9. 1 Reihe	200	250	300	350	400	500
I. Rang Logen 6 bis 9. 2 Reihe	100	130	150	180	200	250
I. Rang Festlogen 1 Reihe	200	250	300	350	400	500
I. Rang Festlogen 2 Reihe	100	130	150	180	200	250
II. Rang Logen 1 bis 5. 1 Reihe	80	100	120	140	160	200
II. Rang Logen 1 bis 5. 2 Reihe*	40	50	60	70	80	100
II. Rang Logen 6 bis 9. 1 Reihe	120	150	180	210	240	300
II. Rang Logen 6 bis 9. 2 Reihe	60	80	90	110	120	150
III. Rang Logen 1 bis 5. 1 Reihe	60	80	90	110	120	150
III. Rang Logen 1 bis 5. 2 Reihe*	20	25	30	35	40	50
III. Rang Logen 6 bis 9. 1 Reihe	80	100	120	140	160	200
III. Rang Logen 6 bis 9. 2 Reihe	40	50	60	70	80	100
1. Mittelrang 1. bis 3. Reihe	150	190	230	260	300	380
1. Mittelrang 4. bis 8. Reihe	100	130	150	180	200	250
1. Mittelrang 4. bis 8. Reihe*	20	25	30	35	40	50
2. Mittelrang 1. bis 3. Reihe	100	130	150	180	200	250
2. Mittelrang 4. bis 7. Reihe	60	80	90	110	120	150
2. Mittelrang 4. bis 7. Reihe*	20	25	30	35	40	50
Galerie Mitte 1. Reihe	80	100	120	140	160	200
Galerie Mitte 2. bis 5. Reihe	60	80	90	110	120	150
Galerie Mitte 6. bis 9. Reihe	40	50	60	70	80	100
Galerie Seite 1. Reihe	40	50	60	70	80	100
Galerie Seite 2. Reihe	20	25	30	35	40	50
Galerie ganz Seite 1. Reihe	20	25	30	35	40	50
Parterre Stehplätze	10	10	10	10	10	10
Galeriestehplätze	6	6	6	6	6	6
Rollstuhl- und Begleitsitze	40	40	40	40	40	40

*) Sitze mit schlechter Sicht

1339 Sitzplätze
172 Stehplätze
2 Rollstuhlplätze
2 Begleitersitze

AKADEMIETHEATER

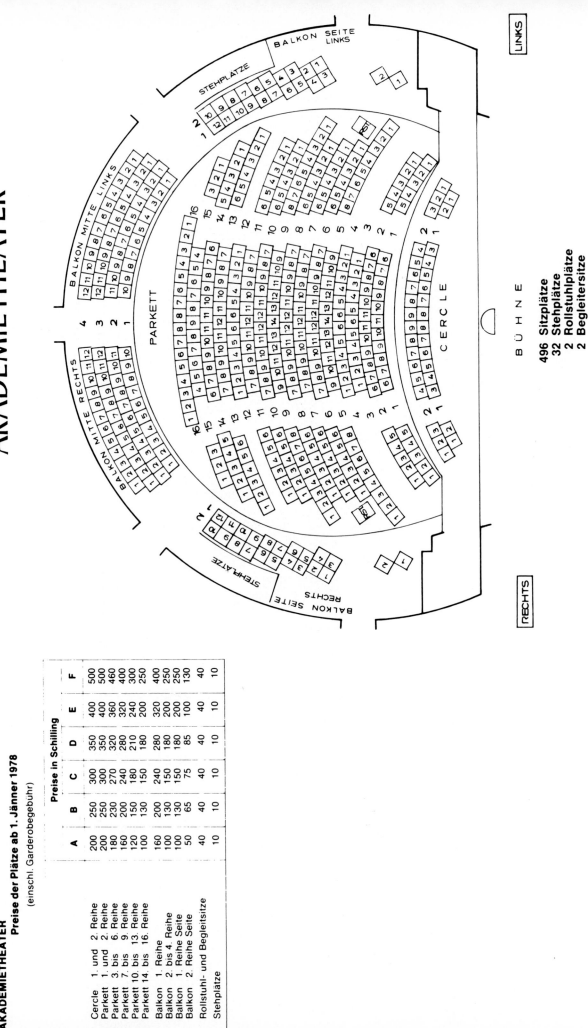

AKADEMIETHEATER
Preise der Plätze ab 1. Jänner 1978
(einschl. Garderobegebühr)

	Preise in Schilling					
	A	B	C	D	E	F
Cercle 1. und 2. Reihe	200	250	300	350	400	500
Parkett 1. und 2. Reihe	200	250	300	350	400	500
Parkett 3. bis 6. Reihe	180	230	270	320	360	460
Parkett 7. bis 9. Reihe	160	200	240	280	320	400
Parkett 10. bis 13. Reihe	120	150	180	210	240	300
Parkett 14. bis 16. Reihe	100	130	150	180	200	250
Balkon 1. Reihe	160	200	240	280	320	400
Balkon 2. bis 4. Reihe	100	130	150	180	200	250
Balkon 1. Reihe Seite	100	130	150	180	200	250
Balkon 2. Reihe Seite	50	65	75	85	100	130
Rollstuhl- und Begleitsitze	40	40	40	40	40	40
Stehplätze	10	10	10	10	10	10

Fig. 186. Seating plan and price list for the Akademietheater, 1978 (Bundestheaterverband)

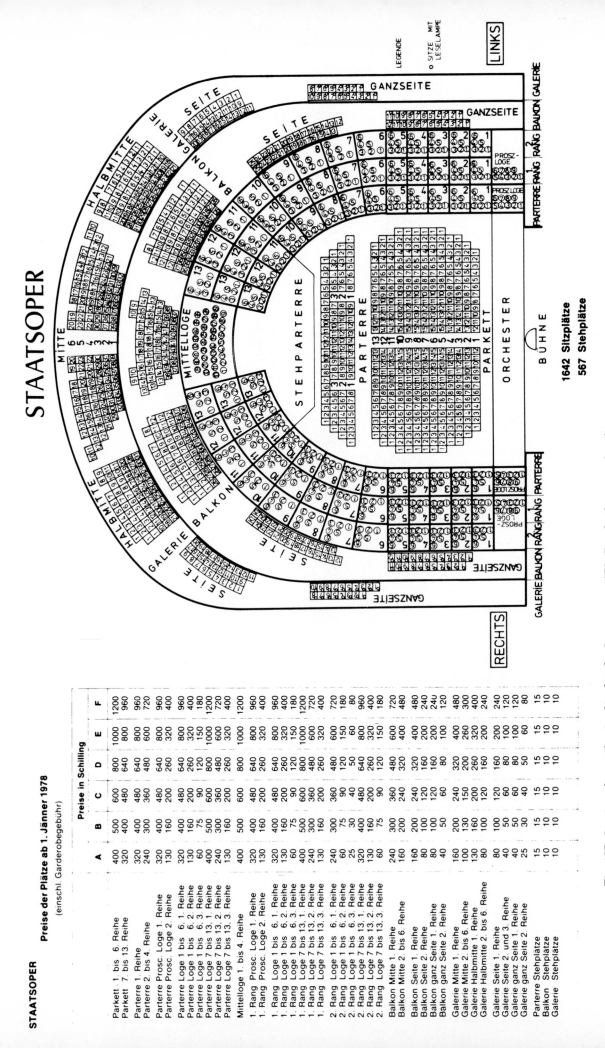

Fig. 187. Seating plan and price list for the Staatsoper, 1978 (Bundestheaterverband)

VOLKSOPER

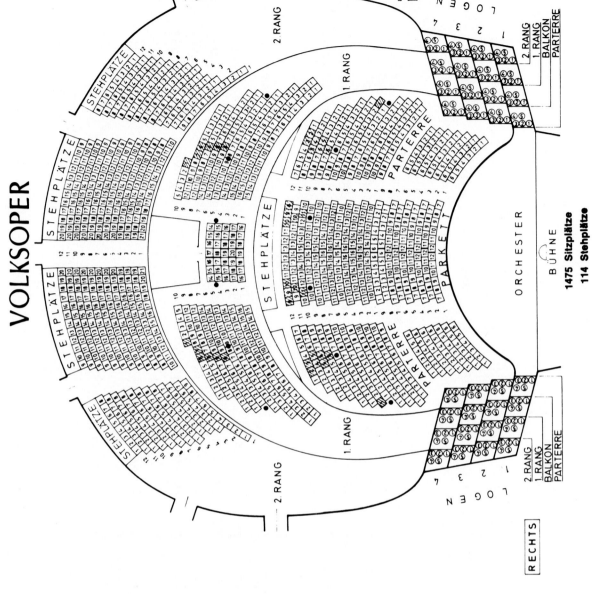

Fig. 188. Seating plan and price list for the Volksoper, 1978 (Bundestheaterverband)

VOLKSOPER **Preise der Plätze ab 1. Jänner 1978**

(einschl. Garderobegebühr)

Preise in Schilling

		A	B	C	D	E	F
Parterre	Loge 1. Reihe	120	150	180	240	300	360
Parterre	Loge 2. Reihe	40	50	60	80	100	120
Balkon	Loge 1. Reihe	120	150	180	240	300	360
Balkon	Loge 2. Reihe	40	50	60	80	100	120
I. Rang	Loge 1. Reihe	80	100	120	160	200	240
I. Rang	Loge 2. Reihe	20	25	30	40	50	60
II. Rang	Loge 1. Reihe	40	50	60	80	100	120
II. Rang	Loge 2. Reihe	20	25	30	40	50	60
Parkett	1. bis 9. Reihe	140	180	220	280	360	440
Parterre	1. bis 7. Reihe	110	140	180	220	280	360
Parterre	8. bis 12. Reihe	80	100	120	160	200	240
Parterre	Säulensitze	40	50	60	80	100	120
1. Rang	1. Reihe	140	180	220	280	360	440
1. Rang	2. bis 5. Reihe	100	130	160	200	260	320
1. Rang	6. bis 10. Reihe	60	75	90	120	150	180
1. Rang	Säulensitze	40	50	60	80	100	120
2. Rang	1. Reihe	100	130	160	200	260	320
2. Rang	2. bis 7. Reihe	60	75	90	120	150	180
2. Rang	8. bis 12. Reihe	40	50	60	80	100	120
Parterre	Stehplätze	10	10	10	10	10	10
2. Rang	Stehplätze	6	6	6	6	6	6

YEAR	1969	1970	1971	1972	1973	1974	1975	1976	1977
VALUE OF SCHILLING	4.0¢	4.1¢	4.2¢	5.0¢	5.8¢	6.0¢	6.5¢	6.8¢	7.0¢
EXPENSES									
Salaries and performance fees	$ 395,454,000	$ 430,207,000	$ 469,700,000	$ 536,043,000	$ 631,718,000	$ 699,571,000	$ 773,685,000	$ 845,741,000	$ 934,754,000
Scene and costume design costs	10,853,000	42,758,000	16,069,000	17,930,000	1,203,000	16,096,000	21,841,000	30,111,000	32,959,000
Other costs	70,986,000	46,818,000	112,904,000	121,456,000	164,069,000	163,833,000	182,057,000	200,334,000	224,811,000
TOTAL	$ 477,293,000	$ 519,783,000	$ 598,673,000	$ 675,429,000	$ 796,990,000	$ 879,500,000	$ 977,581,000	$ 1,076,186,000	$ 1,192,524,000
INCOME									
Single ticket and sub- scription sales	$ 112,219,000	$ 109,489,000	$ 119,422,000	$ 127,280,000	$ 119,328,000	$ 133,243,000	$ 150,329,000	$ 173,606,000	$ 199,064,000
Cloakroom and program sales	5,022,000	4,963,000	7,689,000	8,265,000	8,682,000	10,055,000	7,638,000	5,732,000	6,549,000
Other income	21,124,000	28,501,000	26,862,000	25,614,000	38,476,000	41,396,000	40,577,000	45,834,000	43,072,000
TOTAL	$ 138,365,000	$ 142,953,000	$ 153,973,000	$ 161,159,000	$ 166,486,000	$ 184,694,000	$ 198,544,000	$ 225,172,000	$ 248,685,000
TAX SUBSIDY	$ 338,928,000	$ 376,830,000	$ 444,700,000	$ 514,270,000	$ 630,504,000	$ 694,806,000	$ 779,037,000	$ 851,014,000	$ 943,839,000
SUBSIDY PERCENTAGE	71.0%	72.5%	74.3%	76.1%	79.1%	79.0%	79.7%	79.1%	79.1%

Fig. 189. Expenses and income for the four Viennese national theaters, 1969–77 (Deutscher Bühnenverein, Köln)

Ausgaben (Beträge in Schilling)

	BURGTHEATER		STAATSOPER		VOLKSOPER		GENERALSEKRETARIAT UND ZENTRALE BETRIEBE		BUNDESTHEATER-VERBAND	
	1977	1976	1977	1976	1977	1976	1977	1976	1977	1976
Aktivitätsaufwand										
Solisten	42,496.794	39,048.056	76,363.200[1]	65,935.250	27,051.869	27,123.109	—	—	145,911.863	132,106.415
Regie und szenischer Dienst	12,321.084	11,951.849	31,225.050	27,317.816	12,695.033	12,578.568	—	—	56,241.167	51,848.233
Orchester	—	—	38,835.652	37,599.384	19,792.126	19,174.734	—	—	58,627.778	56,774.118
Bühnenmusik	—	—	—	—	—	—	7,294.208	7,298.566	7,294.208	7,298.566
Chor	—	—	20,717.041	19,464.038	12,188.357	11,177.406	—	—	32,905.398	30,641.444
Tanzsolisten	—	—	4,469.048	4,541.799	1,876.711	1,663.465	—	—	6,345.759	6,205.264
Ballett	—	—	11,966.333	11,365.590	5,857.367	5,243.579	—	—	17,823.700	16,609.169
Technisches Personal	58,300.947	57,551.848	63,187.367	62,842.010	38,203.351	37,322.516	64,901.360	55,558.629	224,593.025	213,275.003
Mehrleistungen und sonstige Entschädigungen[2]	9,923.771	10,570.092	20,610.707	12,984.767	11,453.391	8,769.737	14,433.185	9,636.246	56,421.054	41,960.842
Verwaltung	1,402.279	662.116	1,707.069	1,965.233	980.724	651.742	31,493.737[3]	28,638.157[3]	35,583.809	31,917.248
Dienstgeberbeiträge	12,877.094	12,070.614	25,496.094	21,749.293	13,493.098	12,269.681	12,630.875	10,583.145	64,497.161	56,672.733
Summe	137,321.969	131,854.575	294,577.561	265,765.180	143,592.027	135,974.537	130,753.365	111,714.743	706,244.922	645,309.035
Pensionsaufwand										
Künstlerisches Personal	28,633.595	24,295.517	89,853.212	79,639.060	27,640.151	23,682.404	885.987[4]	112.623	147,012.945	127,729.604
Technisches Personal	29,284.664	26,332.327	26,920.020	23,978.686	13,033.175	11,890.583	1,214.154[4]	474.417	70,452.013	62,676.013
Adm. Personal	65,756	165,814	136,064	182,933	52,853	63,892	4,836.935	4,599.431	5,091.608	5,012.070
Dienstgeberbeiträge	1,585.002	1,370.263	3,019.263	2,547.077	1,144.800	954.253	203.602	143.097	5,952.667	5,014.690
Summe	59,569.017	52,163.921	119,928.559	106,347.756	41,870.979	36,591.132	7,140.678	5,329.568	228,509.233	200,432.377
Sachaufwand										
Entgelte an Gäste, Exter-nisten, Statisten, Substituten	21,750.714	24,881.131	39,524.895	33,129.294	7,227.000	7,249.549	—	—	68,502.609	65,259.974
Tantiemen[5]	4,844.622	2,711.455	5,954.240	3,812.112	3,874.099	3,469.992	—	—	14,672.961	9,993.559
Materialaufwand[6]	8,489.566	9,637.933	16,219.592	10,935.280	7,950.017	5,602.802	6,130.825	3,934.977	38,790.000	30,110.992
Instandhaltungskosten[7]	7,644.792	11,526.641	11,207.041	8,159.473	8,925.224	6,826.728	11,590.219	7,844.257	39,367.276	34,357.099
Sonstiger Aufwand[8]	18,738.578	19,242.565	29,736.401	24,449.105	12,800.487	8,908.013	12,706.337	8,798.717	73,981.803	61,398.400
Baumaßnahmen	88,835	590.467	2,404.996	2,198.625	1,669.563	109.014	429.657	842.279	4,593.051	3,740.385
Sonstige Anlagen	4,026.762	12,772.274[9]	2,999.720	1,715.805	3,548.478	1,742.802	7,257.283[10]	9,353.137[10]	17,832.243	25,584.018
Summe	65,583.869	81,362.466	108,046.885	84,399.694	45,994.868	33,908.900	38,114.321	30,773.367	257,739.943	230,444.427
Gesamtaufwand	262,474.855	265,380.962	522,553.005	456,512.630	231,457.874	206,474.569	176,008.364	147,817.678	1.192,494.098	1.076,185.839

[1] Die Steigerung bei dieser Position ergibt sich durch ein vermehrtes Engagement von Spitzenstars, dessen Auswirkung sich bei den Einnahmen der Staatsoper deutlich niederschlägt.
[2] Die sonstigen Entschädigungen beinhalten die Entschädigungen für Gastspiele und den Opernball.
[3] Bei dieser Post werden auch die Bediensteten der Werkstätten, soweit sie nicht dem technischen Personal zugehören, verrechnet.
[4] Das Ansteigen dieser Post resultiert aus verrechnungstechnischen Maßnahmen im Zusammenhang mit der Zentralisierung der Werkstätten.
[5] Der Mehraufwand wurde zum Großteil durch die Anhebung der Tantiemensätze bzw. durch Mehrennahmen verursacht.
[6] in dieser Summe sind u. a. die Aufwendungen für Neuinszenierungen und für Instandhaltungsmaterial enthalten.
[7] Die Erhöhung dieses Aufwandes resultiert aus notwendiger Instandhaltung der Gebäude und Bühneneinrichtungen.
[8] Dieser Aufwand schließt die Kosten für Fremdarbeit, Druckkosten, elektrische Energie und für Gastspiele im Burgtheater ein
[9] Diese Position enthält die Anschaffungskosten einer neuen Bühnenlichtanlage im Burgtheater
[10] Diese Position enthält die Kosten einer neuen automatischen Telefonzentrale für die gesamten Bundestheater

Fig. 190. Expenses for the Burgtheater, Staatsoper, Volksoper, and Generalsekretariat of the Bundestheaterverband, 1976 and 1977 (Bundestheaterverband Bericht, 1977/78)

Einnahmen (Beträge in Schilling)

	Burgtheater		Akademietheater		Staatsoper		Volksoper		Bundestheaterverband	
	1977	1976	1977	1976	1977	1976	1977	1976	1977	1976
Freier Kartenverkauf	18,092.934	17,686.794	10,140.838	10,222.749	84,633.266	69,598.056	27,681.698	26,113.826	140,548.736	123,621.425
Abonnements	7,960.915[1]	8,735.528	3,071.593[1]	3,340.806	15,435.076[1]	16,539.667	4,372.663[1]	4,398.028	30,840.247	33,014.029
Geschlossene Vorstellungen	4,921.551	3,900.727	1,580.086	1,118.633	5,372.175	3,624.513	5,890.731	6,102.971	17,764.543	14,746.844
Gastspiele[2]	376.022	956.979	—	—	8,438.481	33.635	888.535	1,233.156	9,703.038	2,223.770
	31,351.422	31,280.028	14,792.517	14,682.188	113,878.998	89,795.871	38,833.627	37,847.981	198,856.564	173,606.068
Programme und sonstige Druckwerke	1,583.001	1,412.752	633.357	535.833	3,087.081	2,503.055	1,615.009	1,280.304	6,918.448	5,731.944
Führungen	49.318	115.421	—	—	1,342.212	1,471.074	—	—	1,391.530	1,586.495
Opernball	—	—	—	—	6,858.943	6,078.438	—	—	6,858.943	6,078.438
Pensionsbeiträge[3]	4,770.993	6,242.536	497.505	461.026	9,518.166	11,406.885	7,467.797	7,202.111	22,254.461	25,312.558
Sonstige Einnahmen	1,929.682	2,134.963	236.757	150.470	1,991.813	2,171.451	897.554	897.208	5,055.806	5,354.092
	39,684.416	41,185.700	16,160.136	15,829.517	136,677.213	113,426.774	48,813.987	47,227.604	241,335.752	217,669.595
Einnahmen des Generalsekretariats und der zentralen Betriebe (Pensionsbeiträge und sonstige)									7,349.063	7,502.219
									248,684.815	225,171.814

1) Die Reduktion der Abonnementeinnahmen ergab sich durch die Verringerung der Vorstellungsanzahl pro Abonnement.
2) Arbeiterkammer-Tourneen in den Bundesländern und Auslandsgastspiele laut Übersicht auf den Seiten 97 ff. und 334 ff.
3) Die Erfolgsziffern beinhalten auch die Überweisungsbeträge nach dem ASVG.

Fig. 191. Income for the Bundestheaterverband, 1976 and 1977 (Bundestheaterverband Bericht, 1977//78)

278

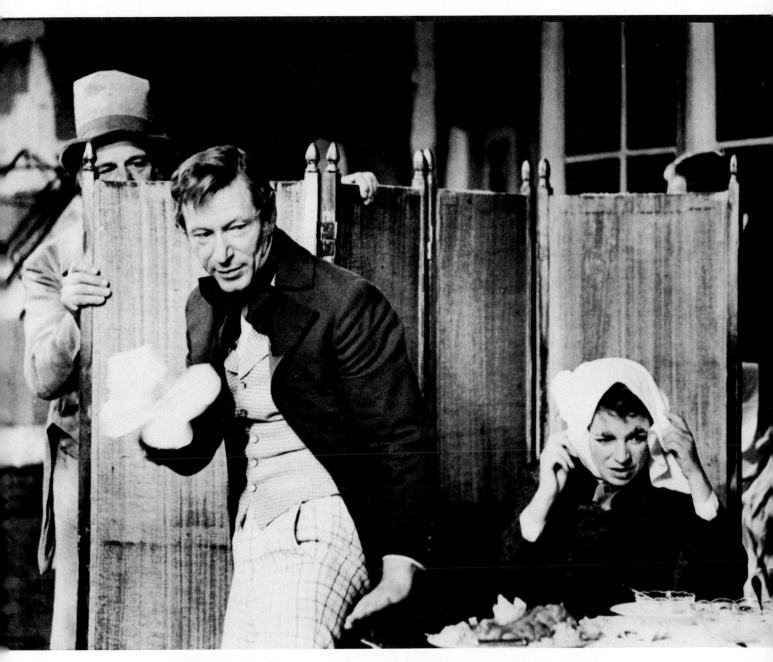

Fig. 192. Nestroy's farce with music *Einen Jux will er sich machen,* source of Thornton Wilder's *The Matchmaker* and the musical *Hello Dolly!* at the Burgtheater, directed by Axel von Ambesser and designed by Lois Egg. Melchior (Hugo Gottschlich) observes Weinberl (Josef Meinrad) and Christopherl (Inge Konradi) (Foto Hausmann/Burgtheater)

Fig. 193. The confrontation scene from Schiller's *Maria Stuart* at the Burgtheater. Queen Elizabeth (Hilde Krahl) listens contemptuously to Maria (Aglaja Schmid) as Leicester (Sebastian Fischer) looks on (Foto Hausmann/Burgtheater)

Fig. 194. *Herr Puntila und sein Knecht Matti,* Brecht's folk play about a rich man with a split personality, his daughter, and his chauffeur, was performed in the Akademietheater. Puntila (Attila Hörbiger) confronts Matti (Heinz Reincke) and other members of his household as he emerges from the outdoor bathhouse . . . (Foto Hausmann/Burgtheater)

Fig. 195. . . . Matti and Eve (Elsa Ludwig) plan a joke to play on her father (Foto Haus-
mann/Burgtheater)

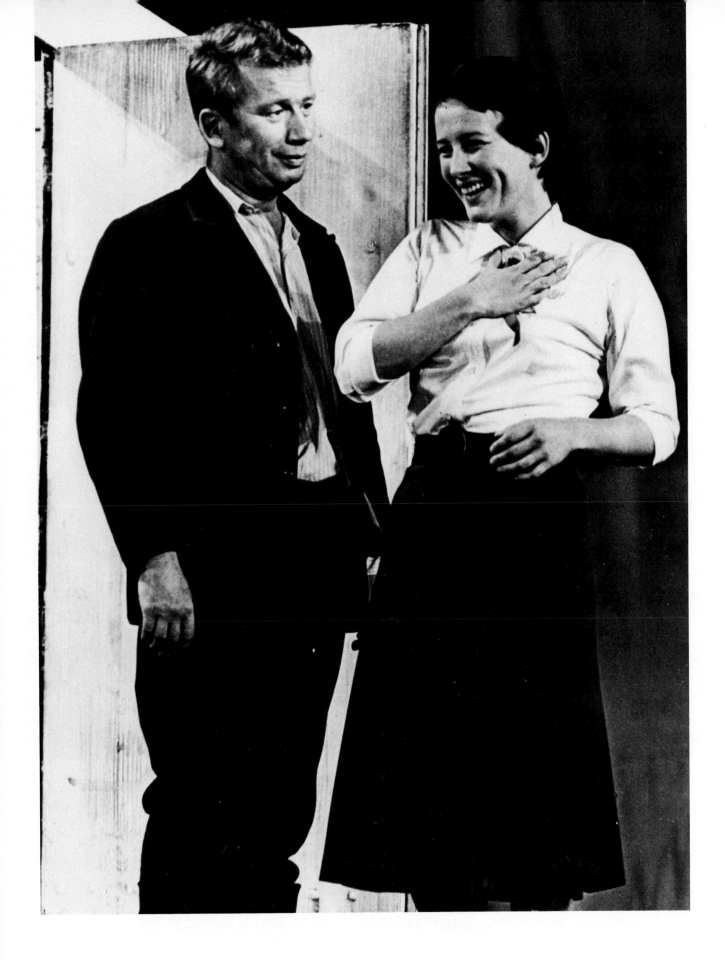

Fig. 196. Janáček's *Jenufa* at the Staatsoper, directed by Otto Schenk and designed by Günther Schneider-Siemssen. From left, Sena Jurinac as Jenufa, Elizabeth Höngen as Grandmother Buryja and Waldemar Kmentt as Laca (Foto Fayer/Staatsoper)

Fig. 197. Hans Pfitzner's musical legend *Palestrina* in a production directed by Hans Hotter and designed by Günter Schneider-Siemssen. Act II, the Council of Trent (Foto Fayer/Staatsoper)

Fig. 198. Alban Berg's seminal opera *Lulu* was performed recently at the Staatsoper in a production directed by Otto Schenk and designed by Günther Schneider-Siemssen. In the first scene, the Tierbändiger (Gerd Nienstedt) prepares the audience for his human menagerie . . . (Foto Fayer/Staatsoper)

Fig. 199. . . . Lulu (Anja Silja) descends the stairway past her portrait as Pierrot, to greet Rodrigo (Oskar Czerwenka) and Schigolch (Hans Hotter) below . . . (Foto Fayer/Staatsoper)

Fig. 200. . . . With the ghosts of two dead husbands at the table, Lulu drinks wine with
Alwa (Waldemar Kmentt) . . . (Foto Fayer/Staatsoper)

Fig. 201. . . . Lulu entertains Schigolch . . . (Foto Fayer/Staatsoper)

Fig. 202. . . . The Countess Geschwitz (Martha Mödl) finishes out Lulu's term in prison
for her lover (Foto Fayer/Staatsoper)

Fig. 203. James King as Bacchus and Gundula Janowitz as Ariadne in a recent production
of *Ariadne auf Naxos* by Hugo von Hofmannsthal and Richard Strauss. The production
was directed and designed by Filippo Sanjust and conducted by Karl Böhm (Foto Fayer/
Staatsoper)

Fig. 205. Leonard Bernstein's *West Side Story* at the Volksoper in a production translated by Marcel Prawy, directed by Alan Johnson and designed by Wolfram Skalicki. Arline Woods as Anita sings "Schön ist es hier in Amerika" (Foto Hausmann/Volksoper)

Fig. 204. Puccini's *Der Mantel* at the Volksoper, directed by Andre Diehl and designed by Roman Weyl. Marilyn Zschau as Georgette and Ion Buzea as Luigi (Foto Hausmann/Volksoper)

IX. HAMBURG, GERMANY

Hamburgische Staatsoper

The free Hanseatic city-state of Hamburg provides perhaps the best answer to the theory that appreciation of opera and drama in Germany is the result of court theaters and royal subsidies. Theater activity in Hamburg goes back more than three hundred years, and all the present national theaters in the city began as people's theaters, organized by businessmen for the edification and entertainment of the general public. Thus, they began as theaters supported by gifts from prosperous citizens and are today theaters supported by taxes collected from all the citizens.

The city of Hamburg was fortunate in its geographic location and its position as Germany's leading seaport to escape the horrors of the Thirty Years' War, which had such a devastating effect on the rest of the country. During the 17th century it became a wealthy city, leader of the Hanseatic League, and home for thousands of refugees from other parts of Germany and Austria. Theater and opera developed about the same time, and the first building erected by the citizenry for public theatrical entertainment, at the intersection of Jungfernstieg and Gänsemarkt, was called the Opern-Theatrum. It was designed by the Italian architect Girolamo Sartorio and was opened on January 2, 1678, with the Singspiel *Adam und Eva,* also called *Der erschaffene, gefallene und wieder aufgerichtete Mensch,* with text by Christian Richter and music by Johann Theile. Music, dance, speech, and morality thus set the tone for the further development of the theatrical arts in Hamburg. The content of the morality plays was particularly helpful in appeasing the Lutheran clergy, which, like its counterpart in London, routinely attacked the theater on the grounds of immorality.

For quite a long time there was no particular separation of "theater" from "opera" in Hamburg. A morality play one night was followed by an opera the next in the Opern-Theatrum. Only gradually did the actors who performed the plays and the singers, dancers, and orchestra musicians who performed the operas begin to form themselves into separate companies, and not until the 19th century did it become common for them to perform in separate theater buildings.

From 1678 to 1738 the Opern-Theatrum was the scene of a good deal of opera activity along with the development of morality plays into Singspiele. The operas of

Mattheson and Telemann and some early pieces by Händel contributed to the emergence of a German style in opera, quite different from Italian models, a style that underwent further development later in the work of Gluck, Mozart, Beethoven, and Weber. In 1738 the Hamburg Senate ceased to support the performance companies, and the building was rented to visiting opera and drama companies. Caroline Neuber took over the management of the house and renamed it the Comödienhaus am Gänsemarkt, suggesting that only plays were performed in it, but such was not the case—performances of operas by visiting companies took up a good share of the performance schedule.

The policy of renting the theater to various managements went on for quite some time. When a new manager took over the operations of the theater, he often changed its name. In 1741, J. F. Schönemann called it the Deutsche Schaubühne and, with Pietro Mingotti, offered the public their first experiences of operas by Pergolesi, Gluck, Graun, and Hasse. Konrad Ackermann took over the management and in the year 1765 put up a new building that replaced the old one on the same site. Ackermann called it the Comödienhaus again, but in 1767, when Lessing, Ekhof, Seyler, and F. L. Schröder formed a new company, the house took on the title Deutsches National-theater. It was not a true national theater, however, as it was privately financed, and, in fact, the managers were forced to dissolve their partnership two years later due to lack of a proper subsidy. Lessing wrote his *Hamburgische Dramaturgie* at this time, however, and his discussion of the need for a stable, tax-supported German national theater was studied in many European cities. In 1776 the Burgtheater in Vienna was reorganized as a national theater with a tax subsidy, and in 1809 the Hamburg Senate finally recognized the validity of Lessing's arguments and established a permanent subsidy. In honor of the new arrangement, which guaranteed stability and artistic growth of the opera and drama companies, the theater was renamed the Hamburg-isches Stadt-Theater.

It was now possible for the managers to plan their seasons well in advance, to engage actors, singers, dancers, and musicians on a relatively stable basis, and to try out new works without the fear that an expensive failure might close them down. Audiences became accustomed to seeing plays by Lessing, Goethe, and Schiller and operas by Mozart and Beethoven, along with boulevard comedies, concerts, and ballets. In 1827 the city built a new theater on Dammtorstrasse, the site of the present Staats-oper. Called the Neues Stadttheater, it was designed by Karl Friedrich Schinkel and was opened on May 3 with a performance of Goethe's *Egmont,* with the incidental music Beethoven composed for the earlier Burgtheater production.

The theater has proved to be remarkably durable. It was remodeled in 1873 and given a new facade, designed by Martin Haller, as well as a new auditorium. In 1926 the stage machinery was redesigned by Adolf Linnebach and a new stage house was built. The auditorium was burned out during World War II, but the iron curtain saved the stage, which was in good enough condition to permit temporary use of the facility again in 1946. The theater was completely redesigned and rebuilt under the direction of the architect Gerhard Weber and opened yet again on October 15, 1955, with a performance of Mozart's *Die Zauberflöte.*

Fig. 206. Hamburg's Opern-Theatrum, designed by Girolamo Sartorio, which served the theatergoing public from its opening in 1678 until 1763, when it was torn down to make room for a new theater (Hamburgische Staatsoper)

Fig. 207. The Ackermannsches Comödienhaus, built by Konrad Ackermann in 1765 on the site of the old Opern-Theatrum. Designed by David Fischer, it seated 1,600 people on the main floor, the loges, and two balconies. To suggest the variety of productions done in this theater, the opening performance consisted of a short piece, *Die Comödie in dem Tempel der Tugend*, a ballet, *Die Kornärndte*, and a tragedy, *Zelmire*. The theater bears a surprising resemblance to the Barter Theater of Virginia (Hamburgische Staatsoper)

Fig. 208. The Neues Stadttheater, erected on Dammtorstrasse by the city of Hamburg in 1827. Designed by Carl Friedrich Schinkel, the theater seated 2,800 persons in a main floor section, three loges, and a balcony (Hamburgische Staatsoper)

Wir sind beglückt! wir sind entzückt! die Lind hat uns den Kopf verrückt.

Fig. 209. A cartoon of the 1840's satirizing the Jenny Lind craze in Hamburg at the time
(Hamburgische Staatsoper)

Fig. 210. The redesigned facade of the Neues Stadttheater, which dates from 1874. The designer also provided a new foyer and rebuilt the interior of the auditorium. The new furnishings were inaugurated on September 16, 1974, with a performance of Wagner's *Lohengrin* (Hamburgische Staatsoper)

Since the end of World War II, the Hamburg Staatsoper has become one of the world's leading lyric theaters. Under the capable management of Günther Rennert, Rolf Liebermann, Heinz Tietjen, and August Everding, the singing, dancing, and orchestra ensembles have been greatly strengthened. The repertory has been expanded to include many works from the 17th and 18th centuries, and the world of modern opera has been diligently explored.

The effort to make opera over into genuine music drama has continued unceasingly and has been a goal of all the Intendants. Today it is a widely accepted practice in German theaters to place stage directors at the head of both opera and spoken drama companies. Over the years the German theater has shown that there need be no distinction between directors of spoken drama and directors of opera, and as a result such stage directors as Rennert, Everding, Tietjen, Götz Friedrich, Jean-Pierre Ponnelle, Hans Neugebauer, Oskar Fritz Schuh, Hansgünther Heyme, Werner Düggelin, Hans Neuenfels, and Otto Schenk have regularly worked in both media.

Above all, the Hamburg Staatsoper has led the way in commissioning and performing new works for the lyric theater. It is the responsibility of the wealthier theaters to try to replenish what is being withdrawn, or the art of the opera will die out. It is hard to add a new work to the repertory. It must compete with the masterpieces of the form by Monteverdi, Mozart, Beethoven, Wagner, Verdi, Puccini, and Richard Strauss. It takes years to compose an opera, and since this is by far the most expensive form of theatrical art to stage, the chances for first-class production of an untried work are slim. Yet new works have to be found to replace what is being played out, and the Hamburg Staatsoper has done more than its fair share. There follows a list of new operas recently given their world premieres by the company:

1953–54 Boshuslav Martinu: *Die Heirat*
1954–55 Marcel Mihalovici: *Die Heimkehr*
1955–56 Ernst Krenek: *Pallas Athene weint*
1958–59 Richard Mohaupt: *Der grüne Kakadu*
1959–60 Hans Werner Henze: *Der Prinz von Homburg* (commissioned)
1962–63 Giselher Klebe: *Figaro lässt sich scheiden* (commissioned)
1963–64 Ernst Krenek: *Der goldene Bock* (commissioned)
1964–65 Gottfried von Einem: *Der Zerissene* (commissioned)
         Antonio Bibalo: *Das Lächeln am Fuss der Leiter*
1965–66 Giselher Klebe: *Jacobowsky und der Oberst* (commissioned)
         Boris Blacher: *Zwischenfälle bei ener Notlandung* (commissioned)
1966–67 Gunther Schuller: *The Visitation* (commissioned)
         Alexander Goehr: *Arden muss sterben* (commissioned)
1967–68 Humphrey Searle: *Hamlet* (commissioned)
1968–69 Gian-Carlo Menotti: *Hilfe, Hilfe, die Globolinks* (commissioned)
         Lars Johan Werle: *Die Reise* (commissioned)
         Krysztof Penderecki: *Die Teufel von Loudun* (commissioned)
1969–70 Milko Kelemen: *Der Belagerungszustand* (commissioned)

Ernst Krenek: *Das kommt davon oder Wenn Sardakai auf Reisen geht* (commissioned)

1970–71 Paul Burkhard: *Ein Stern geht auf aus Jaakob* (commissioned)

Mauricio Kagel: *Staatstheater* (commissioned)

1971–72 Josef Tal: *Ashmedai* (commissioned)

1972–73 Nicolas Schöffer/Pierre Henry: *Kyldex I* (commissioned)

Walter Steffen: *Unter dem Milchwald* (commissioned)

1974–75 Günter Bialas: *Der gestiefelte Kater, oder Wie man das Spiel spielt*

Diether de la Motte: *So oder so*

1976–77 Hans-Jürgen von Bose: *Blutbund* (commissioned)

1977–78 Manfred Niehaus: *Die Abendteuer des Tartarin aus Tarascon* (commissioned)

Heinz Holliger: *Kommen und Gehen* (commissioned)

Technical aspects of the Hamburgische Staatsoper are as follows:

Seating capacity: 1,675 seats.

Architect: Gerhard Weber.

Opened: October 15, 1955, with Mozart's *Die Zauberflöte,* directed by Günther Rennert.

Proscenium size: 12 meters wide by 8 meters high.

Stage size: 37 meters wide by 26.6 meters deep.

Side stages: 11 meters wide by 7.5 meters deep.

Technical equipment: Revolving stage 14.8 meters in diameter, full stage wagons, full stage double-decked hydraulic lifts, lighting control over 360 silicon control rectifier dimmers, 40 large projection units, and an elaborate sound control system used for special effects, not to amplify voices.

Orchestra pit: Three lifts with an area of 129 square meters for 125 musicians.

The principal Besucherorganisationen that support the Hamburgische Staatsoper are the Hamburger Volksbühne e.V. and the Kulturring der Jugend. The company tours to various cities and also visits foreign countries on an exchange basis.

The Staatsoperintendant of the Hamburgische Staatsoper is Christoph von Dohnányi. During 1976–77 the personnel of the company numbered as follows:

Artistic direction	39
Principal singers	36
Ballet dancers	60
Chorus singers	83
Orchestra musicians	132
Technical personnel	334
Administrative personnel	50
House personnel	100
Total	834

Fig. 211. The Hamburgische Staatsoper on Dammtorstrasse in the heart of the city (Hamburgische Staatsoper)

Fig. 212. Auditorium of the Staatsoper, designed by Gerhard Weber. The boxes of old are replaced by flying balconies, a motif expanded on by Wilhelm Riphan in his Grosses Haus at Cologne. Several lighting bridges are installed in the ceiling of the auditorium (Hamburgische Staatsoper)

Public performances, attendance, and percentages of house capacity were as follows:

	PERFORMANCES	ATTENDANCE	PERCENT OF CAPACITY
Operas	234	366,795	92.8%
Ballets	64	106,995	96.8%
Guest companies	5	(included above)	
Totals	303	473,790	94.8%

During the season 1978–79 the following opera and ballet productions were offered:

Operas

New Productions   Ligeti: *Le Grand Macabre* (first German production)
Von Einem: *Kabale und Liebe* (first German production)
Bernstein: *West Side Story*
Tschaikowsky: *Eugen Onegin*
Puccini: *Manon Lescaut*
Massenet: *Le Cid* (concert performance)
Beethoven: *Fidelio*

Revivals   Mozart: *Die Zauberflöte*
Così fan tutte
Die Entführung aus dem Serail
Die Hochzeit des Figaro
Don Giovanni
Weber: *Der Freischütz*
Donizetti: *Der Liebestrank*
Viva la Mamma
Rossini: *Der Barbier von Sevilla*
Berg: *Lulu*
Wagner: *Der fliegende Holländer*
Parsifal
Lohengrin
Verdi: *Nabucco*
Der Troubadour
Othello
Don Carlos
Ein Maskenball
Rigoletto
La traviata
Debussy: *Pelléas und Mélisande*
Strauss, J.: *Die Fledermaus*

Gluck: *Orpheus und Euridike*
Strauss, R.: *Der Rosenkavalier*
              Die Frau ohne Schatten
Puccini: *La Bohème*
              Madame Butterfly

Ballets

New Productions   Scarlatti/Stolze/Cranko: *Der Widerspenstigen Zähmung*
                      Strauss/Neumeier: *Josephs Legende*
Revivals   Britten/Neumeier: *Tanz für den Anfang*
                      Crumb/Neumeier: *Die Stille*
                      Genzmer/Neumeier: *Trauma*
                      Gluck/Neumeier: *Don Juan*
                      Mahler/Neumeier: *Dritte Sinfonie von Gustav Mahler*
                      Mahler/Neumeier: *Vierte Sinfonie von Gustav Mahler*
                      Mahler/Neumeier: *Rückert-Lieder*
                      Mahler/Neumeier: *Epilog*
                      Mendelssohn/Ligeti/Neumeier: *Ein Sommernachtstraum*
                      Musikcollage/Neumeier: *Rondo*
                      Prokofieff/Neumeier: *Romeo und Julia*
                      Ravel/Neumeier: *Daphnis und Chloë*
                      Schubert/Neumeier: *Streichquintett C-Dur von Franz Schubert*
                      Schumann/Neumeier: *Kinderszenen*
                      Skrjabin/Neumeier: *Dämmern*
                      Skrjabin/Neumeier: *Désir*
                      Strawinsky/Neumeier: *Le Sacre*
                      Strawinsky/Cranko: *Jeu de cartes*
                      Strawinsky/Neumeier: *Petruschka-Variationen*
                      Strawinsky/Robbins: *Les Noces*
                      Strawinsky/Balanchine: *Agon*
                      Tschaikowsky/Neumeier: *Illusionen—wie Schwanensee*
                      Tschaikowsky/Neumeier: *Der Nussknacker*
                      Tschaikowsky/Neumeier: *Dornröschen*
                      Williams/Neumeier: *Tanz für den Schluss*

There follow a seating plan and a price list for the 1978–79 season (Figs. 213 and 214, pp. 307–308.

Fig. 215, p. 309, shows a nine-year summary of the finances of the Staatsoper.

Scenes from recent productions at the Staatsoper are shown in Figs. 216–228, pp. 310–322.

Preisgruppe	Platzgattung	Kassenpreise					Premieren-preise	Opern-abonnement			B-Premieren-abonnement		Premieren-abonnement		Sonder-abonnement		
		D	C	B	A	S		Einzelpreis	Gesamtpreis für 10 Auff.	Bei Ratenzahlung	Erste Vorstellung nach der Premiere	Bei Ratenzahlung	8 Aufführungen Gesamtpreis	Bei Ratenzahlung	Einzelpreis	Gesamtpreis für 10 Konzerte	Bei Ratenzahlung
		DM	DM	DM	DM	DM	DM	DM	DM	DM	DM	DM	DM	DM	DM	DM	DM
1	Parkett 1. bis 3. Reihe Parkett 4. und 5. Reihe Pl. 5 bis Mitte 1. Rang Balkon 1. und 2. Reihe 1. Rang Loge 2 bis 5, Plätze 3/4	30,-	35,-	44,-	53,-	75,-	86,- 106,-	30,-	300,-	120,- / 90,- / 90,-	556,-	208.50 / 208.50 / 139,-	808,-	303,- / 303,- / 202,-	20,-	200,-	80,- / 60,- / 60,-
2	Parkett 6. und 7. Reihe Pl. 5 bis Mitte Parkett 11. Reihe Pl. 5 bis Mitte Parkett 12. Reihe Pl. 4 bis Mitte Parkett 13. Reihe Pl. 3 bis Mitte Parkett 14. Reihe Pl. 2 bis Mitte Parkett 15. Reihe 1. Rang Balkon 3. und 4. Reihe 1. Rang Loge 2 bis 5, Pl. 1/2	28,-	32,-	40,-	48,-	70,-	80,- 96,-	28,-	280,-	112,- / 84,- / 84,-	516,-	193.50 / 193.50 / 129,-	736,-	276,- / 276,- / 184,-	18,-	180,-	72,- / 54,- / 54,-
3	Parkett 8. Reihe Pl. 7 bis Mitte Parkett 9. Reihe Pl. 7 bis Mitte Parkett 10. Reihe Pl. 6 bis Mitte 1. Rang Balkon 5. Reihe 1. Rang Loge 1, Pl. 3/4	26,-	29,-	35,-	43,-	65,-	76,- 88,-	25,-	250,-	100,- / 75,- / 75,-	476,-	178.50 / 178.50 / 119,-	680,-	255,- / 255,- / 170,-	16,-	160,-	64,- / 48,- / 48,-
4	Parkett 4. Reihe Pl. 1–4 Parkett 5. Reihe Pl. 1–4 Parkett 6. Reihe Pl. 1–4 Parkett 7. Reihe Pl. 1–4 Parkett 8. Reihe Pl. 1–6 Parkett 9. Reihe Pl. 1–6 Parkett 10. Reihe Pl. 1–5 Parkett 11. Reihe Pl. 1–4 Parkett 12. Reihe Pl. 1–3 Parkett 13. Reihe Pl. 1 2 Parkett 14. Reihe Pl. 1 Parkett 16. bis 21. Reihe 1. Rang Loge 1, Pl. 1/2 2. Rang Balkon 1. Reihe	23,-	26,-	32,-	39,-	58,-	68,- 78,-	22,-	220,-	88,- / 66,- / 66,-	426,-	159.75 / 159.75 / 106.50	604,-	226.50 / 226.50 / 151,-	14,-	140,-	56,- / 42,- / 42,-
5	Parkett 22. bis 25. Reihe 2. Rang Balkon 2. Reihe 2. Rang Loge 2 bis 5, Pl. 2–4	20,-	23,-	28,-	35,-	48,-	54,- 70,-	20,-	200,-	80,- / 60,- / 60,-	358,-	134.25 / 134.25 / 89.50	528,-	198,- / 198,- / 132,-	12,-	120,-	48,- / 36,- / 36,-
6	2. Rang Balkon 3. Reihe 2. Rang Balkon 4. Reihe Pl. 1–6 2. Rang Loge 1, Pl. 2–4 3. Rang Balkon 1. Reihe 3. Rang Loge 2 bis 5, 1. Reihe Pl. 3/4 – kein Abonnement –	17,-	20,-	24,-	30,-	42,-	48,- 60,-	17,-	170,-	68,- / 51,- / 51,-	312,-	117,- / 117,- / 78,-	456,-	171,- / 171,- / 114,-	10,-	100,-	40,- / 30,- / 30,-
7	2. Rang Balkon 4. R. Pl. 7 bis Mitte 2. Rang Loge 1 bis 5, Pl. 1 3. Rang Balkon 2. und 3. Reihe 3. Rang Loge 2–5, 2. u. 3. R. Pl. 3/4 – kein Abonnement –	14,-	17,-	20,-	25,-	36,-	40,- 50,-	13,-	130,-	52,- / 39,- / 39,-	266,-	99.75 / 99.75 / 66.50	380,-	142.50 / 142.50 / 95,—	8,-	80,-	32,- / 24,- / 24,-
8	3. Rang Loge 1 Pl. 3/4 4. Rang Balkon 1. und 2. Reihe	11,-	13,-	16,-	20,-	30,-	32,-/ 40,-										
9	3. Rang Loge 1 bis 5, Pl. 2 4. Rang Loge 1 bis 5, Pl. 3/4	8,-	10,-	12,-	16,-	20,-	20,-/ 21,-										
10	3. Rang Loge 1–5, Pl. 1 (Sichtbeh.) 4. Rang Loge 1 bis 5, Pl. 1/2	5,-	6,-	7,-	10,-	12,-	12,-/ 13,-										
11	Steh- und Hörplätze	3,-	3,-	5,-	5,-	6,-	6,-/ 7,-										

Die Kassenpreise können bei besonderen Vorstellungen erhöht werden. Die Abo-Preise bleiben in jedem Fall konstant.

Fig. 213. Ticket prices and subscription opportunities for the Hamburgische Staatsoper for 1978–79. There are subscriptions for ten performances in the regular schedule, eight premieres, eight second-night premieres, and ten concerts. Although the box office, single-ticket price can be raised for certain performances, the subscription prices remain constant (Hamburgische Staatsoper)

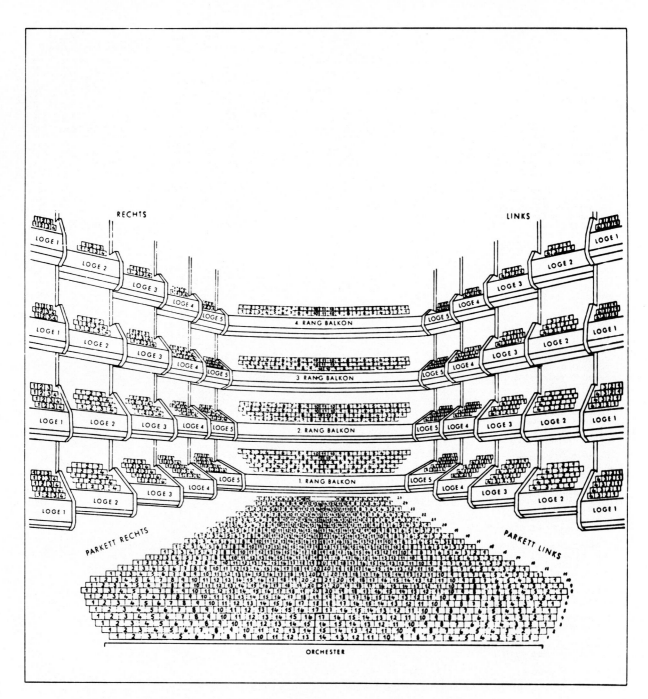

Fig. 214. Seating plan for the Hamburgische Staatsoper (Hamburgische Staatsoper)

YEAR	1969	1970	1971	1972	1973	1974	1975	1976	1977
VALUE OF DEUTSCHE MARK	28¢	29¢	30¢	34¢	40¢	42¢	44¢	48¢	50¢
EXPENSES									
Artists' salaries	DM 13,367,000	DM 15,724,000	DM 16,920,000	DM 18,187,000	DM 19,618,000	DM 20,793,000	DM 21,335,000	DM 24,079,000	DM 23,878,000
Technical salaries	5,478,000	5,896,000	6,706,000	7,075,000	8,245,000	8,680,000	9,575,000	10,221,000	10,852,000
Administration	1,119,000	1,311,000	1,505,000	2,141,000	1,960,000	2,586,000	2,603,000	2,737,000	2,908,000
Other personnel	1,850,000	2,193,000	2,530,000	2,333,000	3,273,000	3,197,000	3,570,000	4,169,000	4,276,000
Pension funds	---	---	---	891,000	1,338,000	952,000	945,000	955,000	1,413,000
Production costs	5,332,000	5,487,000	5,472,000	6,427,000	7,261,000	9,166,000	7,873,000	9,507,000	11,653,000
Loan payments	---	---	---	---	---	593,000	853,000	3,446,000	3,354,000
Building maintenance	---	---	---	---	---	330,000	---	389,000	1,187,000
TOTAL	DM 27,146,000	DM 30,611,000	DM 33,133,000	DM 37,054,000	DM 41,695,000	DM 46,297,000	DM 46,752,000	DM 55,503,000	DM 59,521,000
INCOME									
Single tickets	DM 1,740,000	DM 2,156,000	DM 2,401,000	DM 2,965,000	DM 2,774,000	DM 3,500,000	DM 4,070,000	DM 4,678,000	DM 4,319,000
Subscriptions	2,957,000	3,025,000	3,398,000	3,654,000	3,639,000	3,308,000	3,988,000	4,141,000	4,754,000
Children's theater subscriptions	487,000	446,000	485,000	275,000	333,000	354,000	---	---	---
Visitor groups	655,000	551,000	494,000	373,000	391,000	433,000	586,000	716,000	591,000
Cloakroom charges	316,000	303,000	291,000	287,000	282,000	286,000	326,000	342,000	381,000
Radio and TV fees	918,000	532,000	9??,000	560,000	---	8,000	379,000	24,000	27,000
Touring	48,000	144,000	241,000	148,000	471,000	568,000	457,000	643,000	638,000
Guest performances by other companies	---	15,000	---	---	---	59,000	21,000	107,000	2,032,000
Program sales	186,000	215,000	218,000	245,000	249,000	331,000	322,000	338,000	380,000
Other income	745,000	786,000	501,000	584,000	566,000	446,000	659,000	1,137,000	2,195,000
TOTAL	DM 8,052,000	DM 8,173,000	DM 8,973,000	DM 9,091,000	DM 8,705,000	DM 9,293,000	DM 10,808,000	DM 12,126,000	DM 15,317,000
TAX SUBSIDY	DM 19,094,000	DM 22,438,000	DM 24,160,000	DM 27,963,000	DM 32,990,000	DM 37,004,000	DM 35,944,000	DM 43,377,000	DM 44,204,000
SUBSIDY PERCENTAGE	70.3%	73.3%	72.9%	75.5%	79.1%	79.9%	76.9%	78.2%	74.3%

Fig. 215. Expenses and income for the Hamburgische Staatsoper, 1969-77 (Deutscher Bühnenverein, Köln)

Fig. 216. Hugo von Hofmannstahl's fairy tale opera *Die Frau ohne Schatten,* set to music by Richard Strauss, at the Hamburgische Staatsoper. The final scene of reconciliation: Eva Marton and René Kollo as the Empress and the Emperor and below them, Donald McIntyre and Birgit Nilsson as Barak and his wife. In the background, the children, waiting to be born. The production was directed by Kurt Horres, designed by Hanna Jordan, and conducted by Christoph von Dohnányi (Hamburgische Staatsoper/Gert von Bassewitz)

Fig. 217. The scene of the auto-da-fé, in which the Inquisition burns people alive in public, in Verdi's *Don Carlos.* Center, Bernd Weikl as Marquis Posa and Sylvia Sass as Queen Elizabeth of Spain. The production was designed and directed by Jean-Pierre Ponnelle (Hamburgische Staatsoper/Gert von Bassewitz)

Fig. 218. Scenes from a new production of *Die Fledermaus*. Dr. Falke (William Workman) plans his revenge on Eisenstein before the shadowy image of a huge bat wing . . . (Hamburgische Staatsoper/Gert von Bassewitz)

Fig. 219. . . . At a party given by Prince Orlofsky (Hanna Schwarz)—who is really Count Dracula in disguise, having some fun in Vienna—Falke promises an amusing evening to his host and the assembled vampire and transvestite guests . . . (Hamburgische Staatsoper/Gert von Bassewitz)

Fig. 220. . . . Under the silver palm trees, Eisenstein (Donald Grobe) plans an affair with his masked wife, Rosalinde (Teresa Zylis-Gara) . . . (Hamburgische Staatsoper/Gert von Bassewitz)

Fig. 221. . . . In Act III, a prison that strongly resembles a Viennese drawing room is the scene of merriment led by Falke and, to his left, Orlofsky/Dracula. The production was directed by Götz Griedrich and designed by Andreas Reinhardt (Hamburgische Staatsoper/Gert von Bassewitz)

Fig. 222. Alban Berg's *Lulu* in a production directed by Luc Bondy and designed by Rolf and Marianne Glittenberg in which the action is moved up to the 1920's. Lulu (Anja Silja) poses in her extravagant head piece for Dr. Schön (Günther Reich) . . . (Hamburgische Staatsoper/Gert von Bassewitz)

Fig. 223. . . . From the filthy backyard of a bordello, Lulu watches as Jack the Ripper lights a Christmas tree in his tiny room (Hamburgische Staatsoper/Gert von Bassewitz)

318 · NATIONAL THEATERS IN GERMAN AND AUSTRIAN CITIES

Fig. 225. . . . Before a background of military crosses, Wesener (Harald Stamm) fails to recognize his daughter Marie (Gabriella Fuchs) . . . (Hamburgische Staatsoper/Gert von Bassewitz)

Fig. 224. Three scenes from Zimmermann's epochal *Die Soldaten,* directed by Götz Friedrich and designed by Josef Svoboda. The Gräfin de la Roche (Carol Wyatt) questions her son (Heinz Kruse) about Marie . . . (Hamburgische Staatsoper/Gert von Bassewitz)

Fig. 226. . . . and finally, with the dead body of Marie in the foreground, a masked chorus sings the final military commands as the projection of a broken doll fills the background (Hamburgische Staatsoper/Gert von Bassewitz)

Fig. 227. Tschaikowsky's ballet *Dornröschen* as choreographed by John Neumeier. From left, Eduardo Bertini, François Klaus, Lynne Charles, and Eugen Ivanics (Hamburgische Staatsoper/Gert von Bassewitz)

Fig. 228. The ballet *Streichquintett C-Dur von Franz Schubert* as choreographed by John Neumeier. Marianne Kruuse and Lynn Charles in the center spotlight (Hamburgische Staatsoper/Gert von Bassewitz)

Deutsches Schauspielhaus

There are two spoken drama national theaters in Hamburg, the Deutsches Schauspielhaus on Kirchenallee and the Thalia Theater not far away on Gerhart-Hauptmann-Platz. Planning is under way to combine the two theaters under one management to reduce expenses.

The Deutsches Schauspielhaus was founded in 1900 by a group of private citizens who thought Hamburg needed a theater for serious plays, a "Burgtheater an der Alster." They raised sufficient funds for a handsome building and hired a former member of the Burgtheater staff, Alfred Freiherr von Berger, as Intendant. The theater developed a good reputation under Berger and such other Intendants as Carl Hagemann, Max Grube, Paul Eger, Erich Ziegel, and Albert Lippert, producing plays by Lessing, Goethe, Schiller, Shakespeare, Hauptmann, Gozzi, Ibsen, Strindberg, and Brecht. In 1933 the theater's status as a private corporation was changed to that of a public theater with a tax subsidy.

Possibly the best-known Intendant in the theater's history was Gustaf Gründgens, one of the half dozen leading director-actors of the past half century. He took over the theater in 1955 and remained there until his death in 1963. During that time he directed and acted in many significant productions including some world premieres, as follows:

1955   *Das kalte Licht* by Carl Zuckmayer (world premiere); directed.

1956   *Herrenhaus* by Thomas Wolfe; directed and played General Ramsay.
          Thomas Chatterton by Hanns Henny Jahn (world premiere); directed.
          Nichts Neues aus Hollywood by Curt Goetz (world premiere); directed and played Cliff Clifford.

1957   *Faust I* by Goethe; directed and played Mephistopheles. This production was seen at the New York City Center in February of 1961.
          Der Entertainer by John Osborne (first production in Germany); played Archie Rice.

1958   *Faust II* by Goethe; directed and played Mephistopheles.

1959   *Die heilige Johanna der Schlachthöfe* by Bertolt Brecht (world premiere); directed.
          Sappho by Lawrence Durrell (world premiere); directed.

1960   *Von Bergamo bis morgen früh* by Dieter Waldmann (world premiere); directed.

1961   *Actis* by Lawrence Durrell (world premiere); directed.

1962   *Don Carlos* by Schiller; directed and played Philip II.

1963   *Hamlet* by Shakespeare; directed.

The company operates in a main theater and a studio theater. Technical aspects of these theaters are as follows:

Deutsches Schauspielhaus

Seating capacity: 1,519 seats.

Architect: Firma Fellner und Hellmer.

Opened: September 15, 1900, with Goethe's *Iphigenie auf Tauris* under the direction of Alfred Freiherr von Berger.

Proscenium size: 11 meters wide by 5.8 meters high.

Stage size: 17.5 meters wide by 15 meters deep.

Technical equipment: Revolving stage, lighting control over 200 dimmers (System AEG).

Orchestra pit: Hydraulic lift; may be used as a pit for 12 musicians or as a forestage.

Studiobühne Malersaal

Seating capacity: Multiform; about 300 seats.

Opened: April 8, 1971, with Edward Bond's *Die Hochzeit des Papstes*.

Playing area: 15 meters by 20 meters. Ceiling height is 4 meters.

Technical equipment: No fixed lighting layout. Control console with 20 circuits (System Strand Electric).

The Generalintendant of the Deutsches Schauspielhaus is Ivan Nagel. Personnel of the theater during 1976–77 numbered as follows:

Artistic direction	25
Actors and actresses	40
Technical personnel	173
Administrative personnel	37
House personnel	59
Total	334

During the same season the company's performance, attendance, and percent-attendance record was as follows:

	PERFORMANCES	ATTENDANCE	PERCENT OF CAPACITY
Adult plays	374	301,805	56.5%
Children's plays	23	29,017	85.7%
Guest companies	69	(included above)	
Totals	466	330,822	71.1%

During 1978–79 the Deutsches Schauspielhaus presented the following works:

Shakespeare: *Das Wintermärchen*
 Othello
 Ein Sommernachtstraum
 Hamlet

Fig. 229. The Deutsches Schauspielhaus on Kirchenallee in Hamburg, across the street from the main railway station (Deutsches Schauspielhaus)

Deutsches Schauspielhaus
in Hamburg.

Eröffnungs-Vorstellung: Sonnabend, den 15. September.

PROLOG von Alfred Freiherrn von Berger.

„Die Weihe des Hauses" von Beethoven.

Iphigenie auf Tauris
Schauspiel in fünf Aufzügen von Goethe.

Iphigenie	Stella Hohenfels a. G.
Thoas, König der Taurier	Carl Bender
Orest	Carl Wagner
Pylades	Heinrich Stillfried
Arkas	Max Montor

Schauplatz: Hain vor Dianens Tempel.

Regie: Oberregisseur Cord Hachmann.

Die Dekoration ist aus dem Atelier der Hof-Theatermaler Brüder Kautsky & Rottonara in Wien.
Die Costüme sind von der Rheinischen Costüm-Fabrik Cahn & David, Düsseldorf, geliefert.

Erhöhte Preise der Plätze für diese Vorstellung:

Der Gesammtertrag wird ohne jeden Abzug der Gründung einer „Pensions-Anstalt des Deutschen Schauspielhauses" zur Verfügung gestellt.

Proscenium-Logen.

	incl. Garderobe und Programm				incl. Garderobe und Programm	
		der Platz				der Platz
Fremdenloge (Balcon rechts Loge No. 1) (5 Personen)	ℳ 45.—	30 ₰	ℳ 46.50	Ein Sitz I. Rang 1. 2. Reihe	ℳ 7.—	30 ₰ „ 7.30
Eine Loge im Parquet (5 Personen)	„ 37.50	30 „	„ 39.—	„ „ 3. 7.	„ 6.—	30 „ „ 6.30
(4 Personen)	„ 30.—	30 „	„ 31.20	„ „ 8.—11.	„ 5.—	30 „ „ 5.30
Eine Loge im Balcon (5 Personen)	„ 37.50	30 „	„ 39.—	„ Parquet	„ 6.—	30 „ „ 6.30
(4 Personen)	„ 30.—	30 „	„ 31.20	„ zweites Parquet	„ 5.—	30 „ „ 5.30
Eine Loge im I. Rang (5 Personen)	„ 30.—	30 „	„ 31.50	„ Parterre-Sperrsitz	„ 3.—	25 „ „ 3.25
(4 Personen)	„ 24.—	30 „	„ 25.20	„ II. Rang 1. 2. Reihe	„ 3.—	25 „ „ 3.25
Eine Loge im II. Rang (4 Personen)	„ 12.—	25 „	„ 13.—	„ „ 3. 7.	„ 2.25	25 „ „ 2.50
(3 Personen)	„ 9.—	25 „	„ 9.75	„ „ 8.—13.	„ 1.50	25 „ „ 1.75
				II. Rang Stehplätze	„ 0.75	15 „ „ 0.90

Die Logen werden nur im Ganzen verkauft und einzelne Plätze nicht abgegeben.

Billets sind von Dienstag, den 4. September ab täglich an der Tageskasse (Eingang von der Kirchenallee) zu haben.

Die Vorstellungen vom Sonntag, den 16. Sept. bis Sonntag, den 30. Sept. finden außer Abonnement statt. Den Abonnenten werden ihre Plätze für die betreffenden Tage reservirt und können die Billets zu den hier folgenden Kassen-Preisen gegen Vorzeigung der Abonnementsquittung bis Montag, den 10. Sept. 2½ Uhr, an der Tages-Kasse (Eingang von der Kirchenallee) in Empfang genommen werden.

Preise der Plätze:

Proscenium-Logen.

	incl. Garderobe und Programm				incl. Garderobe und Programm					incl. Garderobe und Programm	
		der Platz				der Platz					der Platz
Fremdenloge (Balcon rechts Loge No. 1) (5 Pers.)	ℳ 30.—	30 ₰	ℳ 31.50	Eine Loge im II. Rang (4 Personen)	ℳ 8.—	25 ₰	ℳ 9.—	Ein Sitz Parquet	ℳ 4.—	30 ₰	ℳ 4.30
Eine Loge im Parquet (5 Personen)	25.—	30	26.50	(3 Personen)	6.—	25	6.75	„ zweites Parquet	3.50	30	3.80
(4 Personen)	20.—	30	21.20	Die Logen werden nur im Ganzen verkauft und einzelne Plätze nicht abgegeben.				„ Parterre-Sperrsitz	2.—	25	2.25
Eine Loge im Balcon (5 Personen)	25.—	30	26.50					„ II. Rang 1.—2. Reihe	2.—	25	2.25
(4 Personen)	20.—	30	21.20	Ein Sitz I. Rang 1.—2. Reihe	4.50	30	4.80	„ „ 3.—7.	1.50	25	1.75
Eine Loge im I. Rang (5 Personen)	20.—	30	21.50	„ „ 3.—7.	4.—	30	4.30	„ „ 8.—13.	1.—	25	1.25
(4 Personen)	16.—	30	17.20	„ „ 8.—11.	3.50	30	3.80	II. Rang Stehplätze	—.50	15	—.65

Die Bureaux befinden sich von Montag, den 3. September ab im Schauspielhause.

Die Ausgabe der bestellten Abonnementbillets ist bis zum 13. September im Bureau der Tageskasse von 10—2½ Uhr, Eingang von der Capellenstraße, woselbst auch noch Neuanmeldungen auf Abonnements entgegengenommen werden.

Fig. 231. Playbill announcing the world premiere of Gerhart Hauptmann's tragedy *Veland* and the 25th anniversary season of the Deutsches Schauspielhaus in Hamburg (Deutsches Schauspielhaus)

Offenbach: *La Périchole*
Molière: *Der eingebildete Kranke*
Lessing: *Emilia Galotti*
Ibsen: *Hedda Gabler*
Strindberg: *Der Vater*
Savary/Wilms/Kuntzsch: *In 80 Tagen um die Welt* (world premiere)
Fo: *Dario Fo Spektakel*
Kipphardt: *März* (world premiere)
Schröder/Heising: *Traum-Mörder*
Anski: *Der Dibbuk*
Dorst: *König Arthur und die Tafelrunde* (world premiere)
Kilty: *Geliebter Lügner*
Osborne: *Blick zurück im Zorn*
Müller: *Gundlings Leben* (world premiere)

A summary of prices for single tickets and subscriptions is shown in Figs. 232 and 233, p. 331.

Fig. 234, p. 332, shows a nine-year financial summary.

Scenes from recent productions at the Hamburg Deutsches Schauspielhaus are shown in Figs. 235–239, pp, 333–338.

Thalia Theater

The Thalia Theater was founded in 1843 as a private theater by Chérie Maurice and began receiving regular subsidies from the city of Hamburg after World War I. The original theater building was located on the Pferdemarkt, but in 1912 a new structure was erected directly across from the site of the old one by the architectural firm of Lundt and Kallmorgen. It opened August 31, 1912, with four short works, *Der Einzug* by Otto Ernst, *Die Laune des Verliebten* by Goethe, *Unter Brüdern* by Paul Heyse, and Wedekind's *Der Kammersänger*. The auditorium seated 1,300 spectators.

During a bombing attack in April, 1945, the theater was partly destroyed, but enough of it remained so that it could be reopened, with 669 seats available, on September 29, 1946, with Shakespeare's *Was ihr wollt*. The company performed temporarily during 1959 and 1960 in the Theater am Besenbinderhof while its own theater was completely redesigned and rebuilt on what is now Gerhart-Hauptmann-Platz. When

Fig. 232 *(Top right)*. Prices for single tickets and for subscriptions to seven performances, which include the program, the coat-check charge, a contribution to the theater's pension plan, and the theater's monthly magazine. Subscription performances take place Tuesday through Saturday evenings, Saturday afternoons, and Sunday afternoons. This rate schedule was established for the Spielzeit 1978–79 (Deutsches Schauspielhaus)

Fig. 233 *(Bottom right)*. Seating plan for the Deutsches Schauspielhaus, Hamburg (Deutsches Schauspielhaus)

Platz-Gruppe	Plätze	Abend Kassenpreise DM	Nachmittag Kassenpreise DM	Abend Abonnementspreise DM	Nachmittag Abonnementspreise DM	Scheckheft DM	Scheckheft Gesamtpreis DM
1	Parkett 1.–9. Reihe I. Rang 1.–3. Reihe Parkett-, Balkonlogen	29,–	26,–	23,50 = 164,50	19,– = 133,–	25,–	150,–
2	Parkett 10.–14. Reihe	25,–	22,–	20,– = 140,–	16,50 = 115,–	21,50	129,–
3	Parkett 15.–19. Reihe I. Rang 4. + 5. Reihe	21,–	18,–	16,50 = 115,50	13,50 = 94,50	18,–	108,–
4	I. Rang 6.–8. Reihe I. Rangloge II. Rang 1.–3. Reihe	17,–	14,–	13,50 = 94,50	10,50 = 73,50	14,50	87,–
5	Parkett 20.–22. Reihe I. Rang 9.–11. Reihe	13,–	11,–	10,50 = 73,50	8,50 = 59,50	11,–	66,–
6	II. Rang 4.–7. Reihe II. Rangloge II. Rang Seite 1. + 2. Reihe	9,–	8,–	7,50 = 52,50	6,50 = 42,50	7,50	45,–
7	II. Rang 8.–11. Reihe Logenrücksitze Sichtbehinderte Plätze	7,–	5,–	5,– = 35,–	4,– = 28,–	6,–	36,–

Vorstellungen inkl. Programm, Garderobenablage, Altersversorgungsabgabe und Theaterzeitung

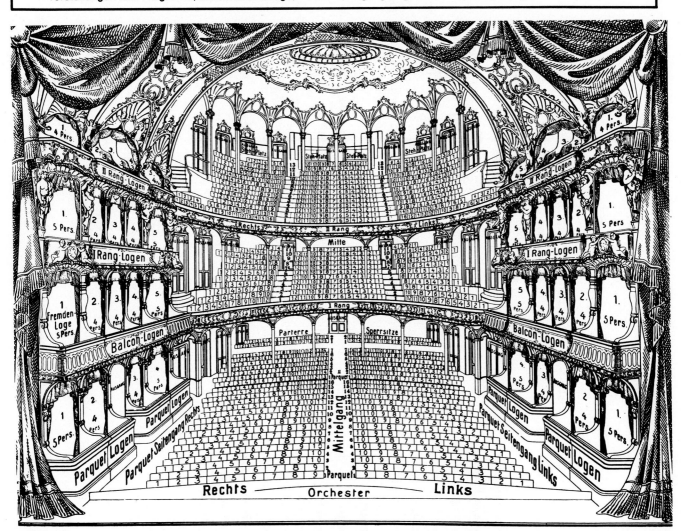

Deutsches Schauspielhaus, Hamburg

YEAR	1969	1970	1971	1972	1973	1974	1975	1976	1977
VALUE OF DEUTSCHE MARK	28¢	29¢	30¢	34¢	40¢	42¢	44¢	48¢	50¢
EXPENSES									
Artists' salaries	DM 3,237,000	DM 3,627,000	DM 4,482,000	DM 4,467,000	DM 4,490,000	DM 5,461,000	DM 5,639,000	DM 6,106,000	DM 6,576,000
Technical salaries	3,095,000	3,462,000	4,071,000	4,491,000	4,989,000	5,777,000	6,120,000	6,518,000	6,837,000
Administration	904,000	962,000	1,134,000	1,361,000	1,565,000	1,720,000	1,759,000	1,773,000	1,934,000
Other personnel	185,000	237,000	148,000	139,000	154,000	160,000	181,000	167,000	189,000
Pension funds	248,000	276,000	348,000	428,000	601,000	671,000	687,000	678,000	709,000
Production costs	1,854,000	2,014,000	2,362,000	2,865,000	3,295,000	3,686,000	4,032,000	4,295,000	4,325,000
Loan payments	---	---	---	---	---	104,000	90,000	141,000	225,000
Building maintenance	---	134,000	---	---	---	26,000	53,000	13,000	---
TOTAL	DM 9,523,000	DM 10,712,000	DM 12,545,000	DM 13,751,000	DM 15,094,000	DM 17,605,000	DM 18,561,000	DM 19,691,000	DM 20,795,000
INCOME									
Single tickets	DM 557,000	DM 870,000	DM 1,051,000	DM 782,000	DM 1,075,000	DM 1,042,000	DM 1,960,000	DM 1,921,000	DM 1,989,000
Subscriptions	1,479,000	1,077,000	975,000	1,083,000	1,024,000	989,000	1,203,000	1,056,000	951,000
Children's theater subscriptions	361,000	366,000	459,000	504,000	574,000	764,000	---	217,000	244,000
Visitor groups	375,000	287,000	368,000	205,000	69,000	89,000	101,000	99,000	111,000
Cloakroom charges	245,000	226,000	231,000	218,000	235,000	235,000	---	---	---
Radio and TV fees	183,000	218,000	107,000	423,000	14,000	227,000	317,000	663,000	321,000
Touring	109,000	148,000	71,000	99,000	217,000	330,000	236,000	412,000	288,000
Guest performances by other companies	---	64,000	100,000	204,000	372,000	320,000	700,000	548,000	341,000
Program sales	151,000	122,000	124,000	215,000	263,000	302,000	71,000	65,000	101,000
Other income	136,000	145,000	127,000	129,000	164,000	190,000	227,000	514,000	194,000
TOTAL	DM 3,574,000	DM 3,525,000	DM 3,613,000	DM 3,862,000	DM 4,007,000	DM 4,488,000	DM 4,815,000	DM 5,495,000	DM 4,520,000
TAX SUBSIDY	DM 5,949,000	DM 7,189,000	DM 8,932,000	DM 9,889,000	DM 11,087,000	DM 13,117,000	DM 13,746,000	DM 14,198,000	DM 16,275,000
SUBSIDY PERCENTAGE	62.5%	67.1%	71.2%	71.9%	75.5%	74.5%	74.1%	72.1%	78.5%

Fig. 234. Expenses and income for the Deutsches Schauspielhaus, Hamburg from 1969 through 1977 (Deutscher Bühnenverein, Köln)

Fig. 235. Two scenes from one of the Deutsches Schauspielhaus's most famous productions, Goethe's *Faust I,* directed by Gustaf Gründgens. Mephistopheles (Gründgens) counsels Faust (Will Quadflieg) . . . and . . . (Rosemarie Clausen)

Fig. 236. . . . in the Walpurgisnacht sequence, a rejuvenated Faust dances with one of the witches (Rosemarie Clausen)

Fig. 237. The first production of Brecht's *Die heilige Johanna der Schlachthöfe* took place at the Deutsches Schauspielhaus under the direction of Gustaf Gründgens. Joan harangues the Chicago gamblers, speculators, and hog barons (Rosemarie Clausen)

Fig. 238. Peter Zadek's controversial production of Shakespeare's *Othello* in Hamburg. Ulrich Wildgruber as a knockabout Moor and Eva Mattes as a hippy Desdemona (Deutsches Schauspielhaus/Gisela Scheidler)

Fig. 239. John Osborne's *Blick zurück im Zorn,* directed by Arie Zinger. Heinrich Giskes as Jimmy Porter and Ilse Ritter as Allison (Deutsches Schauspielhaus/Gisela Scheidler)

the new Thalia Theater was finished, the company returned, and the theater has been in continuous operation ever since as part of Hamburg's national theater complex. Technical aspects of the building are as follows:

Seating capacity: 1,104 seats.
Architect: Werner Kallmorgen.
Opened: December 3, 1960, with Shaw's *Die heilige Johanna.*
Proscenium size: 7.65 meters high by 9.8 meters wide.
Stage size: 16 meters wide by 14.5 meters deep.
Technical equipment: Revolving stage unit with lifts 12.5 meters in diameter, lighting control over 120 magnetic amplifier dimmers (ELA-Anlage). A small experimental stage is also in use.

The Generalintendant of the Thalia Theater is Boy Gobert. Personnel of the company during 1976–77 numbered as follows:

Artistic direction	20
Actors and actresses	38
Technical personnel	141
Administrative personnel	31
House personnel	80
Total	310

Public performance, attendance, and percentage of capacity business were as follows:

	PERFORMANCES	ATTENDANCE	PERCENT OF CAPACITY
Musicals	39	37,745	95.5%
Adult plays	396	305,507	84.9%
Children's plays	36	11,742	85.8%
Guest companies	12	(included above)	
Totals	483	354,994	88.7%

Altogether, the three national theaters in Hamburg played to 1,159,666 people during 1976–77, or about 68 percent of the population of this large north German city-state.

During 1977–78, the Thalia Theater performed the following plays:

Synge: *Ein wahrer Held*
Gorki: *Kinder der Sonne*
Fosse/Kander: *Chicago* (first German production)
Hacks: *Das Jahrmarktsfest zu Plundersweilern*
  Ein Gespräch im Hause Stein über den abwesenden Herrn von Goethe

Nestroy: *Einen Jux will er sich machen*
Bond: *Der Irre* (first German production)
Wedekind: *Der Marquis von Keith*
Ionesco: *Die Stühle*
Arrabel: *Klau mir eine kleine Milliarde* (first German production)
Molière: *Don Juan*
Griffiths: *Komiker* (first German production)
Pinter: *Der Hausmeister*
Schiller: *Kabale und Liebe*
Shakespeare: *Hamlet*

Fig. 241, p. 342, shows a nine-year financial summary.

Scenes from recent productions at the Thalia Theater are shown in Figs. 242–244, pp. 343–345.

Fig. 240. Subscription prices for a series of eight performances during the season 1978–79 at the Thalia Theater (Thalia Theater)

Abonnementspreise für die Spielzeit 1978/79

Preisgruppe		Nachmittags- und Abendpreise bei 8 Vorstellungen	
		Gesamt	Raten
A	Parkett 1.–7. Reihe Ranglogen	192,—	72,— 72,— 48,—
B	Parkett 8.–11. Reihe	156,—	58,50 58,50 39,—
C	Parkett 12.–15. Reihe Mittelrang 1.–2. Reihe	124,—	46,50 46,50 31,—
D	Parkett 16.–18. Reihe Mittelrang 3.–5. Reihe Oberrang 1.–2. Reihe	92,—	34,50 34,50 23,—
E	Parkett 19.–21. Reihe Oberrang 3.–8. Reihe	64,—	24,— 24,— 16,—

Rechnungen und Abonnements-Platzkarten werden zusammenhängend etwa Mitte August 1978 verschickt. Sollten sie bis Anfang September 1978 nicht bei Ihnen eingegangen sein, bitten wir um Benachrichtigung.

YEAR	1969	1970	1971	1972	1973	1974	1975	1976	1977
VALUE OF DEUTSCHE MARK	28¢	29¢	30¢	34¢	40¢	42¢	44¢	48¢	50¢
EXPENSES									
Artists' salaries	DM 2,554,000	DM 3,236,000	DM 3,252,000	DM 3,957,000	DM 4,031,000	DM 4,675,000	DM 5,685,000	DM 6,360,000	DM 7,708,000
Technical salaries	2,120,000	2,498,000	2,803,000	3,413,000	4,161,000	4,509,000	4,888,000	5,145,000	5,219,000
Administration	867,000	1,052,000	1,163,000	1,410,000	1,702,000	1,885,000	1,973,000	2,091,000	2,141,000
Other personnel	253,000	259,000	303,000	339,000	358,000	343,000	346,000	337,000	317,000
Pension funds	198,000	220,000	264,000	293,000	383,000	486,000	449,000	449,000	429,000
Production costs	1,808,000	1,721,000	2,035,000	2,161,000	2,236,000	2,492,000	2,862,000	3,169,000	3,324,000
Loan payments	63,000	---	---	---	---	---	278,000	134,000	64,000
Building maintenance	30,000	---	65,000	90,000	---	---	---	---	---
TOTAL	DM 7,893,000	DM 8,986,000	DM 9,885,000	DM 11,663,000	DM 12,871,000	DM 14,637,000	DM 16,481,000	DM 17,685,000	DM 19,202,000
INCOME									
Single tickets	DM 1,212,000	DM 1,226,000	DM 1,139,000	DM 1,262,000	DM 1,070,000	DM 1,225,000	DM 1,360,000	DM 1,562,000	DM 1,521,000
Subscriptions	1,636,000	1,655,000	1,617,000	1,996,000	1,989,000	1,967,000	2,434,000	2,430,000	2,423,000
Children's theater subscriptions	129,000	67,000	85,000	113,000	147,000	189,000	49,000	35,000	28,000
Visitor groups	282,000	342,000	306,000	300,000	346,000	403,000	344,000	442,000	502,000
Cloakroom charges	234,000	232,000	201,000	243,000	232,000	253,000	243,000	249,000	247,000
Radio and TV fees	4,000	134,000	6,000	254,000	91,000	10,000	402,000	310,000	396,000
Touring	19,000	30,000	54,000	39,000	57,000	214,000	246,000	385,000	599,000
Guest performances by other companies	---	51,000	---	17,000	---	114,000	29,000	63,000	140,000
Program sales	117,000	129,000	127,000	158,000	138,000	158,000	175,000	175,000	175,000
Other income	179,000	175,000	196,000	282,000	556,000	194,000	289,000	240,000	356,000
TOTAL	DM 3,812,000	DM 4,041,000	DM 3,731,000	DM 4,664,000	DM 4,626,000	DM 4,727,000	DM 5,571,000	DM 5,891,000	DM 6,387,000
TAX SUBSIDY	DM 4,081,000	DM 4,945,000	DM 6,154,000	DM 6,999,000	DM 8,245,000	DM 9,910,000	DM 10,910,000	DM 11,794,000	DM 12,815,000
SUBSIDY PERCENTAGE	51.7%	55.0%	62.3%	60.0%	64.1%	67.7%	66.2%	66.7%	66.7%

Fig. 241. Expenses and income for the Thalia Theater, 1969–77 (Deutscher Bühnenverein, Köln)

Fig. 242. Peter Zadek's production of *Komiker* by the English playwright Trevor Griffiths. At left, Mr. Challenor (Boy Gobert) argues with the teacher (Heinz Schubert) about what is funny in the theater while the would-be comedians Phil (Uwe Friedrichsen), Ged (Ulrich Wildgruber), and McBrain (Hans-Peter Hallwachs) listen attentively (Hans Meyer-Veden)

Fig. 243. An intense production of Shakespeare's *Hamlet,* directed by Hans Neuenfels. Maria Emo as the Queen, Melanie Horeschovsky as Ophelia II, and Konrad Kraus as Laertes (Thalia Theater)

Fig. 244. The first German production of Edward Bond's *Der Irre,* directed by Gerd Heinz. Ulrich Kuhlmann as the Fool and Monika Baumgartner as his friend (Hans Meyer-Veden)

344 • NATIONAL THEATERS IN GERMAN AND AUSTRIAN CITIES

IX.   HAMBURG, GERMANY • 345

X. WEST BERLIN, GERMANY

It is an unfortunate fact of modern life that Berlin is split into two parts, the police state east and the liberal democratic west. Berliners hope to see their city reunited someday, but it is an irony of history that the city began as two fishing villages on opposite sides of the Spree River, Berlin and Cölln, which for many decades displayed no special desire to be united. In fact, it was the decision of the Elector Frederick II in 1440 to make Berlin his Residenz for purposes of governing the Mark of Brandenburg that finally led to the development of the two towns into an important city.

During the 17th century, the Great Elector, Frederick William, stimulated growth and variety in Berlin. He planned a large Lustgarten to the north of his elaborate palace and laid out the famous avenue Unter den Linden to the west of it. In 1685 he invited the French Huguenots, who were being persecuted in their own country, to settle in Brandenburg, and many families came to Berlin, bringing French culture and ideas with them. The Electorate of Brandenburg became the Kingdom of Prussia in 1701, and the city reflected its new affluence in many fine baroque buildings, the castle, the Zeughaus (Armory), St. Hedwig's Cathedral, and later the imposing museums on an island in the Spree called the Museuminsel.

With the accession to the throne of Frederick the Great in 1740, the Prussian city on the Spree came under the influence of a monarch with a breadth of culture to match his military talent. The King engaged the architect Georg von Knobelsdorff to design a new opera house in classical style, and the building, on Unter den Linden across a courtyard from the Royal Library, was completed in 1742. Frederick, who was an amateur musician and a poet of some skill, took a keen interest in the musical productions staged in his theater. In 1755 he wrote a libretto in French called *Montezuma* for his court composer Karl Heinrich Graun on the subject of the conquest of Mexico by Cortez. He provided for production of drama as well as opera and ballet, although the acting troupes were French and performed only French plays. Frederick the Great took little interest in German drama, as he considered the language barbaric.

Drama and opera continued to develop in Berlin through the reign of the next monarch, Frederick William II. In 1786, following the example of the Emperor Joseph

II in Vienna ten years earlier, he established a Königliches Nationaltheater on the Gendarmenmarkt. Here, finally, August Wilhelm Iffland presented the plays of Lessing, Goethe, and Schiller to the Berlin public. Opera was performed in German as well as Italian, and Mozart saw a production here in 1789 of his *Die Entführung aus dem Serail.* Later, in 1816, the first performance of E. T. A. Hoffmann's opera *Undine* took place. The theater burned down in 1817 but was quickly replaced by an even grander structure on the same site, designed by the architect Karl Schinkel, and opened in 1821 with the first performance of Weber's *Der Freischütz.*

Today, the divided city provides national theater complexes in both sectors. In the east are the Deutsche Staatsoper Unter den Linden, the Komische Oper on Behrenstrasse nearby, the Deutsches Theater on Schumannstrasse, and the Berliner Ensemble in the Theater am Schiffbauerdamm. The West Berlin complex includes the Deutsche Oper Berlin on Bismarckstrasse and the Schiller-Theater not far away on the same street. Under the direction of the Schiller-Theater are also the Schlosspark-Theater on Schlossstrasse and the Schiller-Theater Werkstatt in the main building. West Berlin is one of the 11 West German states and in 1977 had a population of 1,950,706. It receives a large special subsidy from Bonn each year, part of which is used to support its educational and cultural institutions.

Deutsche Oper Berlin

Like the Hamburg Staatsoper, the Deutsche Oper Berlin began as a private theater subsidized by wealthy patrons and then was turned into a national theater subsidized by federal tax revenues. In 1910 a group of opera lovers in the Berlin suburb of Charlottenburg raised sufficient funds to build and endow a new opera house, designed by the architect Heinrich Seelig and named the Deutsches Opernhaus. It seated 2,098 spectators and had a stage 1,300 square meters in size, with all types of scene-shifting machinery available at the time.

The house was opened November 7, 1912, with a performance of *Fidelio* under the Intendant Georg Hartmann. The theater established a good reputation by doing operas not regularly seen at the rival house on Unter den Linden, but after the war inflation brought the company to the verge of bankruptcy. The city of Berlin annexed Charlottenburg and took over responsibility for its opera house, renaming it the Städtische Oper, although people tended to call it the Charlottenburg Oper. Heinz Tietjen became Intendant in 1925 and engaged Bruno Walter as Generalmusikdirektor and Emil Preetorius as principal scene designer. The trend toward placing stage directors at the head of opera companies started in 1931, when one of Max Reinhardt's best actors, Carl Ebert, took over the management of the house. He engaged Rudolf Bing to look after the artistic administration of the theater and devoted most of his own energies to directing the opera productions as though they were plays in a spoken drama house. With the help of his principal conductor, Fritz Busch, and the scene designer Caspar Neher, Ebert worked toward the elusive Wagnerian ideal of the Gesamtkunstwerk, productions in which the expressive elements of music, language, pantomime, dance, and scenic investiture are blended into a single, unified artistic

Fig. 245. Frederick the Great's Königlisches Opernhaus on Unter den Linden, as it appeared before World War II. This theater is presently operated by the East Berlin Communist government (Allgemeine Elektricitäts-Gesellschaft)

Fig. 246. The Schauspielhaus on the Gendarmenmarkt, designed in 1820–21 by Karl Friedrich Schinkel. Badly damaged during the war, it is currently being restored by the East German government as a theater for chamber opera and concerts with a seating capacity of about 600 (Allgemeine Elektricitäts-Gesellschaft)

representation of the dramatic poem in the theater. In addition to directing himself, he invited other established stage directors such as Jürgen Fehling and Gustaf Gründgens to stage operas for him, and by 1933, when the Nazis dismissed the entire top management of the theater, he had laid the groundwork for the modern practice of placing final responsibility for opera production in the hands of the stage director rather than the conductor.

During 1943 the theater was totally destroyed in a bombing raid, but the company was reassembled after the war and operated in the relatively undamaged Theater des Westens until 1961, when it was able to move back into its completely redesigned and rebuilt theater, now renamed the Deutsche Oper Berlin.

The stage director Gustav Rudolf Sellner became Generalintendant in 1961 and staged the opening production, *Don Giovanni,* on September 24 of that year. Under his administration and those of his successors, the theater has become one of the leading opera houses of the western world. Not only are standards of performance very high and the repertory exceptionally broad, but also, like its counterpart in Hamburg, the Deutsche Oper Berlin has made a sustained effort to develop and perform new operas in the interest of replenishing a very limited repertory of genuine world masterpieces. There follows a list of the new operas given their world premieres by the company since its reopening in 1961:

1961	Giselher Klebe: *Alkmene* (commissioned)
1963	Darius Milhaud: *Oreste* (premiere of entire work)
1964	Roger Sessions: *Montezuma*
1965	Isang Yun: *The Dream of Liu-Tung* (commissioned)
	Hans Werner Henze: *Der junge Lord* (commissioned)
1966	Roman Haubenstock-Ramati: *Amerika*
1968	Luigi Dallapiccola: *Ulisse* (commissioned)
1969	Boris Blacher: *200,000 Taler* (commissioned)
1970	Thomas Kessler: *Nationale Feiertage* (commissioned)
1971	Aribert Reimann: *Melusine*
1972	Wolfgang Fortner: *Elizabeth Tudor*
	Sylvano Bussotti: *Apology* (commissioned)
1973	Nicholas Nabokov: *Love's Labour's Lost* (commissioned)
	Klaus Huber: *Jot* (commissioned)
1975	Mauricio Kagel: *Mare Nostrum*
1976	Karl Heinz Wahren: *Fettklösschen* (commissioned)
	Toshiro Mayuzumi: *Kinkakuji* (commissioned)

Opportunities to see the important German and Austrian theater companies in America are few, as it costs so much to tour, but theatergoers in the Washington area were able to judge the quality of the work of the Deutsche Oper Berlin for themselves during a two-week stand in November, 1975, at the Kennedy Center. The company performed *Lohengrin* as staged originally by Wieland Wagner and conducted by Lorin Maazel; *Tosca,* directed by Boleslaw Barlog and conducted by Maazel; and

Così fan tutte, which was directed by Otto Schenk and conducted by Karl Böhm. Critical response in the American papers was favorable, as was a review in the British magazine *Opera.* The project was carried out by the American and West German governments at a cost of DM 1,300,000 (about $600,000), with each country paying about half, in honor of the American Bicentennial. The American soprano Anabelle Bernard made her United States debut at the time, singing Fiordiligi.

Technical aspects of the theater are as follows:

Seating capacity: 1,903 seats.

Architect: Fritz Bornemann.

Opened: September 24, 1961, with Mozart's *Don Giovanni,* staged by the Intendant, Gustav Rudolf Sellner.

Proscenium size: 14.5 meters wide by 8 meters high.

Stage size: 28 meters wide by 19 meters deep. Rear and side stages triple the main stage area.

Technical equipment: Four main stage lifts, of which two are double-decked; two side stage wagons and one rear stage wagon, the latter carrying a turntable 17 meters in diameter; two movable tormentors with lighting platforms, lighting bridge, and overhead bridges for horizon lighting units, Wickel-Horizont; 50 scene projection machines, including two Xenon units; a 240-dimmer lighting control unit that uses magnetic amplifiers and card presets; and a sound system that permits amplification of backstage sound effects and communication throughout the theater. There is also a TV control center and several TV cameras permanently installed. Several seats in the auditorium have apparatus for the hard of hearing.

Orchestra pit: Four double-decked lifts with an area of 15 meters by 8 meters for 120 musicians.

The Besucherorganisationen that support the West German theaters are the Freie Volksbühne, the Theatergemeinde e.V., the Theater der Schulen, the Berliner Theaterclub e.V., and the Berliner Besucherring.

The Generalintendant of the Deutsche Oper Berlin is Siegfried Palm. During the 76–77 season the company numbered as follows:

Artistic direction	43
Principal singers	53
Ballet dancers	52
Chorus singers	113
Orchestra musicians	138
Technical personnel	358
Administrative personnel	58
House personnel	85
Total	900

Fig. 247. The modernistic Deutsche Oper Berlin, rebuilt after the war on Bismarckstrasse, site of the former Charlottenburg Opera (Deutsche Oper Berlin)

Fig. 248. Auditorium of the Deutsche Oper Berlin, showing part of the orchestra pit, the typically continental seating, and the flying boxes cantilevered out from the walls, which replace the traditional box seats of the Italian opera houses (Deutsche Oper Berlin)

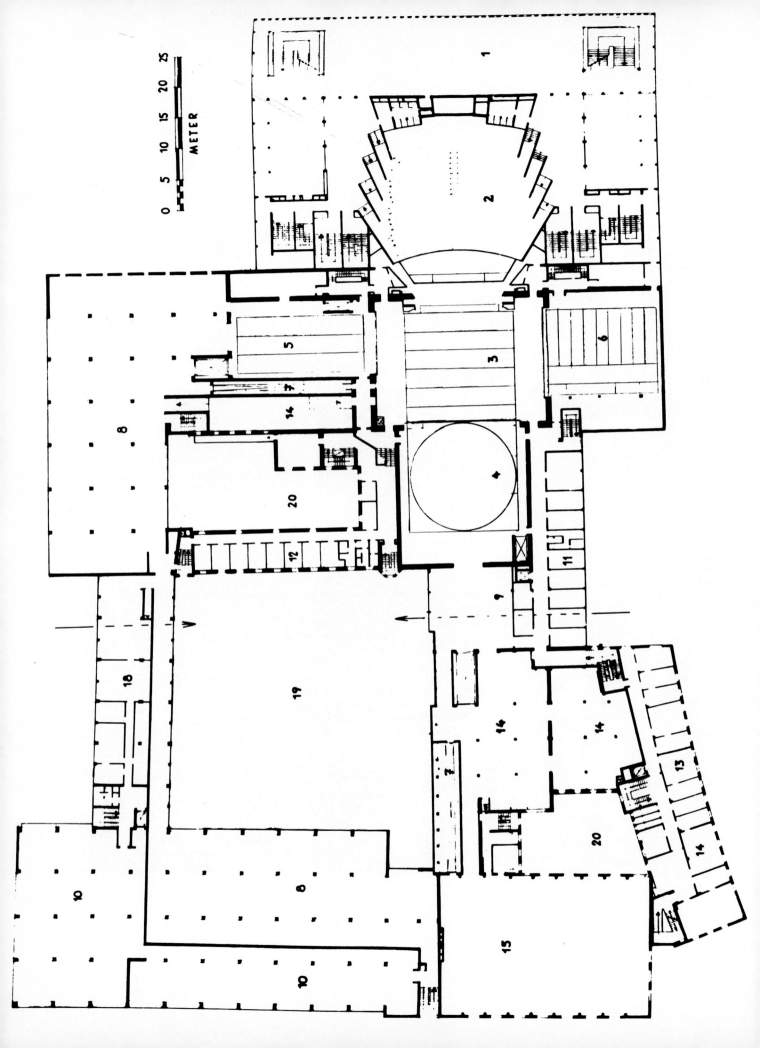

Fig. 249. Ground plan of the Deutsche Oper Berlin: (1) lobby area; (2) auditorium; (3) main stage; (4) rear stage over large rehearsal stage; (5) side stage left; (6) side stage right; (7) drop storage—see *Figure 250*; (8) scene storage; (9) rear projection room over ballet rehearsal stage; (10) costume storage over large painting studio; (11) women's dressing rooms; (12) men's dressing rooms; (13) administration offices; (14) scene storage over rehearsal room; (15) scene shop; (18) costume shop; (19) parking; (20) garden (Bühnentechnische Rundschau)

Fig. 250. A view of the inside of the drop storage area beneath the right side stage. Back-
drops are rolled up, put on the elevator, and lowered between long bins in which the
drops are stored. The drops being struck are rolled off the elevator into the bins, and
the drops needed for the next production are rolled out of the bins onto the elevator
floor. They are then lifted to stage level, where they are unrolled, fastened to battens,
and flown (Deutsche Oper Berlin)

During the same season the company established the following performance, attendance, and house percentage record:

	PERFORMANCES	ATTENDANCE	PERCENT OF CAPACITY
Operas	247	385,577	82.1%
Ballets	50	82,741	87.1%
Operettas	13	24,369	98.6%
Totals	310	492,687	89.3%

During the 1978–79 season the Deutsche Oper Berlin staged the following opera and ballet productions:

Operas

New Productions	Tschaikowsky: *Pique Dame*
	Mozart: *Die Hochzeit des Figaro*
	Verdi: *Nabucco*
	Strauss: *Capriccio*
	Bizet: *Carmen*
Revivals	Beethoven: *Fidelio*
	Berg: *Wozzeck*
	Blacher: *Preussisches Märchen*
	Hindemith: *Cardillac*
	Humperdinck: *Hänsel und Gretel*
	Janáček: *Jenufa*
	Leoncavallo: *Der Bajazzo*
	Lortzing: *Der Wildschütz*
	Mascagni: *Cavalleria rusticana*
	Mozart: *Die Entführung aus dem Serail*
	Don Giovanni
	Così fan tutte
	Titus
	Die Zauberflöte
	Mussorgski: *Boris Godunow*
	Offenbach: *Hoffmanns Erzählungen*
	Die Banditen
	Pfitzner: *Palestrina*
	Ponchielli: *La Gioconda*
	Puccini: *Manon Lescaut*
	La Bohème
	Tosca
	Madame Butterfly
	Der Mantel

Schwester Angelika

Gianni Schicchi

Rossini: *Der Türke in Italien*

Der Barbier von Sevilla

Aschenbrödel

Smetana: *Die verkaufte Braut*

Strauss, J.: *Die Fledermaus*

Strauss, R.: *Salome*

Elektra

Der Rosenkavalier

Ariadne auf Naxos

Die Frau ohne Schatten

Arabella

Tschaikowsky: *Eugene Onegin*

Verdi: *Attila*

Rigoletto

Der Troubadour

La traviata

Die sizilianische Vesper

Ein Maskenball

Don Carlos

Aida

Otello

Falstaff

Wagner: *Der fliegende Holländer*

Tannhäuser

Lohengrin

Tristan und Isolde

Die Meistersinger von Nürnberg

Das Rheingold

Die Walküre

Siegfried

Götterdämmerung

Parsifal

Weber: *Der Freischütz*

Ballets

New Production   Schostakowitsch/Panov: *Der Idiot*

Revivals   Adam/Coralli/Tudor: *Giselle*

Armbruster/Schortemeier/Baumann: *3 und 16*

Beethoven/van Manen: *Adagio Hammerklavier*

Bizet/Balanchine: *Symphonie in C*

Boerman/van Dantzig: *Monument für einen gestorbenen*
Jungen
Cage/van Manen: *Twilight*
Cohen/Jooss: *Der grüne Tisch*
Delibes/Parés: *Coppelia*
Glasunow/Gsovsky/Beriozoff: *Raymonda*
Henry/Schaeffer/Béjart: *Symphonie für einem einsamen*
Menschen
Hindemith/Balanchine: *Die vier Temperamente*
Lesur/van Manen: *Metaforen*
Prokofieff/Bojartschikow: *Romeo und Julia*
Prokofieff/Panov: *Cinderella*
Prokofieff/Tudor: *Gala Performance*
Ravel/Balanchine: *La Valse*
Ravel/Jooss: *Pavane auf den Tod einer Infantin*
Ravel/van Manen: *Daphnis und Chloë*
Ravel/Béjart: *Bolero*
Schirren/Lommel: *Evolutio*
Strawinsky/Fokine/Cranko: *Der Feuervogel*
Strawinsky/Taras: *Petruschka*
Strawinsky/Panov: *Le Sacre du Printemps*
Strawinsky/Balanchine: *Apollon Musagète*
Agon
Tschaikowsky/MacMillan nach Iwanow und Petipa:
Schwanensee
Dornröschen
Tschaikowsky/Balanchine: *Serenade*
Webern/Béjart: *Opus 5*

Subscription and single-ticket price lists for the season 1977–78 are shown in Figs. 251 and 252, pp. 360–361.

Fig. 253, p. 362, shows a nine-year summary of the finances of the Deutsche Oper Berlin follows:

There follows a more detailed financial summary for the theater covering the years 1975–77. The 1975 figures are final whereas those for the two subsequent years are estimates, showing how a major German theater plans its budgets two years in advance (Figs. 254–257, pp. 363–366).

Scenes from recent productions by the Deutsche Oper Berlin are shown in Figs. 258–277, pp. 367–386.

Platzart		Abonnementspreise (bei Ratenzahlung)	Ermäßigte Abonnementspreise bei ganzjähriger Vorauszahlung	Preise des freien Kartenverkaufs		
				A–Preise	B–Preise	C–Preise
Parkett						
1. – 2. Reihe		25,00 DM	23,70 DM	31,20 DM	39,20 DM	47,20 DM
3. – 6. Reihe		21,00 DM	19,90 DM	26,20 DM	33,20 DM	40,20 DM
7. – 12. Reihe		17,80 DM	16,90 DM	22,20 DM	28,20 DM	34,20 DM
13. – 19. Reihe		15,40 DM	14,60 DM	19,20 DM	24,20 DM	29,20 DM
20. – 22. Reihe		11,40 DM	10,80 DM	14,20 DM	18,20 DM	22,20 DM
Hochparkett						
23. – 24. Reihe				10,20 DM	13,20 DM	16,20 DM
25. – 26. Reihe				9,20 DM	11,20 DM	13,20 DM
Logen Mitte				9,20 DM	11,20 DM	13,20 DM
Logen A, B, C	1. Reihe			31,20 DM	39,20 DM	47,20 DM
	2. – 3. Reihe			26,20 DM	33,20 DM	40,20 DM
	4. Reihe			10,20 DM	13,20 DM	16,20 DM
1. Rang						
1. Reihe				40,20 DM	50,20 DM	60,20 DM
2. Reihe		25,00 DM	23,70 DM	31,20 DM	39,20 DM	47,20 DM
3. – 5. Reihe		15,40 DM	14,60 DM	19,20 DM	24,20 DM	29,20 DM
6. – 9. Reihe		8,20 DM	7,70 DM	10,20 DM	13,20 DM	16,20 DM
Mittelloge				10,20 DM	13,20 DM	16,20 DM
Logen A, B, C				14,20 DM	18,20 DM	22,20 DM
Loge D	1. Reihe	25,00 DM	23,70 DM	31,20 DM	39,20 DM	47,20 DM
	2. – 3. Reihe			26,20 DM	33,20 DM	40,20 DM
	4. Reihe			10,20 DM	13,20 DM	16,20 DM
2. Rang						
1. Reihe		8,20 DM	7,70 DM	10,20 DM	13,20 DM	16,20 DM
2. – 3. Reihe		7,40 DM	6,90 DM	9,20 DM	11,20 DM	13,20 DM
4. – 5. Reihe				7,20 DM	9,20 DM	11,20 DM
6. – 9. Reihe				5,20 DM	7,20 DM	9,20 DM
Loge A				10,20 DM	13,20 DM	16,20 DM
Schwerbeschädigtenplätze (4 Pl.)				9,20 DM	11,20 DM	13,20 DM

Fig. 251. Price lists for the Deutsche Oper Berlin, 1977–78. Subscriptions are sold in groups of ten performances only. Thus, a subscription in the first or second row of the Parkett would cost DM 250 if paid for in installments and DM 237 if paid for all at once. As at other theaters, subscription prices are fixed, but individual prices in the same location vary according to the expense of the production (Deutsche Oper Berlin)

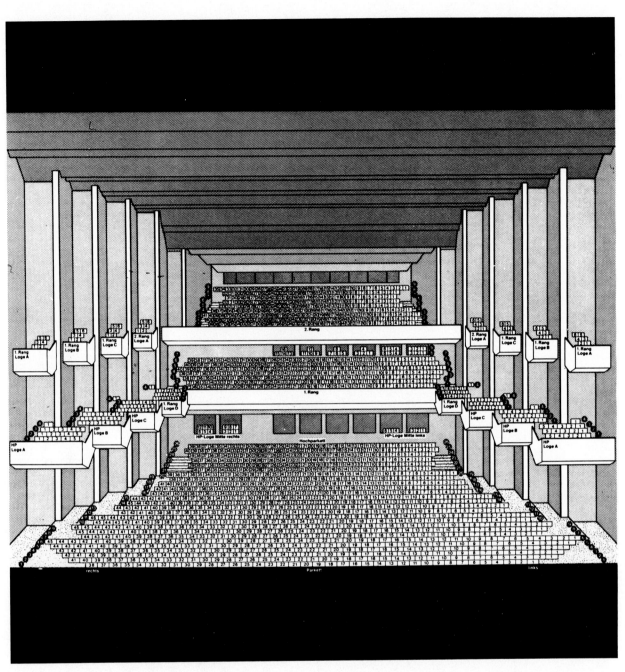

Fig. 252. Seating plan for the auditorium of the Deutsche Oper Berlin (Deutsche Oper Berlin)

YEAR	1969	1970	1971	1972	1973	1974	1975	1976	1977
VALUE OF DEUTSCHE MARK	28¢	29¢	30¢	34¢	40¢	42¢	44¢	48¢	50¢
EXPENSES									
Artists' salaries	DM 15,187,000	DM 17,026,000	DM 19,188,000	DM 20,327,000	DM 23,776,000	DM 24,934,000	DM 26,960,000	DM 27,916,000	DM 28,776,000
Technical salaries	5,109,000	6,228,000	7,579,000	7,773,000	7,151,000	12,430,000	13,828,000	13,870,000	14,676,000
Administration	2,200,000	2,045,000	2,489,000	3,002,000	5,629,000	2,041,000	2,110,000	2,250,000	2,559,000
Other personnel	133,000	698,000	160,000	131,000	64,000	102,000	89,000	82,000	98,000
Pension funds	1,341,000	1,404,000	---	2,405,000	2,820,000	316,000	417,000	2,477,000	2,562,000
Production costs	3,741,000	8,100,000	3,926,000	4,042,000	4,596,000	4,710,000	6,114,000	4,773,000	5,447,000
Loan payments	---	---	---	---	---	150,000	209,000	98,000	87,000
Building maintenance	83,000	284,000	907,000	1,127,000	1,714,000	3,302,000	3,308,000	3,233,000	4,798,000
TOTAL	DM 27,794,000	DM 35,785,000	DM 34,249,000	DM 38,807,000	DM 45,750,000	DM 47,985,000	DM 53,035,000	DM 54,699,000	DM 59,003,000
INCOME									
Single tickets	DM 2,016,000	DM 1,756,000	DM 2,097,000	DM 2,167,000	DM 2,447,000	DM 2,535,000	DM 2,948,000	DM 3,111,000	DM 4,086,000
Subscriptions	1,537,000	1,464,000	1,386,000	1,406,000	1,449,000	1,600,000	1,543,000	1,712,000	2,421,000
Children's theater subscriptions	101,000	63,000	114,000	139,000	170,000	144,000	---	---	---
Visitor groups	829,000	775,000	820,000	905,000	978,000	900,000	940,000	1,053,000	1,149,000
Cloakroom charges	238,000	215,000	247,000	280,000	278,000	290,000	315,000	298,000	317,000
Radio and TV fees	14,000	139,000	1,000	1,000	27,000	238,000	---	371,000	168,000
Touring	120,000	1,695,000	251,000	273,000	378,000	186,000	831,000	135,000	79,000
Guest performances by other companies	---	---	---	---	---	---	---	---	---
Program sales	188,000	195,000	259,000	265,000	304,000	351,000	376,000	347,000	452,000
Other income	135,000	65,000	160,000	194,000	75,000	57,000	58,000	104,000	65,000
TOTAL	DM 5,178,000	DM 6,367,000	DM 5,335,000	DM 5,630,000	DM 6,106,000	DM 6,301,000	DM 7,011,000	DM 7,131,000	DM 8,737,000
TAX SUBSIDY	DM 22,616,000	DM 29,418,000	DM 28,914,000	DM 33,177,000	DM 39,644,000	DM 41,684,000	DM 46,024,000	DM 47,568,000	DM 50,266,000
SUBSIDY PERCENTAGE	81.4%	82.2%	84.4%	85.5%	86.7%	86.9%	88.8%	87.0%	85.2%

Fig. 253. Expenses and income for the Deutsche Oper Berlin, 1969–77 (Deutscher Bühnen-verein, Köln)

Teilplan Hauptverwaltung

Deutsche Oper Berlin

Wirtschafter: Senator für Wissenschaft und Kunst
Wirtschaftsstelle: Deutsche Oper Berlin

Vorbemerkung:
Die Deutsche Oper Berlin hat die Aufgabe, das musikalische Theater zu pflegen und weiterzuentwickeln.

Einnahmen

Haushalts-stelle	Einnahmen	Funktion	Ansatz 1977 DM	1976 DM	Rechnung 1975 DM
111 20	Entgelte für die Teilnahme an Lehrgängen und Kursen	181	6 000	7 000	5 112,00
111 22	Eintrittsgelder	181	5 975 000	5 825 000	5 177 386,20
111 80	Erstattungen für Dienst- und Sachleistungen aus anderen Abschnitten	181	283 000	290 000	254 079,50
113 01	Verkauf von Altmaterial und ausgesonderten Sachen	181	8 000	8 000	7 410,00
119 02	Ablieferung von Einnahmen aus Nebentätigkeit	181	—	10 000	—
119 06	Ersatz von Post- und Fernsprechgebühren	181	2 000	2 000	1 796,94
119 79	Verschiedene Einnahmen	181	20 000	25 000	17 245,34
124 01	Mieten für Grundstücke, Gebäude und Räume	181	46 400	43 800	32 691,59
124 03	Mieten für Maschinen, Geräte und Ausstattungsgegenstände	181	3 000	3 000	2 274,09
125 04	Entgelte für Dienstleistungen für andere	181	320 000	330 000	315 122,20
125 06	Programme	181	450 000	380 000	358 520,50
125 07	Einnahmen aus Gastspielreisen	181	100 000	100 000	830 962,49
125 08	Entgelte für Übertragungen und Aufnahmen	181	120 000	120 000	6 787,10
125 11	Verkaufserlöse	181	7 000	7 000	1 498,50
132 01	Verkauf von Fahrzeugen	181	—	2 000	851 126,00
251 90	Zuweisungen vom Bund für laufende Zwecke	181	2 000	—	12 826,07
332 01	Investitionszulage	181	5 000	10 000	—
	Summe der Einnahmen		**7 345 400**	**7 162 800**	**7 874 888,52**

Ausgaben

Haushalts-stelle	Ausgaben	Funktion / Direktion	Ansatz 1977 DM	1976 DM	Rechnung 1975 DM
422 01	Dienstbezüge der planmäßigen Beamten	181	187 000	182 000	171 787,31
425 01	Vergütungen der planmäßigen Angestellten und des planmäßigen künstlerischen Personals	181	19 496 000	18 416 000	18 947 288,44
425 11	Vergütungen der nichtplanmäßigen Angestellten	181	280 000	133 000	79 591,11
426 01	Löhne der planmäßigen Arbeiter	181	10 146 000	9 917 000	9 968 718,09
426 11	Löhne der nichtplanmäßigen Arbeiter	181	695 000	684 000	642 183,83
427 01	Ausgaben für das künstlerische Personal	181	13 363 000	12 732 000	13 078 206,86
427 90	Ausgaben für das künstlerische Personal aus Zuwendungen	181	—	—	R 8 000,00
441 00	Beihilfen und Unterstützungen für Dienstkräfte	181	81 000	83 700	80 960,24
453 00	Trennungsgeld und Umzugskostenvergütungen	181	9 000	18 400	8 934,97
459 02	Kassenverlustentschädigungen	181	1 200	1 200	975,69
459 03	Prämien für besondere Leistungen	181	200	300	200,00
511 01	Geschäftsbedarf	181	170 000	170 000	143 929,12
511 80	Erstattungen für Geschäftsbedarf	181	10 000	10 000	16 156,45
512 01	Bücher und Zeitschriften	181	5 500	5 500	5 550,61
512 03	Noten und Textbücher	181	20 000	20 000	17 062,29
512 04	Programme und Eintrittskarten	181	360 000	350 000	359 000,00
513 01	Post- und Fernmeldegebühren	181	85 000	82 000	93 899,56
514 01	Haltung von Fahrzeugen	181	—	—	8 962,27
514 03	Sonstige Ausgaben für die Haltung von Fahrzeugen	181	7 000	9 000	—
515 01	Büromaschinen und -einrichtungen	181	15 000	15 000	13 573,61
515 03	Geräte, technische Einrichtungen und Ausstattungen	181	75 000	63 000	57 826,44
515 12	Geräte, technische Einrichtungen und Ausstattungen für den künstlerischen Betrieb	181	1 800 000	1 600 000	1 651 339,55
515 26	Wäsche	181	500	500	497,40
516 01	Dienst- und Schutzkleidung	181	35 000	35 000	38 000,00
517 01	Bewirtschaftung der Grundstücke, Gebäude und Räume	181	—	—	1 014 818,31
517 02	Heizung	181	338 000	245 000	—
517 21	Strom	181	281 000	250 000	—
517 23	Wasser	181	14 500	18 000	—
517 24	Entwässerung	181	16 200	22 000	—
517 25	Straßenreinigung	181	17 600	18 000	—
517 26	Müllabfuhr	181	18 500	13 000	—
517 27	Hausreinigung und Desinfektion	181	250 000	235 000	—
517 28	Steuern und Versicherungen für Grundstücke	181	195 000	195 000	—
517 29	Sonstige Ausgaben für die Bewirtschaftung der Grundstücke, Gebäude und Räume	181	31 000	50 000	1 289,61
517 81	Erstattungen für Hausreinigung und Desinfektion	181	1 500	1 500	1 498,50
518 01	Mieten für Grundstücke, Gebäude und Räume	181	2 200	63 500	62 431,20
518 02	Mieten für Fahrzeuge	181	140 000	180 000	204 413,53
518 03	Mieten für Maschinen, Geräte und sonstige Gegenstände für den künstlerischen Betrieb	181	220 000	200 000	172 234,25
519 10	Kleiner Unterhaltungsbedarf	181	25 000	20 000	—
522 52	Verbrauchsmittel für die Datenverarbeitung	181	10 000	10 000	—
522 79	Allgemeine Verbrauchsmittel	181	4 500	3 000	4 329,30
524 01	Lehrmittel und Unterrichtsmaterial	181	1 000	1 000	450,00
526 02	Sitzungsgelder und Unkostenentschädigungen	181	1 200	1 200	—
527 00	Dienstreisen	181	200 000	195 000	199 417,97
529 05	Repräsentationsmittel	181	—	2 500	1 717,69
531 08	Besucherbetreuung	181	2 000	—	688,10
533 01	Kränze, Blumenspenden und Nachrufe	181	300	300	—
540 20	Versicherungsbeiträge	181	2 000	2 000	2 295,48
540 24	Entgelte für Aufführungsrechte und Kompositionsaufträge	181	640 000	360 000	324 685,06

Fig. 254. Income and outgo for the years 1975–77. The figures for 1976 and 1977 are estimates based on fixed amounts from 1975. The numbers in the left margin are account numbers, explained in the next pages (Deutsche Oper Berlin)

08 40 / 1977

Ausgaben

Haushalts-stelle		Funktion	Ansatz 1977 DM	Ansatz 1976 DM	Rechnung 1975 DM
540 48	Sächliche Ausgaben für Gastspielreisen	181	70 000	70 000	1 114 048,07
540 79	Verschiedene Ausgaben	181	500	500	41,00
540 90	Sächliche Ausgaben für Gastspielreisen aus Zuwendungen	181	—	—	612 443,66 / R 235 767,01
681 70	Stipendien, Ausbildungs- und Erziehungsbeihilfen	181	5 000	5 000	—
685 79	Mitgliedsbeiträge	181	1 200	1 100	1 129,40
701 00	Neubau eines Magazingebäudes	181	2 630 000	4 806 000*)	3 308 494,72 / 973,34 R
811 79	Fahrzeuge	181	—	12 000	18 111,26
812 01	Büro-Computer	181	—	—	163 425,03 / R 11 564,97
812 79	Geräte, technische Einrichtungen und Ausstattungen (Investitionen)	181	121 000	75 000	26 629,26
	Summe der Ausgaben		52 080 600	51 583 200*)	52 617 693,74 / R 251 245,32

Abschluß

		Ansatz 1977 DM	Ansatz 1976 DM	Rechnung 1975 DM
Einnahmen		7 345 400	7 162 800	7 874 838,52
Ausgaben		52 080 600	51 583 200*)	52 868 939,06
Fehlbetrag		44 735 200	44 420 400*)	44 994 100,54

*) einschließlich Nachtragshaushaltsplanes.

Erläuterungen zu den Haushaltsstellen

111 20

Das Ballettschulgeld beträgt 15 DM monatlich.
Weniger in Anlehnung an die Rechnung 1975.

111 22

Die Eintrittspreise werden auf Vorschlag der Deutschen Oper Berlin von den Senatoren für Wissenschaft und Kunst und für Finanzen festgesetzt.

Platzgruppen in der Deutschen Oper Berlin:

Platzart/Reihe	Zahl der Plätze	A-Preise DM	B-Preise DM	C-Preise DM
Parkett				
1—2	79	33,00	42,00	50,00
3—6	174	28,00	35,00	42,00
7—12	269	23,00	29,00	35,00
13—19	297	20,00	25,00	30,00
20—22	116	15,00	19,00	23,00
Hochparkett				
23—24	77	10,50	13,50	16,50
25—26	79	9,50	12,00	14,50
Loge Mitte rechts	12	9,50	12,00	14,50
Loge Mitte links (Versehrtenloge)	4	9,50	12,00	14,50
Logen A, B, C	30	33,00	42,00	50,00

noch 111 22

Platzart/Reihe	Zahl der Plätze	A-Preise DM	B-Preise DM	C-Preise DM
2—3	60	28,00	35,00	42,00
4	6	10,50	13,50	16,50
I. Rang				
1	36	43,00	64,00	65,00
3—5	37	33,00	42,00	50,00
6—9	117	20,00	25,00	30,00
Mittelloge	91	10,50	13,50	16,50
Logen A, B, C	16	10,50	13,50	16,50
Loge D	36	15,00	19,00	23,00
1	10	33,00	42,00	50,00
2—3	20	28,00	35,00	42,00
4	2	10,50	13,50	16,50
II. Rang				
1	39	10,50	13,50	16,50
2—3	81	9,50	12,00	14,50
4—5	71	7,50	9,50	11,50
6—9	130	5,50	7,00	9,00
Loge A	12	10,50	13,50	16,50
	1 901			
Davon Dienstplätze	14			
	1 887			

noch 111 22

Für Premieren und besondere Veranstaltungen werden die B- bzw. C-Preise erhoben.

Im Höchstfall mögliche Abendeinnahme:
A-Preise: rd. 35 700 DM; B-Preise: rd. 45 000 DM; C-Preise: rd. 54 200 DM.

Zahl der Vorstellungen:
Vom 1. Januar 1977 bis 31. Dezember 1977 .... 365 Kalendertage
davon ab:
Ferien einschließlich Vorprobenzeit ... 49 Tage
1 Festtag (24. Dezember) ... 1 Tag — 50 spielfreie Tage
verbleiben 315 Vorstellungen.

Dazu treten zusätzliche Nachmittagsvorstellungen und Matineen.

Presse-, Ehren- und sonstige Freikarten (insbesondere nach Bühnenbrauch) dürfen durchschnittlich bis zu 3 v. H. der verfügbaren Eintrittskarten abgegeben werden. Dies entspricht unter Zugrundelegung eines Kartenpreises von durchschnittlich 26 DM — im 1977 einer nominellen Einnahme von rd. 464 000 DM. Darüber hinaus können im Einzelfall vor allem an Personengruppen in ungünstigen sozialen Verhältnissen Eintrittskarten kostenlos abgegeben werden, wenn kein Einnahmeausfall damit verbunden ist.

Für die gemeinnützigen Besucherorganisationen, das Theater der Schulen und den Veranstaltungsdienst des Senators für Familie, Jugend und Sport für verbilligte Plätze vorgesehene Platzkontingente:
Gemeinnützige Besucherorganisationen ... 190 000 Plätze
Theater der Schulen ... 40 000 Plätze
Veranstaltungsdienst des Senators für Familie, Jugend und Sport ... 3 780 Plätze

Es werden folgende Einnahmen erwartet:
Kassenverkauf ... 3 220 000 DM
Abonnement (12 000 Abonnenten) ... 1 650 000 DM
Gemeinnützige Besucherorganisationen ... 1 280 000 DM
Theater der Schulen ... 91 000 DM
Veranstaltungsdienst des Senators für Familie, Jugend und Sport ... 16 640 DM
6 257 640 DM
rd. 6 258 000 DM

Davon entfallen auf die Haushaltsstellen:
111 22 ... rd. 5 975 000 DM
111 80 ... 283 000 DM

Mehr wegen Erhöhung der Eintrittspreise zum Beginn der Spielzeit 1976/1977 um durchschnittlich 5 v. H., der nachgezogenen Erhöhung der Abonnementspreise zum Beginn der Spielzeit 1977/1978 und einer weiteren Erhöhung der Kassenpreise um 5 v. H. zum Beginn der Spielzeit 1977/1978. Bei der Ermittlung des Ansatzes wurde im übrigen das Rechnungsergebnis 1975 zugrunde gelegt.

111 80

Erstattungen für die Abgabe von Eintrittskarten von
03 00, Haushaltsstelle 531 80 ... 237 000 DM
03 30, Haushaltsstelle 531 80 ... 20 000 DM
07 00, Haushaltsstelle 524 80 ... 7 600 DM
08 00, Haushaltsstelle 529 80 ... 1 600 DM
10 00, Haushaltsstelle 671 84 ... 16 640 DM
282 840 DM
rd. 283 000 DM

(vgl. auch Erläuterung zu 111 22).

119 02

Mit Einnahmen aus der Abführung von Einnahmenanteilen der Mitglieder des Chores und des Orchesters aus Nebentätigkeiten unter Verwendung der Bezeichnung »Deutsche Oper Berlin« oder von Dienstinstrumenten ist nach den Erfahrungen der Vergangenheit nicht zu rechnen.

119 79

Insbesondere Rückvergütungen von Versicherungsprämien. Weniger in Anlehnung an die Rechnung 1975.

124 01

Verpachtung des spielfreien Hauses (geschätzt) ... 12 400 DM
Pacht für Büfett (10½ Monate je 3 000 DM) ... 31 500 DM
Miete für Verkaufsstand ... 2 500 DM
46 400 DM
Mehr wegen Erhöhung der Büfett-Pacht und der Miete für den Verkaufsstand.

124 03

Aus der Vermietung von Dekorationen, Kostümen und Requisiten.

125 04

Das Garderobenentgelt beträgt 1,— DM.

125 06

Programmverkauf ... 429 000 DM
Programmeinnahmerate ... 21 000 DM
450 000 DM
Mehr wegen Erhöhung des Programmpreises zum 1. 1. 1977 von 1,50 DM auf 1,90 DM.

125 07

Für kleinere Gastspielreisen ins übrige Bundesgebiet:
Erwartete Einnahmen ... 100 000 DM
Für Gastspielreisen sind folgende Ausgaben veranschlagt:
Haushaltsstelle 427 01 ... 30 000 DM
Haushaltsstelle 540 48 ... 70 000 DM
Insgesamt ... 100 000 DM

125 08

Es soll versucht werden, insbesondere die Berliner Rundfunk- und Fernsehanstalten zu veranlassen, in Zukunft häufiger als bisher Aufführungen der Deutschen Oper Berlin in ihren Programmen auszustrahlen (vgl. auch Erläuterungen zu 425 01 und 427 01).

422 01

Bezeichnung	Bes.-Gr.	Zahl der Stellen 1977	1976	Betrag 1976 DM
Leitender Regierungsdirektor	A 16	1	1	56 000
Amtsrat	A 12	1	1	39 620
Regierung.goberinspektor	A 10	1	1	33 500
Regierungsinspektor/ Regierungsoberinspektor	A 9/A 10	—	1¹)	—
Regierungsinspektor	A 9	1¹)	1¹)	30 330
Regierungshauptsekretär	A 8	1²)	1²)	27 440
		5		186 800
			rd.	187 000

¹) Die Stelle wird bei Freiwerden zu einer Stelle für einen Angestellten der Vergütungsgruppe Vb/IVb.
²) Die Stelle wird bei Freiwerden zu einer Stelle für einen Angestellten der Vergütungsgruppe Vc4.

425 01

Bezeichnung	Verg.-Gr.	Zahl der Stellen 1977	1976	Betrag 1976 DM
Generalintendant	SV	1	1	169 900
Konzertmeister	Srgl.	3	3	244 000
Zweiter Konzertmeister	Srgl.	2	2	150 360
Solocellist	Srgl.	2	2	152 120
Solobratschist	Srgl.	2	2	138 080

Fig. 255. Summary of income, outgo, and the deficits for 1975 and 1977. Explanations of account numbers 111-20 through 425-01. (Deutsche Oper Berlin)

08 40
1977

noch 425 01

Bezeichnung	Verg.-Gr.	Zahl der Stellen 1977	1976	Betrag DM
Orchestermitglied	Srgl.[1]	128	128	7 883 550[9]
Chorsänger	Srgl.	114	114	4 394 000
Ballettmeister (Gruppe)	Srgl.	38	40	1 381 880
Technischer Direktor	Srgl.	1	1	74 160
Technischer Oberinspektor	Srgl.	1	1	53 210
Leiter des Beleuchtungswesens	Srgl.	—	1	—
Direktor des Kostümwesens	Srgl.	1	1	64 180
Chef-Maskenbildner	Srgl.	2	2	116 060
Maskenbildner	Srgl.	20	20	781 190
Künstlerischer Leiter des Malersaales	III	1	1	47 070
Orchesterdirektor	III	1	1	47 070
Angestellter	IVb	2	2	80 900
Technischer Oberinspektor	IVb	1		40 450
Leiter der Kaschier- und Bildhauerwerkstatt	IVb	1	1	40 450
Angestellter	Vb/IVb	4	4	148 120
Technischer Angestellter (Theatertontechniker)	Va/IVb	2	2	74 060
Beleuchtungsobermeister	Vb	1[14]	2	37 030
Gewandmeister	Vb	2	2	74 060
Kostümzeichner und Assistent	Vb	1		37 030
Angestellter	Vc	1[15]	1	34 540
Theatermaler	Vc	1		34 540
Angestellter	Vc	5[9]	5[9]	172 700
Bühnenmeister	Vc	2		69 080
Beleuchtungsmeister	Vc	3		103 620
Requisitenmeister	Vc	1		34 540
Theatertontechniker	Vc	1		34 540
Meister	Vc	3		103 620
Theaterschuhmachermeister	Vc	1		34 540
Rüstmeister	Vc	1		34 540
Theaterinspektor	Vc	2		69 080
Maschinenmeister	VIb/Vc	2	2	223 730
Angestellter	VIb	7[7]	7[7]	191 820
Angestellter	VIb	6	7	
Angestellter (20 Wochenstunden)	VIb	1		15 990
Ballettkassierer	VIb	3	3	95 910
Bibliotheksangestellter	VIb	1		31 970
Hausinspektor	VIb	1[8]		31 970
Technischer Zeichner	VIb	6	6	191 820
Theatermaler	VIb	1		31 970
Kostümmaler	VIb	1		31 970
Produktionsassistent	VIb	1		31 970
Angestellter (Materialverwalter)	VIb	1		31 970
Modellbauer und Zeichner	VIb	4[9][10]	4[9][10]	127 880
Kostümplastiker	VIb	1[9]	1[9]	31 970
Gewandmeister	VIb	5	5	159 850
Fremdsprachenassistent (Fremdsprachensekretär) 30 Wochenstunden	VII/VIc	1		22 330
Angestellter (zugleich Schreibkraft)	VII/VIb	3	3	89 310
Theatermaler	VII/VIb	5	5	148 850
Bibliotheksangestellter	VII/VIb	3		89 770
Magazinmeister	VII/VIb	3	3	89 310
Kaschier (Theaterplastiker)	VII/VIb	2	2	59 540
Orchestersekretär	VII/VIb	1	1	29 770
Angestellter	VIII/VII	1[11]	1[11]	112 360

noch 425 01

Bezeichnung	Verg.-Gr.	Zahl der Stellen 1977	1976	Betrag DM
Angestellter (zugleich Schreibkraft)	VIII/VII	2	2	56 180
Angestellter im Schreibdienst	VIII/VII	1	1	28 090
Materialverwalter	VIII/VII	1	1	28 090
Theatermaler	VIII/VII	2	2	56 180
Orchesterwart	VIII/VII	4	4	112 360
Fornsprecher	IXb,/VII	2	2	51 720
Angestellter	IXb/IXa	2	2	51 720
Kassenbote	IXb	1	1	25 860
Beleuchter im Stellwerk	X/IXb	10[12]	10[12]	248 200
Pförtner	X/IXb	3[13]	3[13]	74 460
Bote				
Aufwandszulage (1000 DM monatlich für den Generalintendanten)				12 000
Übertragungshonorare (vgl. nachstehende bindende Erläuterung)				40 000
		438	440	19 495 300
				rd. 19 496 000

Besonders zu veranschlagende Beträge

1) Tarifvertrag für die Musiker in Kulturorchestern.
2) Im Rahmen des Betrages stehen bis zu 50 000 DM für die Zahlung von Vorschüssen zum Ankauf von wertvollen Musikinstrumenten zur Verfügung.
3) Der Stelleninhaber ist in Vergütungsgruppe IIb eingruppiert.
4) Der Stelleninhaber ist in Vergütungsgruppe Va eingruppiert.
5) Der Stelleninhaber ist in Vergütungsgruppe IVb eingruppiert.
6) Zwei Stelleninhaber sind in Vergütungsgruppe Va eingruppiert.
7) Fünf Stellen fallen nach Inbetriebnahme der MDT-Anlage bei Freiwerden weg.
8) Der Stelleninhaber ist in Vergütungsgruppe Vc eingruppiert.
9) Ein bzw. der Stelleninhaber ist in Vergütungsgruppe Vb eingruppiert.
10) Ein Stelleninhaber ist in Vergütungsgruppe VIa eingruppiert.
11) Eine Stelle fällt mit der Übernahme der Wirtschaftsbuchführung durch den Senator für Finanzen (Landeshauptkasse) bei Freiwerden weg.
12) Die Stelleninhaber sind mindestens für die Dauer der tariflichen Bewährungszeit als Lohnempfänger zu beschäftigen.

Ausgaben für Übertragungshonorare dürfen, soweit nicht im Einzelfall aus besonderen kulturpolitischen Erwägungen eine Ausnahme zugelassen wird, höchstens in dem Umfang geleistet werden, in dem Einnahmen bei der Haushaltsstelle 12508 eingegangen sind oder auf Grund rechtlicher oder tatsächlicher Sicherung eingehen werden.

425 11

1 (1) Angestellter als Ersatzkraft für ein vom Dienst freigestelltes Mitglied des Personalrats — Vergütungsgruppe Vb/IVb — — 37 030 DM
Aushilfsangestellte .... — 16 220 DM
2 (2) Maskenbildner-Volontär .... — 43 170 DM
1 (1) Volontär-Kostümabteilung .. — 14 130 DM
3 (—) Theatermaler/Theaterplastiker-Volontär ... — 62 660 DM
3 (—) Balletttänzer (Anfänger) ... — 72 070 DM

Lehrpersonal
Operstudio
4 (4) Stundenlehrkräfte — Bühnenfach —
49 (49) Wochen für 7 (7) Wochenstunden je 17 DM .... — 23 330 DM
1 (1) Stundenlehrkraft — Sprache — (nur Italienisch)
49 (49) Wochen für 3 (3) Wochenstunden je 17 DM .... — 2 500 DM
1 (1) Stundenlehrkraft — Pianist —
49 (49) Wochen für 4 (4) Wochenstunden je 15 DM .... — 2 940 DM
Arbeitgeberanteile zur Sozialversicherung ... — 4 670 DM
279 320 DM / rd. 280 000 DM

Mehr auf Grund von Tariferhöhungen und für 3 Theatermaler sowie für 3 Balletttänzer (Anfänger) unter gleichzeitigem Wegfall von 2 Stellen für Balletttänzer bei der Haushaltsstelle 425 01 und Wegfall der Mittel für Materiallehrlinge bei der Haushaltsstelle 426 11.

426 11

4 (4) Bühnenarbeiter/Bühnenhandwerker — Lohngruppe III/IVa — als Ersatzkraft für ein vom Dienst freigestelltes Mitglied des Personalrats — — 121 160 DM
1 (1) Arbeiter — Lohngruppe III/IVa — als Ersatzkraft für ein vom Dienst freigestelltes Mitglied des Personalrats — — 30 290 DM
(1) Tischler — Lohngruppe V/Va — als Ersatzkraft für ein vom Dienst freigestelltes Mitglied des Gesamtpersonalrats — — DM
5 (5) Garderobenfrauen (stundenweise) — 80 510 DM
18 (18) Platzanweiser — 235 440 DM
7 (7) Kartenkontrolleure — 57 690 DM
(3) Materiallehrlinge — — DM
Aushilfsarbeiter — 131 190 DM

Besonders zu veranschlagender Betrag
Provision für Platzanweiser für Programmverkauf (10 v.H. der anteiligen Einnahmen aus Programmverkauf einschließlich der Arbeitgeberanteile) — 38 700 DM
694 980 DM / rd. 695 000 DM

Weniger wegen Verlagerung von 3 Beschäftigungspositionen für Materiallehrlinge zur Haushaltsstelle 425 11 und des Wegfalls der Beschäftigungsposition für einen Tischler.

426 01

Bezeichnung	Lohn-gr.	Zahl der Stellen 1977	1976	Betrag DM
Oberplatzanweiser/Obergarderobenfrau (stundenweise)	Srgl.	2	2	40 960
Garderobenfrau (stundenweise)	Srgl.	9	9	155 180
Probenmeister	VII	1	1	35 370
Oberbeleuchter	VII	2	2	70 740
Maschinenmeister	VII	1	1	35 370
Maschinist	VI	4[*]	4[*]	136 600
Beleuchter im Stellwerk	VI	5	5	170 750
Elektriker	VI	5	5	170 750
Seitenmeister	VI	3	3	109 450
Tischler	VI	11	11	375 650
Schlosser	VI	2	2	68 300
Elektriker	VI	2	2	68 300
Kostümmaler	VI	1	1	34 150
Bühnenmaschinist	V/VI	6	6	197 880
Maschinist	V/Va	1	1	32 980
Fahrstuhlmonteur	V/Va	2	2	65 960
Rohrleger/Klempner	V/Va	15	15	494 700
Tischler	V/Va	1	1	32 980
Buchbinder	V/Va	26	26	857 480
Beleuchter/Elektriker	V/Va	31	31	1 022 380
Schlosser/Schweißer	V/Va	10	10[*]	329 800
Tapezierer	V/Va	13	13	428 740
Farbenreiber	V/Va	2	2	65 960
Schuhmacher	V/Va	1	1	32 980
Kostümplastiker	V/Va	2	2	65 960
Rüstgehilfe	V/Va	2	2	
Theaterplastiker	V/Va	1	1	
Knecht/Fahrer (PKW, Pauschallohn)	IV/VIa	1	1	31 380
Kraftfahrer (LKW)	IV/VIa	1	1	31 380
Requisiteur	IV/V	3	3	94 140
Kostümweißnäher	IV/V	3	3	94 140
Bühnenarbeiter/Bühnenhandwerker	III/VIa	76	76	2 302 040
Ankleider	III/IVa	30	30	908 700
Magazinwart	III/IV	1	1	30 290
Hilfarbeiter	III	4	4	117 040
Dekorationsnäher	II/III	4	4	117 040
Wächter	II	4	4	117 040
Hausarbeiter	II	2	2	58 520
Transportarbeiter	II	2	2	58 520
Magazinarbeiter	II	2	2	58 520
Reinigungsfrau	Ia	33	33	933 240
Reinigungsfrau (24 Wochenstunden)	Ia	1	1	16 970
		327	328	10 145 950
				rd. 10 146 000

Besonders zu veranschlagender Betrag
Provision für Platzanweiser für Programmverkauf (10 v.H. der anteiligen Einnahmen aus Programmverkauf einschließlich der Arbeitgeberanteile) .... — 4 300

*Eine Stelle ist bis zur Inbetriebnahme des Magazingebäudes gesperrt.

427 01

(Klammerzahlen = durchschnittliche Zahlen der Mitglieder des ständigen Ensembles)

Gesangsolisten		
Soliston (NV-Solo)	(52)	5 017 000
Gäste		3 845 000 / 8 862 000
Bühnenvorstände		
Chefdramaturg	(1)	56 430
Künstlerischer		
Betriebsdirektor	(1)	71 240
Ständige Dirigenten	(4)	445 200
Erster Spielleiter, Abendregisseur		
Regieassistenten		
Disponent	(7)	191 120
Bühnenbildner und Ausstattungsleiter, Assistent der Ausstattungsleitung, Leiter der Entwurfsabteilung		
Chordirektor, Stellvertreter des Chordirektors	(3)	139 130
Leiter des Balletts, Leiter der Ballettschule, Leiter der Ballettschule	(2)	133 580
Studienleiter, Solo-Repetitoren, Chor-Repetitor	(4)	271 590
Ballett-Repetitoren	(13)	421 830
Inspizient, Souffleure	(7)	248 540
Leiter der Statisterie	(1)	35 620
Assistent des Direktors des Kostümwesens, Assistent des Technischen Direktors	(2)	96 830
Referent für Presseangelegenheiten, Public Relations	(1)	36 730
Gäste (Regisseure, Bühnenbildner, Dirigenten)	(20)	876 050 / 3 023 890
Ballett		
Balletsolisten (NV-Solo)		846 000
Aushilfen, Gäste		116 000 / 962 000
Operstudio (Regieassistent, Korrepetitor)	(1)	33 600
Imgesamt	(119)	

Fig. 256. Explanations of account numbers 425-01 through 427-01, including a listing of salaries by positions (Deutsche Oper Berlin)

noch 427 01

Knabenchor, Zusatzchor	71 700 DM
Verstärkungen, Aushilfen, Krankheitsvertretungen für das Orchester	190 500 DM
Statisterie	103 000 DM
Vergütungen für das künstlerische Personal für Gastspielreisen (vgl. Erläuterungen 125 07 und 540 48)	30 000 DM
Übertragungshonorare (vgl. nachstehende bindende Erläuterung)	80 000 DM
	13 362 690 DM
rd.	13 363 000 DM

Ausgaben für Übertragungshonorare dürfen, soweit nicht aus besonderen kulturpolitischen Erwägungen eine Ausnahme zugelassen wird, höchstens in dem Umfang geleistet werden, in dem Einnahmen bei der Haushaltsstelle 125 08 eingegangen sind oder auf Grund rechtlicher oder tatsächlicher Sicherung eingehen werden.

Mehr in Auswirkung der in 1976 eingetretenen tarifbedingten Gagenerhöhungen sowie einer entsprechenden Erhöhung der frei zu vereinbarenden Gagen.

459 03
Prämien für zwei Kraftfahrer für unfallfreies Fahren.

511 01
In dem Ansatz sind rd. 140 000 DM für Werbung vorgesehen, um den Opernbesuch zu aktivieren.

511 80
Erstattungen an 05 61, Haushaltsstelle 111 80, für die Ausführung von Druckaufträgen.

512 04
Mehr auf Grund erhöhter Papier- und Druckkosten.

514 03
Unterhaltung von 2 Kraftfahrzeugen (1 Personenkraftwagen, 1 VW-Transporter und 2 Dekorationsanhänger).
Weniger durch Wegfall eines Personenkraftwagens.

515 01
Für die Beschaffung von Funktionsmöbeln, Schreibmaschinen sowie Wartungskosten für Büromaschinen.

515 03
Ersatzbeschaffungen für den teilweise überalterten Maschinenbestand sowie zur Verwirklichung der infolge Arbeitszeitverkürzungen unumgänglichen Rationalisierungen, Wartungskosten für die MDT-Anlage.
Mehr insbesondere wegen der Wartungskosten für die MDT-Anlage.

516 01
Unterhaltung und Ersatz der Dienstkleidung für Platzanweiser, Pförtner und Kraftfahrer.

517 02
Mehr durch Inbetriebnahme des Kulissenmagazins und erhöhter Heizkosten.

517 21
Mehr entsprechend dem Bedarf und wegen Inbetriebnahme des Kulissenmagazins.

517 26
Mehr durch Gebührenerhöhung.

517 27
Mehr wegen Tariferhöhungen bei den Reinigungsinstituten und wegen Inbetriebnahme des Kulissenmagazins.

517 29
Weniger entsprechend dem Bedarf.

517 81
Erstattungen an 39 34 (Kreuzberg), Haushaltsstelle 125 80, für Leistungen der Blindenanstalt.

518 01
Mieten für Magazinräume, einschließlich der Kosten für Bewachung und Feuerversicherung.

Mietkosten für Cyclopstraße (1 794 qm)	1 200 DM
Sonstiges	1 000 DM
	2 200 DM

Ferner sind rd. 3 000 qm Kulissenlagerflächen auf dem landeseigenen Grundstück in Berlin 20, Freiheit 14, angemietet.
Weniger, da das Mietobjekt in der Cyclopstraße aufgegeben wird.

518 02
Kulissentransporte zwischen der Oper und den Magazinräumen in Berlin 20, Freiheit 14, sowie Kleintransporte.
Weniger wegen Inbetriebnahme des Kulissenmagazins.

518 03

Miete für Noten	215 000 DM
Miete für Kostüme, Dekorationen, Musikgeräte ...	5 000 DM
	220 000 DM

Mehr wegen erhöhter Mietkosten für Noten.

519 10
Mehr entsprechend dem Bedarf.

522 52
Verbrauchsmittel für den Bürocomputer (geschätzt).

522 79
Ausgaben für den Sanitätsdienst.
Mehr wegen erhöhter Zahlungen an das Deutsche Rote Kreuz.

524 01
Für das Opernstudio.

526 02
Kosten für die Tätigkeit des Personalrats (§40 Abs. 1 Satz 1 PersVG)

527 00

Dienstreisen zur Verpflichtung von Sängern, Regisseuren und anderem Bühnenpersonal	15 000 DM
Vorstellungsreisen zum Abschluß von Engagements, Reisekosten für Gäste	185 000 DM
	200 000 DM

Mehr wegen höherer Reisekosten.

529 05
Insbesondere für Bewirtungen bei Pressekonferenzen und für Ehrengaben aus besonderen Anlässen (bisher veranschlagt bei Haushaltsstelle 529 05).

531 08
Die Ausgaben werden künftig bei der Haushaltsstelle 531 08 nachgewiesen.

540 20
Beiträge zur Garderobenversicherung.

540 24
Von dem Ansatz entfallen auf

Entgelte für Aufführungsrechte	620 000 DM
Kompositionsaufträge	20 000 DM
	640 000 DM

Mehr auf Grund der Neuregelung für die Zahlung von Tantiemen.

540 48
Insbesondere für Tage- und Übernachtungsgelder, Unterbringungskosten, Fahrt- und Flugkosten, Instrumententransport und Versicherung sowie Kulissentransport zur Durchführung und Vorbereitung kleinerer Gastspielreisen ins übrige Bundesgebiet. (vgl. auch Erläuterung zu 125 07 und 427 01).

681 70
Ausbildungsbeihilfen entsprechend den Richtlinien für die Gewährung von Ausbildungsbeihilfen für Schüler des Opernstudios.

685 79
Beitrag für die Mitgliedschaft in der Opernkonferenz und der Internationalen Konferenz der Operndirektoren.

701 00
Das Bauvorhaben soll beendet werden.
Bauplanungsunterlagen vom 19. November 1968 und Ergänzungsunterlagen vom 16. April 1973 liegen vor.

Auf Grund von Lohn- und Stoffpreissteigerungen erhöhen sich die Gesamtkosten um ... 15 000 000 DM	2 386 000 DM
auf insgesamt	17 386 000 DM

Finanzierung:

1971 bis 1974 (nach Abgang von 4 029 000 DM)	6 641 000 DM
1975 (nach Abgang von 191 000 DM)	3 309 000 DM
1976	4 806 000 DM
Ansatz 1977	2 630 000 DM
	17 386 000 DM

Wirtschafter: Senator für Bau- und Wohnungswesen
Wirtschaftsstelle: Senatsverwaltung für Bau- und Wohnungswesen — Abt. Z (Allgemeine Angelegenheiten) —

812 79
Erneuerung von Musikinstrumenten:

1 Flügel	15 000 DM
Erneuerung des Gerätebestands:	
Orchesterstühle	20 000 DM
1 Trenn- und Schneideanlage	20 000 DM
1 automatische Zuschneidekreissäge mit Plattenvorschub	32 000 DM
Erweiterung des Gerätebestands:	
1 Magnetbandeinheit für den Bürocomputer	34 000 DM
	121 000 DM

Fig. 257. Explanations of account numbers 427–01 through 812–79, including rental costs and maintenance on musical instruments (Deutsche Oper Berlin)

Fig. 258. Mozart's *Così fan tutte,* directed by Otto Schenk, designed by Jürgen Rose and conducted by Karl Böhm. From left, Luigi Alva as Ferrando, Pilar Lorengar as Fiordiligi, Brigitte Fassbaender as Dorabella, Erika Köth as Despina, Dietrich Fischer-Dieskau as Don Alfonso, and Barry McDaniel as Guglielmo (Deutsche Oper Berlin/Ilse Buhs)

Fig. 260. Offenbach's *Die Banditen* in a new production directed by Peter Ustinov. Gerti Zeumer as Fiorella, Manfred Röhrl as Pietro, and Donald Grobe as the leader of the bandits, Falsacappa (Deutsche Oper Berlin/Ilse Buhs)

Fig. 259. The wedding sequence from Wieland Wagner's conception of *Lohengrin,* which calls for a chorus that remains immobile throughout and depends to a large extent on projected scenery. Anja Silja as Else von Brabant and Christa Ludwig as Ortrud (Deutsche Oper Berlin/Ilse Buhs)

Fig. 261. Otto Schenk's production of *Die Fledermaus,* designed by Günther Schneider-Siemsen. Eisenstein (Donald Grobe) soothes his nervous wife, Rosalinde (Gundula Janowitz), while his lawyer, Dr. Blind (Karl-Ernst Mercker), plans his next move (Deutsche Oper Berlin/Ilse Buhs)

Fig. 262. Ponchielli's *La Gioconda,* directed and designed by Filippo Sanjust with choreography by Alfonso Catá. Vera Little as Die Blinde and Peter Lagger as Alvise Badoero (Deutsche Oper Berlin/Ilse Buhs)

Fig. 263. Scarpia (Ingvar Wixell) threatens Floria Tosca (Pilar Lorengar) in Boleslaw Barlog's production of Puccini's *Tosca,* designed by Filippo Sanjust (Deutsche Oper Berlin/ Ilse Buhs)

Fig. 264. Lydia Wieder performs the "Dance of the Seven Veils" in a production of *Salome* by Richard Strauss (German Information Center)

Fig. 265. Gustav Rudolf Sellner's production of *Der Rosenkavalier* by Richard Strauss, designed by Filippo Sanjust and conducted by Josef Krips. Octavian (Tatiana Troyanos) nicks the Baron (Franz Mazura) with his sword while Sophie (Edith Mathis) watches in pleased surprise (Deutsche Oper Berlin/Ilse Buhs)

Fig. 266. Scenes from Wolf Volker's expressionistic production of Berg's *Wozzeck*. The doctor (Walter Dicks) listens objectively as Wozzeck (Dietrich Fischer-Dieskau) expresses his fears and hallucinations . . . (Deutsche Oper Berlin/Ilse Buhs)

Fig. 268. . . . The Captain (Helmut Melchert) reassures the Doctor as they listen to strange
sounds by the lake. Marie lies dead in the shadows (Deutsche Oper Berlin/Ilse Buhs)

Fig. 267. . . . Marie (Evelyn Lear) shows her son his reflection in a piece of broken mirror
. . . (Deutsche Oper Berlin/Ilse Buhs)

378 · NATIONAL THEATERS IN GERMAN AND AUSTRIAN CITIES

Fig. 270. The world premiere production of Luigi Dallapiccola's opera *Ulisse (Odysseus)*.
Erik Saeden in the title role with his crew (Deutsche Oper Berlin/Ilse Buhs)

Fig. 269. Hans Werner Henze's satirical opera *Der junge Lord* in its world premiere production by the Deutsche Oper Berlin (German Information Center)

Fig. 272. Scenes from Carl Orff's scenic cantata *Catulli carmina,* directed by Gustav Rudolf Sellner, choreographed by Peter Darrell, and conducted by Eugen Jochum. Eike Walcz as Catullus, Marion Cito as Lesbia, and Falco Kapuste as Caelius (Deutsche Oper Berlin/ Ilse Buhs)

Fig. 271. Stravinsky's ballet *Der Feuervogel,* choreographed by John Cranko, scenery by Jürgen Rose, and conducted by Heinz Wallat. Marcia Haydée as the Firebird and Ray Barra as Ivan Zarewitsch (Deutsche Oper Berlin/Heinz Köster)

Fig. 274. Scenes from the same production team's version of Orff's *Carmina burana,* designed by Teo Otto. Gerd Feldhoff sings one of the baritone solos . . . (Deutsche Oper Berlin/Ilse Buhs)

Fig. 273. Another scene from *Catulli carmina.* From left, Eike Walcz, Katia Dubois as Ipsitilla, Silvia Kesselheim as Ameana, Falco Kapuste, and Marion Cito (Deutsche Oper Berlin/Ilse Buhs)

Fig. 275. . . . The hippies between numbers . . . (Deutsche Oper Berlin/Ilse Buhs)

Fig. 276. . . . Rudolf Betz as a flower child . . . (Deutsche Oper Berlin/Ilse Buhs)

Fig. 277. . . . The dance ensemble. In the foreground, Rudolf Betz, Klaus Beelitz, and Karin Jahnke (Deutsche Oper Berlin/Ilse Buhs)

Schiller-Theater

The spoken drama national theater complex in West Berlin consists of the Schiller-Theater, the Schlosspark-Theater, and the Schiller-Theater Werkstatt, or experimental theater, all under one central management. The main building with the experimental theater is on Bismarckstrasse not far from the Deutsche Oper Berlin, and the Schlosspark Theater is near the Charlottenburg Palace.

The theater was built in 1906 as a private enterprise but, like its sister theater on the same street, was converted after the war into a tax-supported institution for the public good. In recent years its always substantial reputation has been enhanced by the presence in the company of the author Samuel Beckett, who has staged a series of near-definitive productions of his plays. His production of *Warten auf Godot* with Stafan Wigger as Didi, Horst Bollmann as Gogo, Klaus Herm as Lucky, and Carl Raddatz as Pozzo was widely admired in New York when the company visited America in 1977.

Since its reopening in 1951 under the direction of Boleslaw Barlog, the theater has offered many landmark productions to its public, among them Jürgen Fehling's interpretation of Friedrich Schiller's tragedy *Maria Stuart,* Erwin Piscator's adaptation of Tolstoy's *War and Peace,* the world premiere of *Die Verfolgung und Ermordung Jean Paul Marats dargestellt durch die Schauspielgruppe des Hospices zu Charenton unter Anleitung des Herrn de Sade* by Peter Weiss as directed by Konrad Swinarski, and Hansjörg Utzerath's production of the world premiere of *Die Plebejer proben den Aufstand* by Günter Grass. Some interesting productions at the Werkstatt have been *Grosse Schmährede* by Tankred Dorst, *Die bösen Köche* by Günter Grass, *Zoogeschichte* by Edward Albee (world premiere), and Arthur Kopit's *O Vater, armer Vater, Mutter hängt dich in den Schrank und ich bin ganz krank.*

Technical aspects of the theater are as follows:

Seating capacity: 1,103 seats.
Architect: The original Schiller-Theater (1906) was designed by the firm of Heilmann and Littman. After its destruction in World War II, it was redesigned and rebuilt to plans of the firm of Völker and Grosse.
Opened: September 5, 1951.
Proscenium size: From 9.4 meters to 13 meters wide by 7 meters high.
Stage size: 25.5 meters wide by 25 meters deep.
Forestage: 10 meters wide by 3 meters deep.
Technical equipment: Rundhorizont, large turntable 16.7 meters in diameter, three stage lifts, large lighting layout controlled by 220 magnetic amplifier dimmers with card preset control.
The Werkstatt is a free-form area with variable seating capacity. Lighting control by means of a 60-dimmer installation.
The Schlosspark-Theater was opened on November 3, 1945, under the direction of Boleslaw Barlog and seats 478 spectators.

Fig. 278. The Schiller-Theater on Bismarckstrasse. Totally destroyed in World War II, it was redesigned by the architectural firm Völker and Grosse and reopened in 1951 (Schiller-Theater, Berlin)

Fig. 279. The elegant foyer of the Schiller-Theater, which looks out on Bismarckstrasse below (Schiller-Theater, Berlin)

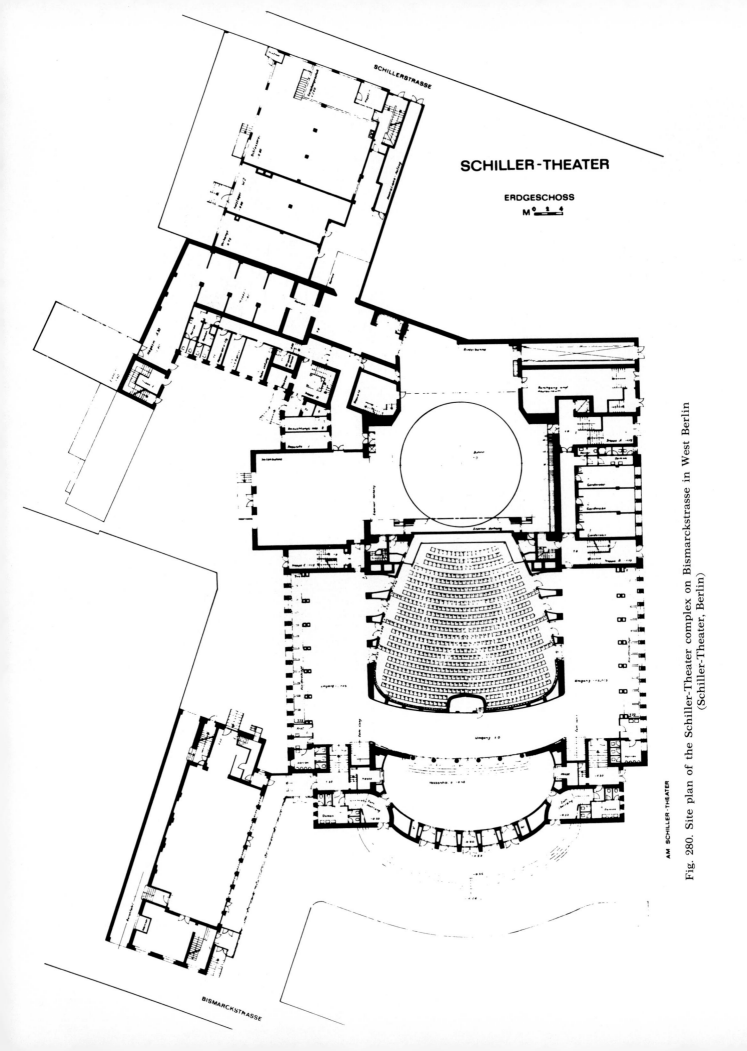

Fig. 280. Site plan of the Schiller-Theater complex on Bismarckstrasse in West Berlin (Schiller-Theater, Berlin)

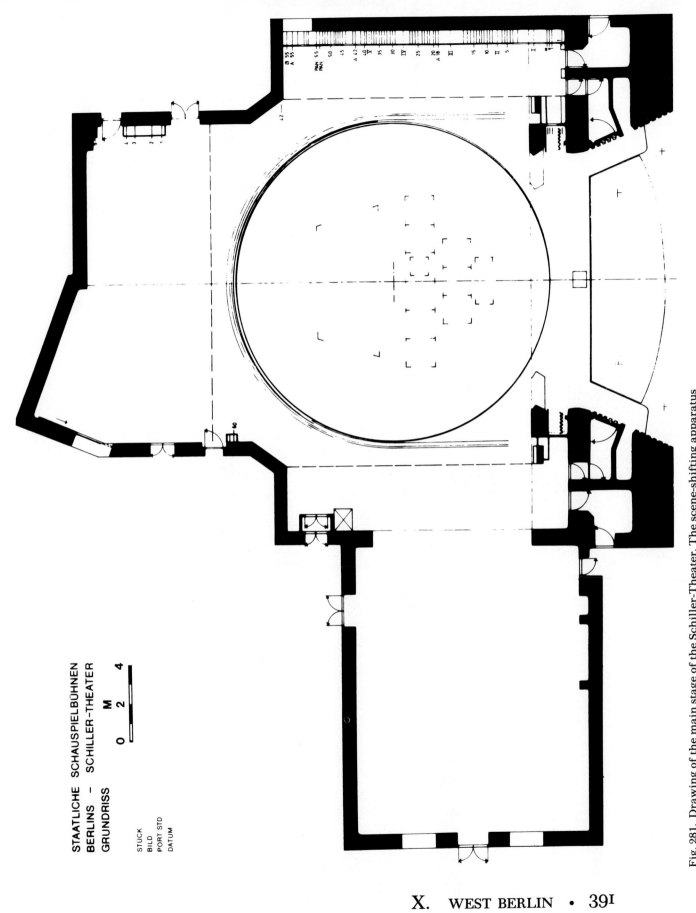

Fig. 281. Drawing of the main stage of the Schiller-Theater. The scene-shifting apparatus consists of full stage wagons, stage lifts, and hand-operated overhead battens (Schiller-Theater, Berlin)

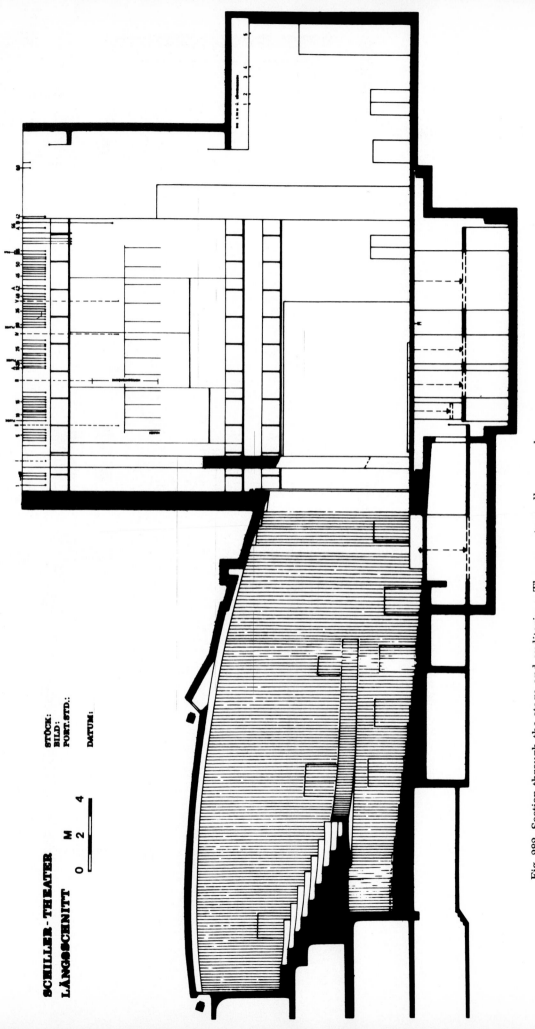

Fig. 282. Section through the stage and auditorium. The rear stage allows ample room for rear projection of scenic effects on the cyclorama. The lifts allow some variety of stage levels but are not as elaborate as those in some German theaters. The forestage permits a limited thrust-stage effect (Schiller-Theater, Berlin)

The Generalintendant of the Schiller-Theater is Hans Lietzau. Personnel of the theater in 1976–77 numbered as follows:

Artistic direction	31
Actors and actresses	91
Technical personnel	223
Administrative personnel	35
House personnel	82
Total	462

During the same season, performances of adult plays were offered to the public as follows:

	PERFORMANCES	ATTENDANCE	PERCENT OF CAPACITY
Schiller-Theater	313	190,249	54.6%
Schlosspark-Theater	296	112,443	80.8%
Werkstatt-Bühne	132	17,672	82.1%
Totals	741	320,364	72.5%

The two national theaters in West Berlin thus played to a total of 813,051 spectators in 1976–77, or about 41.7 percent of the population of the city.

During the season 1977–78 the Schiller-Theater and its two associated theaters presented the following plays:

Molière: *Der Geizige*
         Die Streiche des Scapin
Ibsen: *Hedda Gabler*
Bernhard: *Fest für Boris*
Raimund: *Der Verschwender*
Schiller: *Maria Stuart*
Sternheim: *Die Kassette*
         Die Hose
Kleibich: *Die indische Witwe* (world premiere)
Brecht: *Mann ist Mann*
Pinter: *Der Hausmeister*
Fugard: *Die Insel*
Ostrowski: *Der Wald*
Strindberg: *Der Vater*
O'Casey: *Rote Rosen für mich*
Shakespeare: *Der Sturm*
Brasch: *Lovely Rita* (world premiere)
Horváth: *Glaube, Liebe, Hoffnung*
Bronnen: *Die Exzesse*

Ticket prices and seating plans for the theater are shown in Figs. 283 and 284, pp. 395–396.

Fig. 285, p. 397, shows a nine-year summary of the finances of the Schiller-Theater.

Scenes from recent productions at the Schiller-Theater are shown in Figs. 286–291, pp. 398–403.

Statistical Summary

During the season 1977–78 the following totals were established by the 71 national theater units in West Germany:

Total Performances	
Operas	5,565
Ballets	1,068
Operettas	2,444
Musicals	1,154
Adult plays	15,222
Children's plays	3,333
Concerts by theater orchestras	627
Performances by guest companies	1,577
Total	30,990
Total attendance	17,483,497
Total Employment	25,655
Total Expenditure	DM 1,363,384,000
Total Earned Income	DM 233,024,000
Total Tax Subsidy	DM 1,130,360,000
Subsidy Percentage	82.9%

There is no censorship or interference by government officials in the artistic decisions of the theater managers. The West German Constitution (Grundgesetz), in Article 5, guarantees freedom of opinion, of the press, of art, and of science. Censorship may not take place. Section (3) reads, "Kunst und Wissenschaft, Forschung und Lehre sind frei. Die Freiheit der Lehre entbindet nicht von der Treue zur Verfassung." ("Art and science, research and teaching are free. The freedom to teach does not release one from his loyalty to the Constitution.")

Staatliche Schauspielbühnen Berlins

Schiller-Theater Schloßpark-Theater Werkstatt

EINTRITTSPREISE AB 1. 8. 1977

Schiller-Theater

Platzart	Reihe	Anzahl der Plätze	Einzelpreis DM	bei Premieren DM
Orchester-Sessel	O/A/B	51	26, --	28, 5o
Parkett	1 - 3	79	24, --	26, 5o
Parkett	4 - 6	96	21, --	23, --
Parkett	7 - 1o	14o	19, --	21, --
Parkett	11 - 14	154	17, --	18, --
Parkett	15 - 18	158	13, 5o	16, --
Parkett	19 - 2o	62	11, 5o	12, 5o
Rang	1	48	19, --	21, --
Rang	2 - 3	59	17, --	19, --
Rang	4 - 5	75	13, 5o	14, 5o
Rang	6	45	1o, 5o	11, 5o
Oberrang	1	4o	8, --	9, --
Oberrang	2 - 4	96	6, --	7, --

Schloßpark-Theater im Hebbel-Theater   Stresemannstr. 29, 1 Berlin 61, Kasse 26 o4 29 91

Platzart	Reihe	Anzahl der Plätze	Einzelpreis DM	bei Premieren DM
Parkett	A + B	3o	23, --	25, --
Parkett	1 - 2	33	23, --	25, --
Parkett	3 - 6	9o	21, --	23, --
Parkett	7 - 1o	96	18, --	2o, --
Parkett	11 - 12	43	16, --	18, --
Parkett	13 - 14	32	12, 5o	14, --
Rang	1	22	18, --	2o, --
Rang	2	18	16, --	18, --
Rang	3	17	14, --	16, --
Rang	4	16	12, 5o	14, --
Rang	Seite	45	1o, 5o	12, --
Parkett	Logen	16	6, --	8, --

Für die __Werkstatt-Bühne__ beträgt der Eintrittspreis DM 8, 5o auf allen Plätzen
(Premieren DM 9, 5o).

Auf diese Preise wird ein Zuschlag von DM o, 2o je Eintrittskarte für die Altersversorgungs-abgabe der Künstler erhoben.

Fig. 283. Single-ticket prices for the Schiller-Theater. The five block-booking organizations in Berlin, with over 100,000 members, make their own arrangements with the Schiller-Theater for members' subscriptions (Schiller-Theater, Berlin)

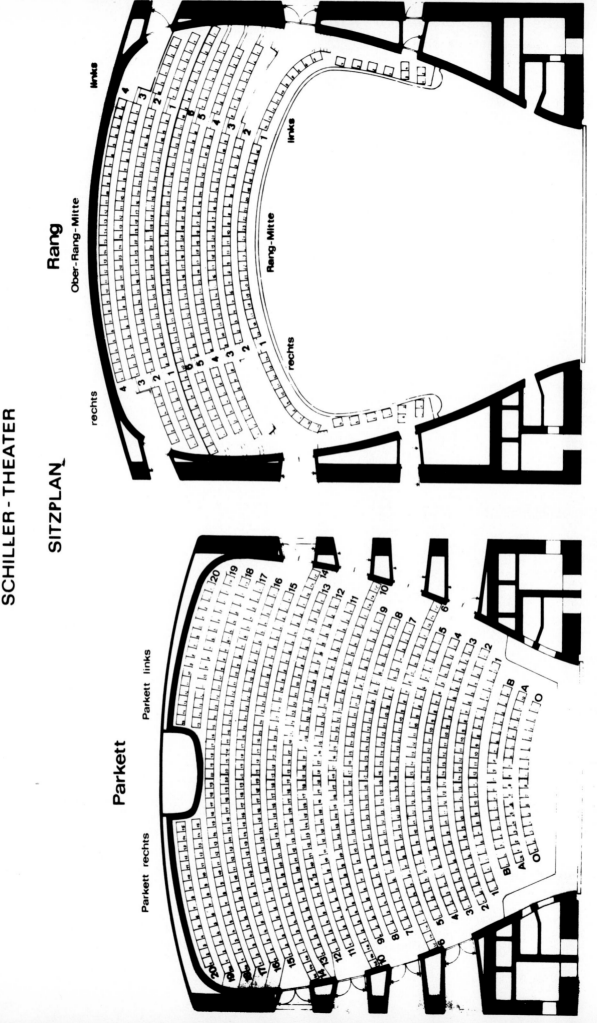

Fig. 284. Seating plans for the Schiller-Theater complex (Schiller-Theater, Berlin)

YEAR	1969	1970	1971	1972	1973	1974	1975	1976	1977
VALUE OF DEUTSCHE MARK	28¢	29¢	30¢	34¢	40¢	42¢	44¢	48¢	50¢
EXPENSES									
Artists' salaries	DM 5,175,000	DM 5,318,000	DM 6,056,000	DM 6,113,000	DM 6,908,000	DM 7,958,000	DM 8,370,000	DM 8,575,000	DM 9,073,000
Technical salaries	1,840,000	1,929,000	2,207,000	6,127,000	6,927,000	8,679,000	9,874,000	10,363,000	10,873,000
Administration	3,691,000	4,309,000	5,073,000	2,134,000	2,547,000	1,698,000	1,661,000	1,743,000	1,835,000
Other personnel	89,000	80,000	69,000	61,000	50,000	42,000	37,000	45,000	59,000
Pension funds	557,000	632,000	---	1,080,000	904,000	---	233,000	1,035,000	1,098,000
Production costs	2,066,000	2,298,000	2,307,000	2,256,000	2,520,000	2,586,000	2,904,000	2,938,000	3,057,000
Loan payments	---	---	---	---	---	---	25,000	76,000	535,000
Building maintenance	370,000	344,000	280,000	619,000	---	---	69,000	205,000	50,000
TOTAL	DM 13,788,000	DM 14,910,000	DM 15,932,000	DM 18,390,000	DM 19,856,000	DM 20,965,000	DM 23,175,000	DM 24,978,000	DM 26,558,000
INCOME									
Single tickets	DM 1,214,000	DM 992,000	DM 1,067,000	DM 1,330,000	DM 1,433,000	DM 1,218,000	DM 1,429,000	DM 1,370,000	DM 1,248,000
Subscriptions	---	---	---	---	---	---	---	---	---
Children's theater subscriptions	108,000	113,000	101,000	185,000	134,000	171,000	---	---	---
Visitor groups	969,000	945,000	879,000	910,000	893,000	857,000	1,010,000	925,000	1,007,000
Cloakroom charges	189,000	171,000	167,000	197,000	195,000	190,000	214,000	189,000	175,000
Radio and TV fees	323,000	220,000	204,000	7,000	7,000	275,000	157,000	323,000	348,000
Touring	196,000	211,000	253,000	82,000	152,000	138,000	217,000	294,000	140,000
Guest performances by other companies	---	---	---	---	---	---	---	---	---
Program sales	89,000	98,000	98,000	122,000	155,000	147,000	163,000	146,000	165,000
Other income	30,000	33,000	83,000	33,000	51,000	144,000	45,000	68,000	44,000
TOTAL	DM 3,118,000	DM 2,783,000	DM 2,852,000	DM 2,804,000	DM 3,018,000	DM 3,140,000	DM 3,235,000	DM 3,315,000	DM 3,125,000
TAX SUBSIDY	DM 10,670,000	DM 12,127,000	DM 13,080,000	DM 15,586,000	DM 16,838,000	DM 17,823,000	DM 19,938,000	DM 21,663,000	DM 23,435,000
SUBSIDY PERCENTAGE	77.4%	81.3%	82.1%	84.8%	84.8%	85.0%	86.0%	86.7%	88.2%

Fig. 285. Expenses and income for the Schiller-Theater, 1969–77 (Deutscher Bühnenverein, Köln)

Fig. 286. Bert Brecht rehearses the uprising in Shakespeare's *Coriolanus* with members of his Berliner Ensemble while outside in the streets of East Berlin the real uprising of June 17, 1953, takes place, in *Die Plebejer proben den Aufstand* by Günter Grass. Rolf Henniger as the Boss (Brecht), Gisela Mattishent as Volumnia (Helene Weigel) and Friedrich Bauschulte as Erwin, the Dramaturg (Erich Engel). The premiere production was directed by Hansjörg Utzerath and designed by H. W. Lenneweit (German Information Center)

Fig. 287. The workers get ready to hang Brecht and Engel from a batten, but the Dramaturg talks them out of it by citing the parable of the belly in *Coriolanus*. When it came time to act, Bert Brecht was prepared only to rehearse (German Information Center)

Fig. 288. Shakespeare's *Der Sturm*, directed by Alfred Kirchner with stage designs by
Axel Manthey. Prospero (Bernhard Minetti) leads Miranda (Angelika Thomas) across a
provocatively bare stage (Schiller-Theater/Ilse Buhs)

Fig. 289. Hedda Gabler (Gisela Stein) glares at her complacent husband Jörgen Tesman (Wolfgang Pampel) in Niels-Peter Rudolph's production of Ibsen's *Hedda Gabler,* with scenic designs by Roger von Möllendorf and costumes by Barbara Bilabel (Schiller-Theater/Anneliese Heuer)

Fig. 290. Samuel Beckett's *Warten auf Godot*, directed by the author. Klaus Herm as Lucky, Horst Bollmann as Estragon, Carl Raddatz as Pozzo, and Stefan Wigger as Vladimir (Schiller-Theater/Anneliese Heuer)

Fig. 291. *Glaube Liebe Hoffnung* by Ödön von Horváth, directed by Günter Krämer and designed by Andreas Reinhardt. Margit Carstensen as Elizabeth and Dadmar von Thomas as the Frau Amstgerichtsrat (Schiller-Theater/Ilse Buhs)

XI. AMERICAN ARTISTS IN THE GERMAN AND AUSTRIAN NATIONAL THEATERS

Darlene Wiley is a young American lyric soprano earning her living as an opera singer in West Germany rather than in America because Germany and Austria are where the jobs are today, and the artists' union, the Genossenschaft Deutscher Bühnen-Angehörigen, does not object to foreigners performing in the German theaters as long as the jobs cannot be filled by native artists. More than 500* Americans are employed in German-language theaters today, and the number is constantly increasing, since year-round employment in America for an opera singer or a ballet dancer is almost unknown.

Fifty years ago the pattern for an American singer was to go to Europe to be trained in voice, musicianship, languages, and repertory and return to America after a few years to begin his or her career. It was thought that only in Europe could one be prepared properly for the operatic and concert stage. For the last 30 years or so, however, the pattern has altered. Musical training and a moderate amount of stage experience can be acquired in American universities and music schools, but the job market in America is too small to accommodate all the artists who have the potential for major careers, so things are now just the opposite: one gets his training over here and looks for work in Germany, Austria, and Switzerland.

Miss Wiley's experience, as recounted in *Rundschau* for April, 1974, is typical of many other American artists these days. She took her undergraduate degree at the College of Wooster in Wooster, Ohio, where she majored in French horn and mi-

---

* According to the federal employment agency Z.B.F. in Frankfurt, there were 455 Americans engaged on year-round contracts in West German theaters during 1978/79: 212 solo singers, 3 actors, 18 solo dancers, 4 choreographers, 137 corps dancers, 51 chorus singers, 5 conductors, 1 Dramaturg, 14 coaches, 2 choral directors, 5 stage directors and 3 scene designers.

nored in voice. She took some German too, but didn't work at it very hard. Later, when she was a graduate student at the University of Illinois, Paul Ulanowsky persuaded her to improve her German diction as he coached her in opera roles and Lieder. She taught for a year at Oberlin Conservatory and then traveled to Germany to join her husband, Gale, who had been drafted and was serving there in the army. They had intended all along that she audition in Germany, so the chance military assignment proved to be a lucky circumstance for them both.

In Germany, Ms. Wiley auditioned for a unique agency, Die Zentrale Bühnen-, Fernseh- und Filmvermittlung der Bundesanstalt für Arbeit, or Z.B.F. for short, which handles most of the actors, singers, and dancers in Germany and Austria. This group is a department of the German federal government, so the artists do not have to pay them anything for finding them jobs in the German theater. There are also several private agents in various cities in West Germany and Austria who do charge commissions.* Ms. Wiley recounts the tensions of her first audition at the Mannheim Nationaltheater, where she sang against 25 other lyric sopranos for the single position of an Anfängerin, or beginner. Finally she obtained a position in the singing ensemble of the Darmstadt Staatstheater, where Rudolf Bing once got some experience as a Disponent, or scheduler, before joining the staff of the Charlottenburg Opera in Berlin.

One of the first facts of life as an American singer in Germany that Ms. Wiley discovered was the need to perfect her German diction and vocabulary. Besides speaking German for many hours of the day and grappling with such things as German income tax forms, she found that the German directors are not "just interested in the voice" to the exclusion of everything else, a common assumption among younger American singers. She listened to another American auditioning at Dortmund, singing Marie's aria from *The Bartered Bride,* a very popular opera in Germany and Austria. The singer had a fine voice but a noticeable American accent, and after a few bars the directors stopped her and told her to come back when her German was better. Then too, like most beginning singers, Ms. Wiley does a certain amount of operetta as all the German houses pay some attention to this popular form, and operetta calls for a good deal of spoken dialogue. If something goes awry and some ad libbing becomes necessary, it is essential to know what another character has just said as he looks at you with a particular kind of gleam in the eye.

Another young American singer who is beginning her career in the German theater is a coloratura soprano from Normal, Illinois, Lesley Manring-Borchers. In response to correspondence she writes:

> I was a voice and violin student at the University of Michigan for four years, graduating in vocal performance. I then sang for three years in New York City with such groups as the Goldovsky Opera and others, but I wanted steady employment as an opera singer and began to look around elsewhere. Germany is the

---

* See *Appendix B* for the names and addresses of the more important agents in West Germany and Austria.

place for steady work and I began in Heidelberg for two years (1975–77), moved up to Bonn for one year (1977–78) and am now in Wuppertal on a two-year contract until the summer of 1980.

My steady roles are Queen of the Night *(Die Zauberflöte)*, Musetta *(La Bohème)*, Oskar *(Ein Maskenball)*, Zerbinetta *(Ariadne auf Naxos)*, Konstanze *(Die Entführung aus dem Serail)*, and a few roles in modern operas such as Miss Wordsworth in Britten's *Albert Herring* and Titania in his *Midsummer Night's Dream*. Next year I sing my first Gilda and my first Rosina. Since I hit Europe I've sung the Queen of the Night 52 times—30 times in Heidelberg and 22 times as of tonight (May 27, 1979) in Wuppertal. And more to come!

I sing two or three nights a week and sometimes have a stretch of a week without performances. My worst month was 14 performances. Ideal is about eight performances a month along with all the daytime rehearsals.

I was fluent in German after my first year over here (that means thinking and dreaming in German), but even today, after five years, I sometimes make mistakes in grammar. The way to get ahead in the German theater, as in life, is to be always musically prepared, be consistent, sing well, and get along with the German stage directors over here. We are in the age of the dictator-Regisseur, who has replaced the hysterical perfectionist conductor of a generation ago. Mr. Goldovsky trained me to think my roles through for myself, and I find it difficult to do every tiny finger movement that a stage director wants, with no chance to try out my own ideas. Unfortunately, few stage directors here draw the character from the music. Many are just looking for gimmicks and are preoccupied with breaking traditions without always being able to replace what is lost with something better.

I have found the German people I have known to be warm and open. I find very few cultural differences between Germans and Americans—we have the same hard-work ethic. In two weeks I am marrying a Berlin-born French horn player in our orchestra, and his family isn't any different from mine. They are open and loving, they accept me, they like rock music, Baskin and Robbins ice cream, and McDonald's. They make me feel like I'm back home in the Middle West!

As I see it, it is more of a possibility in Europe to have a career *and* a family, since you can stay put in one place and have a middle-sized career here. In America, it has to be *career* all the way because of the scarcity of houses and the extreme competition.

Other American singers have had similar experiences. In an exchange of correspondence, Donald Grobe has written as follows:

I am a native of Ottawa, Illinois, born 1929 and attended grade and high school there . . . I won some singing contests and decided to become a musician. I went to Milliken University in Decatur, Illinois, won second prize in the vocal competition of the Chicago Music Festival, and received a scholarship from the

Fig. 292. Darlene Wiley, soprano, as Fiorilla in Rossini's *Der Türke in Italien* at the Staatstheater Darmstadt (Staatstheater Darmstadt)

XI. AMERICAN ARTISTS IN THE NATIONAL THEATERS • 407

Fig. 293. Lesley Manring-Borchers as the insane Queen in *Die Verurteilung des Lukullus,*
text by Bertolt Brecht and music by Paul Dessau, at the Heidelberger Theater (Heidelberger
Theater)

Fig. 294. Ks. Donald Grobe, lyric tenor, as Falsacappa in a recent production of Offenbach's *Die Banditen* at the Deutsche Oper Berlin (Deutsche Oper Berlin)

Chicago Musical College (now part of Roosevelt University). I received my B.M. in performing arts there in 1953. After a summer at the Aspen Festival I went to New York, where I lived for three years, making a living singing everything from requiems to musicals, in synagogues and churches—all the things American singers have to do to survive. Toward the end of those three years I was in *The Saint of Bleecker Street*—sang in the chorus and understudied the lead role, which I sang a couple of times. That showed me that to sing opera I needed experience, and everyone told me the place to get it was in Europe, especially in Germany. I looked for money. Finally, through auditioning, I got a grant from the Searchinger Foundation for an auditioning trip to Europe. I left in February, 1956, and have returned to the U.S. since then only for visits.

My first job was in Krefeld-Mönchen-Gladbach, where I was a lyric tenor for a season and a half. Then to Hannover for three seasons, and from there, in 1960, I came to Berlin. I have remained mainly at the Deutsche Oper Berlin ever since. I have a contract here for seven months out of the year. With the rest of my time I am free to do guest appearances, concerts, TV, and radio. I have sung at most of the festivals around Europe . . . and have guest contracts with the Volksoper in Vienna and with the State Opera in Hamburg. I have over a hundred roles in my repertory and have also sung many concerts. In 1970 Berlin made me a Kammersänger, purely an honor bestowed on people the theater feels deserve it.

The advantages of working in an opera company here would seem to me to be quite apparent: a steady job, without the need to spend most of your time auditioning for things or worrying about where the next dollar is going to come from. Continuous work and the opportunity to work on yourself, your voice, acting, and so forth, and to see the direction you're taking and what you're accomplishing. To do all this, one has to perform, and in a repertory company one performs. Then there is the public attitude toward singers. . . . You are considered a normal part of society here, and not a part of "show biz." You are a professional, doing honorable work within established society.

Learning German took a lot of time, private lessons, and good, hard work. In this matter, it is much more difficult for Americans who come here today. There is more competition from home-grown talent than when I arrived on the scene, so when you come today, you should be proficient in German. Many operas are given in the original Italian or French at the larger houses, but you still have German conductors and stage directors to deal with so one will have to know the language.

How much can you make? That's a broad field! In 1956 I started at Krefeld with DM 800 a month. It was enough to live on. Today I am a well-paid artist with a lot of experience. Last year my taxable income was around $120,000. Taxes take from a third to half your income depending on your tax bracket, dependents, and so forth.

The Germans treat us very well. We fit into their society—Carol, my wife, and I have as much social life as we would like. We enjoy living in Berlin. We find it an exciting city—German, but with many American influences, and we like being in the middle of things.

There is so much work here that, in spite of more and more competition from German singers, talented people will always manage to get work and can have a nice life. The lack of opportunity for performers in America is a thorn in the society of the country, I believe. It's a strange country that will subsidize everything from moon shots to farmers' not growing things on their land, but will not support its own talent in the fine arts. These have never been self-support-ive and never will be. Until the U.S. recognizes this and gives financial support to artists of all kinds to make available to them the opportunity to perform, the country will be considered superficial and un-adult by the rest of the world.

About coming back: I may when I retire—though I will then miss the culture here; but then, it is my homeland and I love it, so—who knows?

In response to the same questions, the mezzo-soprano Carol Wyatt of the Hamburgische Staatsoper and the Deutsche Oper Berlin wrote as follows:

I came to Europe to start a career because I did not know how to start in America. After studying in Italy for five years, Germany was the first country that gave me a concrete offer for work. The advantages of working in regular European companies are many for a beginner. First of all, I had a chance to get to know the stage with many small parts for which I had much preparation. This is the way I feel a singer can get routine on the stage. However, there is a danger of a singer getting in a rut period. If one does not move on to larger European houses and does not get guest offers from other houses, then the routine is to no avail, as one has not moved on. After seven years of working regularly, first in Frankfurt two years and then in Hamburg five years, I have now decided that the time has come to free-lance. Now my goal is to branch out into other European houses and to go back to America as an established artist.

I never planned or wanted to come to Germany. But one evening while I was a student in Italy, I had an espresso with Roberto Bauer and asked him what would be the possibility to start a career and where. I knew of no open doors. I will never forget his answer. At that time he had only one vocal cord, but he managed to pinch out the words from his throat: *Go to Germany!*

Therefore, my first tactic was to find a big European agent who was willing to help an unknown, inexperienced singer. I went to Dr. Rudolf Raab in Vienna, who immediately arranged my first audition—with Christoph von Dohnányi in Frankfurt am Main. He offered me a contract on the spot. I knew no German and was not particularly interested in learning it, as I was interested in singing the Italian roles. I did not care where—I just needed a start.

When I came to Germany, I spoke no German for a year, as most of the people in Frankfurt spoke English with me, whereas in Italy I was babbling Italian after six weeks. The German theaters are very organized, however, and arranged coachings for me twice a day. As a beginner, I had to sing many different kinds of roles. The German roles were not hard to learn. I felt that anybody could learn them with two coachings a day by good German coaches who phonetically corrected my every syllable.

When I started in Germany the money was a little bit more than I would have made in America as a schoolteacher. Social security and so on were all taken out from each monthly paycheck. But as one accumulates roles and experience, one can guest in other theaters and make sometimes almost as much in one evening as one makes in a month in one's own house.

About my family and social life . . . that brings me back to the question about learning the German language. After a little over a year in Frankfurt, I met a man from the orchestra who fortunately at that time spoke no English. We have been together over six years, and now my German is near to perfect as we speak only German together, although he has learned English in the meantime.

I really only have time for my work. Although I would love to get married and have children, there is simply no time to think about it at the moment. What kind of mother would I be to come home for one day and then leave my children again for ten days? I do not think it would be fair.

To relax after I have worked with stage directors like Götz Friedrich, who want blood from you, I resort to long walks in the beautiful green German woods. I think the German stage directors like the spontaneity of American singers. We seem to have a natural quality with our acting that sometimes European singers have trouble capturing. The German houses seem to really appreciate American talent, especially the musical background that most American musicians have.

Winfield Hutton, in an article in *Opera News,* March 20, 1971, entitled "Yankees in Valhalla," makes the same point in regard to the good opinion German stage directors seem to have of American singers. Americans are usually ready to learn more new roles, including more than one in the same opera. Also, the German directors are delighted with the Americans' traditional belief that "the show must go on," a conviction not shared by some of their German colleagues, who are inclined to cancel if they are not in good voice. In one house during a particular season, only three singers sang every scheduled performance, two Americans and a German. One American tenor sang 12 seasons without ever canceling a performance, a fact duly noted by the management when it came time to renew his contract.

In general, of course, American singers are glad of the chance to sing, sing, sing, instead of spending much of their careers teaching other people to sing. The German theaters are directed by artists rather than bureaucrats or businessmen preoccupied with raising money, and artistic values come first. The repertories are very broad, enabling singers to develop a wide range of roles from different styles and periods in the history of music and opera, instead of singing a few standard roles over and over as in America. Further, a good deal of emphasis is placed on making opera productions as dramatically valid as possible, and for this extra rehearsal time is sched-

Fig. 295. The American mezzo-soprano Carol Wyatt as Marina Mnischek in Mussorgski's
Boris Godounov at the Hamburgische Staatsoper (Hamburgische Staatsoper)

XI.   AMERICAN ARTISTS IN THE NATIONAL THEATERS   ·   413

uled. Audiences are younger in the German and Austrian houses and expect the acting level to be equal at least to what they see on their television sets.

Judith Beckmann, a Kammersängerin from North Dakota, has also commented on the matter of dramatic validity in connection with a production of Mozart's *Marriage of Figaro* at the Hamburg Staatsoper, which had been directed by Götz Friedrich. As the Countess, she had been required to play the scene in which she sings the aria "Porgi amor" alone in a large double bed, suggesting the sexual frustration she is experiencing in her present relationship with her husband, the Count. Asked how she felt about this unusual staging, she said that she had been brought up rather conservatively in America and was not entirely comfortable with the scene. Still, she agreed that Friedrich had immense talent as a stage director, that his striving for living characterization, for the genuine feeling, the true-to-life quality helped the opera and helped her. She considered that she was playing a rounded personality, not just a cardboard figure, that she was truly desperate, she truly loved her husband and was truly afraid for him because of his indiscretions. Thus, her characterization was believable, and friends who had seen her do other roles thought that she not only acted better in this production but sang better too.

She is an artist totally immersed in her work, which includes not only performances at Hamburg but also guest appearances with companies in Berlin, Munich, and Vienna. She teaches voice at the Musikhochschule in Hamburg, concertizes widely, and finds time for her husband and two school-age daughters. For relaxation, she works in her garden.

Life can also be interesting and artistically rewarding in the smaller European cities. After growing up in Texas and receiving vocal training and experience with the Westminster Choir College in Princeton, N.J., the lyric tenor William Ingle, who also plays the French horn, received a scholarship to study voice in Italy from 1963 to 1965. Afterward, his agent obtained singing jobs for him at Flensburg, Bremerhaven, Hannover, and Frankfurt am Main. He has been with the Landestheater Linz for several seasons and has written about his career, in an exchange of correspondence, as follows:

Some of the reasons I have stayed in Linz for several years are that I am the leading tenor of the theater and always receive good roles to sing. The pay is very good and I receive an eight-week paid vacation every year. Linz is on the international turnpike, so it is easy for me to get to Vienna or into Germany for guesting. Linz also has an airport, and this is important. Another reason is my family. My wife and daughter have always been with me during my career over here, and we have a good family life in Linz. My daughter will finish high school soon, we have our apartment here, and recently we bought a Landhaus with an orchard not far from Linz. The wooden ceiling in the house is dated 1789. We get along quite well with the Austrians; in fact, our neighbors had to give their O.K. before we could buy our country house, so naturally it made us feel good that they accepted us.

The American singer in Europe has the advantage of the better musical

JUDITH BECKMANN
STAATSOPER HAMBURG

Fig. 296. Ks. Judith Beckmann as Agathe in Weber's *Der Freischütz at the Hamburgische Staatsoper (Hamburgische Staatsoper)*

training in the U.S. The American voice is better trained to cope with all the pressures involved in the opera business. I feel certain that I could write a book about the reasons why Americans are successful here in Europe. It is really too bad that America at this point cannot offer the opera singer what Europe can.

I learned my German in college; however, my first foreign language was Italian. To get started in the opera business in Germany or Austria, one must audition for the agents and be able to speak some German. I sing around 80 opera and operetta performances during a ten-month season. In addition to this comes my guesting and concert work . . . My day is filled with musical solo rehearsals, ensemble rehearsals, or staging. We begin at 10:00 A.M., and big staging rehearsals can last until 14:00. In the afternoon we start at 17:00, and the rehearsal can last three hours. When we have a performance in the evening, we rehearse only a little in the morning, if at all. If we have a guest and have to rehearse just before a performance, this will be paid extra. Things are pretty much routine until my agent calls and I must fly to Germany to sing or drive to Graz to save a performance.

We did a new production of *La traviata* here recently in Italian (instead of German) and it was a big success. Linz is beginning to bring out the Italian operas more and more in the Italian language, and I think this is a trend in Germany also.

The American baritone William Murray also comments on the gradual changeover of the German houses from singing everything in German to performances in the original language of the text:

I used to sing all the roles I presently sing in the original language in German. This is very exciting, I think, because you really feel the audience going with you in the role. When you hear a sob in the audience for "Weine" in *Rigoletto* in the last duet and hear nothing for "Piangi," the inconvenience of having to learn a translation disappears. The American colleges need to offer more language training to voice students than they do now.

One can make a very good salary in Germany if you work hard and are able to guest well in needed roles. This also depends on your nerves and how callous you are to quality, for, as in the U.S., there are not many rehearsals for guests who are "takin' over a role."

The taxes in Germany are high but not as high as in the U.S. According to the new I.R.S. laws, this too will change for the worse in the near future, and the American singer in Europe will be taxed dry from both sides. This is particularly unfair when one considers the high prices in Germany, such as gasoline, which is now (April, 1979) up to 60 cents a quart.

The stage directors I have especially enjoyed working with are Günther Rennert and Otto Schenk, and I have also enjoyed working with the conductors Josef Krips and Josef Keilberth.

William Ingle

Fig. 297. The American lyric-dramatic tenor William Ingle as the Duke in Verdi's *Rigoletto* at the Landestheater Linz (Landestheater Linz)

Fig. 298. The American baritone William Murray as Rigoletto at the Deutsche Oper Berlin
(Deutsche Oper Berlin)

The Heldentenor James King, Kammersänger with the Vienna State Opera, has also noted the high quality of American musical training, in an exchange of correspondence:

Coming to Germany in 1961 brought to me a complete change of life-style and career. From 1952, after getting my M.A. at the University of Kansas City, Missouri, to 1961, I had been a professor of music at the University of Kentucky in Lexington. By studying along with my teaching, I made the change from baritone to tenor and began auditioning in New York as a tenor in 1960. My teacher at that time was Martial Singher.

My musical background is probably as good as any singer's today. American training is as good as one can get. The American problem is that there are too few jobs for singers there after they finish their training. Teachers continue to develop and train more teachers to the point that I really don't think either singers or singing teachers are taken seriously in America.

My first tenor role on any stage was Don José in *Carmen* with the Spring Opera Theater of San Francisco opposite Marilyn Horne. It was her first Carmen. I had done José previously in 1958 in Lexington in a student production, since no student tenor was available. Experience is where you find it.

In 1951, 1952, and 1953 I sang operetta and musicals, chorus parts, and small solo roles in the Kansas City Starlight Theater. This gave me more experience and contact with good musicians, singers, and Broadway stars. The work was hard as hell—performances every night and rehearsals every day for ten weeks in the summer—but I learned a lot. It's a pity that company died out. Perhaps TV did it and people prefer staying at home for their entertainment.

Before leaving for Europe in 1961, I had auditioned five times for the Met. They refused to take me, saying my voice was too small for their house. In October of 1961, I auditioned for the Deutsche Oper Berlin singing these arias in this order: Siegmund's "Spring Song" from *Die Walküre*, the "Flower Song" from *Carmen*, "E lucevan le stelle" from *Tosca*, the "Preislied" from *Die Meistersinger*, and "Che gelida manina" from *La Bohème*. It was a historic event, they tell me. No one had ever before auditioned with such a variety of lyric and dramatic tenor material. My debut there was January 29, 1962, as the Sänger in *Der Rosenkavalier*, and my first big part with the company was Riccardo in *Ballo in Maschera* the following month. I sang 55 performances in Berlin, adding leading roles in *Carmen, Ariadne auf Naxos,* and *Fidelio* to the above. After one of my *Carmen* performances in May of that year, Rudolf Bing walked into my dressing room, asked who I was, where had I been keeping myself, and how soon could I join the Metropolitan Opera in New York? My voice had not changed in just six months.

I wasn't able to accept a contract from him as by then I had many offers and engagements in Germany and Austria. I sang at Salzburg that summer as Achilles in Gluck's *Iphigenie in Aulis* and then expanded my repertory to include Lohengrin, the Kaiser in *Die Frau ohne Schatten,* and Apollo in *Daphne.* In 1965 I made my debut at the Bayreuth Festival in Wieland Wagner's new *Ring* as

Siegmund. By that time I was fully settled in the German way of life and was enjoying living here very much, as do several hundred other Americans who earlier in their careers had been practically jobless singers in America.

I made my Met debut in December, 1965, as Florestan in *Fidelio,* then returned to my home base over here. I don't get to America very often, but when I do I feel depressed at the lack of the great life-affirming instincts that earlier brought our country to great strength and unity of force second to none. America seems to be drying up, growing more and more shallow, like a river two feet deep and a mile wide at the mouth. . . . Pop music rules the media because it makes money and that seems to hold the honored position. I'm not against rock, or pop, or disco—just the monopoly of the media by this musical style, much of it dreadful trash, ludicrous, pornographic, promoting degeneracy. I've often said that we can't live constantly in the presence of defecation without eventually smelling of it.

Our young men talk and act like adolescents. I don't know how long it's been since I heard a bass-voice quality in an American youth. The pop music has succeeded in wiping out the concept of the legitimate, classical singing tone. The American doesn't even sing any more. If he does, his tone is dry and breathy like the pop singer—devoid of any sense of quality. Those who somehow do manage to develop an operatic voice become loners and shut-outs in the process. And then, after all the struggle and training to make artists of themselves, they often give up because of social, economic, and domestic problems connected with lack of job opportunities for professional singers.

Our potential in America is enormous; our opportunities for young singers for post–music school training and experience sadly, tragically lacking. Our country neglects, even seems to curse, some of its finest talent. To my way of thinking, this is a disgrace. I can't understand my own people—how they can be so blind to the great good that the live theater arts can bring, not only to us but to the world.

In Germany I have been treated like a king—literally, as have many other foreign singers who are doing well here. I studied French, Italian, and German at L.S.U. where I was an undergraduate. This foundation has proven invaluable to me in my singing as well as socially in my work in the opera world.

Life in Germany has much to be said for it. This country probably offers more to its people than any other country in the world. I have never seen comparable cities with so much to do and see as those here. Germany is fascinating, enlightening, and it has enriched and blessed my life. The Germans are a great people who have made great mistakes and wrought dreadful evils on the world, but they have also provided us with some of our greatest works of art. We from other parts of the world can be very grateful to them.

The American opera singers of our time would have had no place to go were it not for the hospitality and opportunity offered to them by the Germans. The opera houses have also been open-armed to singers from every other country, as long as they could sing well. In Italy it is quite different. Italian houses never take foreign singers if they can help it.

German singers are again on the rise, but there are still not enough to satisfy the needs of the approximately 60 opera houses in West Germany and Austria. I have a free run of the Heldentenor field here and can almost write my own ticket. I sing 60 to 65 evenings a year throughout the world. My main house is the Vienna State Opera, where for many years I have had a contract for 20 evenings a year. As a sample of my activity, I am booked in February, 1979, for *Lohengrin* at Munich and three *Toscas* in Vienna; in March, for *Lohengrin* and *Fidelio* at Munich and a *Tosca* and two *Pagliaccis* in Vienna; in April, two *Fidelios* and three *Parsifals* in Munich and *Fidelios* in Berlin and in Hannover; in May, a Liederabend in Berlin and one in Vienna, *Ariadne* in Munich, and *Carmen* in Prague; and so it goes. God help me to keep my health. I know how to sing now but have to guard my condition above all things to keep my voice functioning properly.

Costanza Cuccaro was born into and raised by a musical family and, like many singers, studied musical instruments at an early age—in her case, violin and piano. Studying an instrument seems to improve musicality and sight-reading ability. Ms. Cuccaro received her advanced training at the University of Iowa, won first place in the Metropolitan Opera Auditions in 1967–68, won a Fulbright scholarship to study voice in Rome with Luigi Ricci, where she learned Italian, then received her first job offer from the Zürich Opera. She sang leading coloratura roles in Zürich for three years, learned German and French, then went to Berlin, where she has been a leading coloratura with the Deutsche Oper Berlin for several seasons. She has made a debut at the Metropolitan Opera in New York, but the bulk of her singing is done outside the United States.

Brenda Jackson's career has been somewhat similar. Born in St. Louis, she studied at the St. Louis Institute of Music and Washington University in St. Louis, then won the Metropolitan Opera Auditions. These auditions no longer lead to contracts with the Met, but it doesn't hurt to win one. Ms. Jackson went on to Switzerland, where she got experience in both Basel and Zürich. From Switzerland, where she improved her language abilities, she joined the ensemble of the Deutsche Oper Berlin and has been there as a leading lyric coloratura ever since. She too has made an American debut, in New York's Art Park Opera Festival, singing Gilda in Verdi's *Rigoletto*. But the majority of her engagements outside Berlin have been in Vienna, Graz, Kassel, Hannover, Munich, Mannheim, and Frankfurt am Main.

Vera Little-Augustithis, Kammersängerin with the Deutsche Oper Berlin, was born in Memphis, Tennessee. There she attended the Grant Grammar School, where she sang her first role in the theater, the grandmother in the operetta *Tom Sawyer*. She continued her studies at Talladega College in Alabama, where she won a Fulbright scholarship to study music in Paris. From there she made her way to Berlin, where she sang the first black *Carmen* in the company's history. Of this performance the critic for the *Frankfurter Allgemeine* wrote, "This debut is the beginning of a great

Fig. 299. The tenor Ks. James King as Lohengrin at the Vienna State Opera (Staatsoper Wien)

theatrical career for this black singer. She has a first-class talent, a beautiful voice, and a musicality which is far out of the ordinary."

Vittorio Gui heard her in Berlin and invited her to sing before Pope John XXIII in Rome. Again, she was the first of her race to present a recital before the Pope in the Vatican. Since then she has added the roles of Amneris in *Aida*, Ulrica in *Un Ballo in Maschera*, Giulietta in *Hoffmanns Erzählungen*, and other major mezzo-soprano parts to her repertory, roles which she has performed all over Europe. In 1972 the city-state of Berlin made her a Kammersängerin, in honor of her exceptional contributions to the culture of her adopted country.

In addition to singers, the German theaters have shown a good deal of hospitality to dancers. The head of the Hamburg Ballet is an American dancer and choreographer, John Neumeier. Between 1968 and 1978, 28 American dancers have been on the staff of the Hamburgische Staatsoper, including Ray Barra, Lynn Charles, and Marina Eglevsky.

John Neumeier was born in Milwaukee in 1942. He studied dancing there under Sheila Reilly, then continued his studies in Chicago and Copenhagen. Further study at the Royal Ballet School in London led to engagements with the Sybil Shearer Company and with John Cranko at the Stuttgart Ballet. From 1969 to 1973 he was head of the ballet company and chief choreographer for the Ballet Company of the Städtische Bühnen Frankfurt am Main, after which he joined the Hamburg Staatsoper in the same capacity. In addition to his choreographic duties, he established a ballet school in Hamburg in 1978. Recently, one of his most characteristic successes has been his production of Leonard Bernstein's *West Side Story* for the Hamburg company, a show in which he began his professional career in New York when Jerome Robbins directed it in 1957.

American conductors and musicians have also prospered in the German area theaters. Theodore Bloomfield was a regular principal conductor at the Frankfurt Opera for many years, and in 1982 the conductor Lorin Maazel will become Director of the Vienna State Opera, the first American ever to head a major German opera house.

One would suppose that living among a race of people as "foreign" as the Germans are thought to be would impose serious obstacles on American artists in regard to "getting acquainted," being accepted in a stiff and formal culture much older than our own, but such seems not to be the case. Darlene Wiley observes that once the language barrier was gone, things seemed much the same to her over there as here. The Germans are as absorbed as we are in materialism, sports, and news broadcasts. What she began to notice, in fact, was how similar people are everywhere. As she puts it, "the best example of that was the 'little secret' we at the theater all shared when I was singing the old mother of Marie in *The Bartered Bride*. I performed as a stooped and hunched old woman while the German stagehands were winking from the wings because I was actually seven months pregnant under all that costume. Those kinds of experiences make the climb up the ladder of success so much easier, and so much more human . . ."

COSTANZA CUCCARO
GILDA
Bayer. Staatsoper

Fig. 300. Four American artists employed in the German and Austrian national theaters: Costanza Cuccaro as Gilda in *Rigoletto* at the Bayerische Staatsoper . . . (Bayerische Staatsoper, Munich)

Brenda Jackson
OLYMPIA (Hoffmanns Erzählungen)
Deutsche Oper Berlin

Fig. 301. . . . Brenda Jackson as Olympia, the mechanical doll, in Offenbach's *Hoffmanns Erzählungen* at the Deutsche Oper Berlin . . . (Deutsche Oper Berlin)

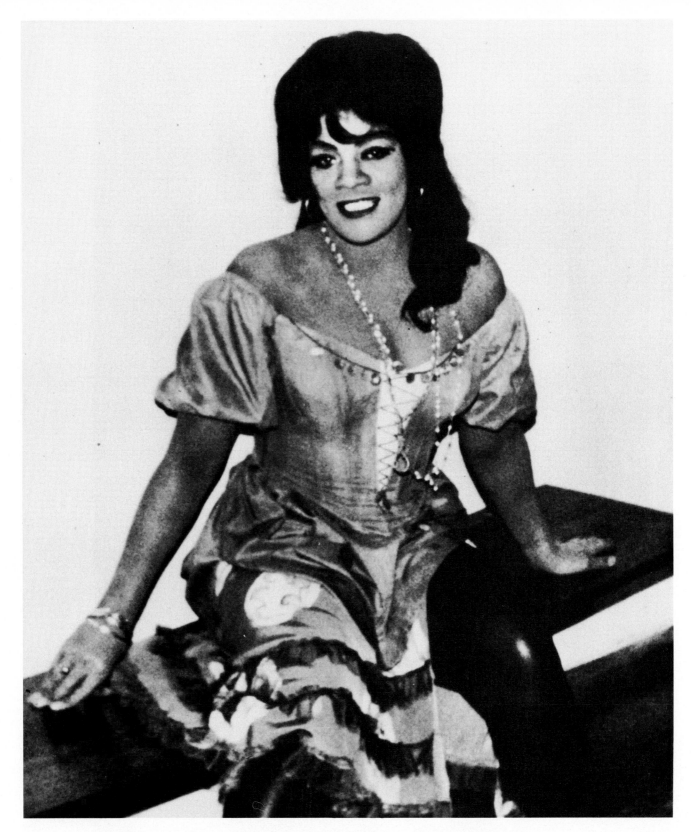

Fig. 302. . . . Ks. Vera Little-Augustithis as Carmen at the Deutsche Oper Berlin . . .
(Deutsche Oper Berlin)

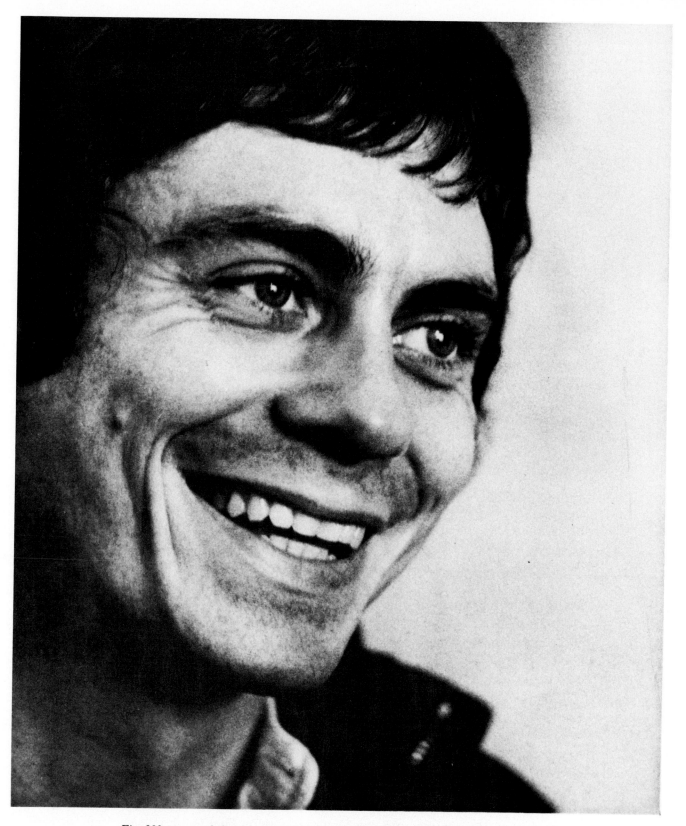

Fig. 303. . . . and the dancer and choreographer John Neumeier, Ballet Director for the Hamburgische Staatsoper (Hamburgische Staatsoper)

XI.   AMERICAN ARTISTS IN THE NATIONAL THEATERS • 427

CONCLUSION

There seem to be quite a few opera companies in America, about 30 with budgets over $500,000 per year, so why are there so few jobs for American opera singers? The reason lies in the fact that most of the American "companies" are not opera companies at all in the European sense of the word. An opera company traditionally is a group of singers, dancers, orchestra musicians, artistic directors, stagehands, and house personnel who produce 20 to 30 operas a year in their own theater on a repertory production basis. Few American companies conform to this definition. The average company does three or four operas a year, rents the theater, rents the orchestra, sometimes rents the scenery and costumes, and rents a chorus if one is needed. The principal singers in the company are all guests, brought in from elsewhere to sing three or four performances and then go their ways. As an example, the Baltimore Opera Company, during the season 1977–78, did four operas in a city of 878,000 population: *Lucia di Lammermoor* October 13, 15, and 17; *The Italian Girl in Algiers* November 17, 19, and 21; Verdi's *Macbeth* February 16, 18, and 20; and *Les Contes d'Hoffmann* April 13, 15, and 17. All the principal singers were different, and all were singing in Baltimore as guests. The company did not perform its four operas in repertory but rather as a small stock company, doing four shows a year at three performances each.

Companies in other cities operate at about the same level, with a few exceptions. According to information published in the Central Opera Service Bulletins during the 1977–78 season, the Opera Company of Boston did three operas at four performances each, the Charlotte Opera Association did six performances of three operas, and the Lyric Opera of Chicago did 50 performances of seven operas. The Chicago company does operate on a repertory basis, and all seven operas were done between September 23 and December 17, a season of about 11 weeks. The principal singers were all in Chicago as guests, however, and one can only wonder what the rest of the company— the comprimario singers, the chorus, the dancers, the stage and musical directors, the stagehands, and the administrative personnel—do during the remaining 41 weeks of the year?

But things are better in Chicago than in a lot of other places: the Cincinnati Opera Association did 12 performances of six operas; the Dallas Civic Opera, 12 performances of four operas; and the Michigan Opera Theatre did 30 performances of five operas in Detroit, a city of 1,387,000 population. Companies in Fort Worth, Honolulu, Houston, Kansas City, Louisville, Memphis, Miami, Milwaukee, New Orleans, Omaha, Philadelphia, Pittsburgh, Portland, San Antonio, San Diego, Seattle, Tulsa, Tucson, and Washington, D.C., operate at about the same level of activity, from Tulsa's four performances of two operas to Houston's 33 performances of six operas and Seattle's 38 performances of nine operas. The San Francisco Opera has developed over many years into a widely respected repertory opera company, performing in its own theater and providing work year round for part of its personnel. The main company did 60 performances of ten operas during 1977–78, and a smaller subsidiary company, the Spring Opera Theater, did 16 performances of four more on tour. Most of the principal singers were engaged for only 11 weeks, however, between September 9 and November 27.

The two New York companies come closer to European standards of operation than do any other companies in America, but neither the New York City Opera nor the Metropolitan Opera performs in its own city for the standard 46 weeks that is routine in Germany and Austria, although not in Italy or France. The New York City Opera performed in New York from August 31 through November 13—11 weeks. It was then in Los Angeles, which has no opera company of its own, from November 16 through December 11—four weeks. The company was on vacation from mid-December until the middle of February, and then began its spring season, which lasted from February 23 through April 30—nine weeks. Two weeks in Washington, D.C., in May rounded out a 26-week season, during which the company gave 202 performances of 24 operas. Most members of the company were free to seek employment elsewhere during the other 26 weeks of the year, however.

The Metropolitan Opera Association provides something close to year-round employment for the 800 or so members of its company. The 1977–78 season began on October 10 and ran continuously through April 15—27 weeks in New York. Eight more weeks on the road brought employment to 35 weeks, during which time the company did 247 performances of 21 operas. The company operates in its own theater at Lincoln Center and during the summer makes extra money renting the building to touring ballet companies.

The employment possibilities for actors and actresses in the American resident professional theaters are little better. The so-called LORT theaters (for the Equity contract designation—League of Resident Theaters) often employ actors on a year-round basis, but many others are "jobbed in" for a specific play and then sent back to New York. With a few exceptions, the LORT theaters too are stock companies rather than repertory companies. A play is put on for about six weeks, then taken off to make room for the next play, which also runs about six weeks, and so on through an average season of 36 to 40 weeks during which the theater does about 200 performances of five, six, or seven plays. The Guthrie Theater in Minneapolis plays rotating repertory, and the company tends to stay together throughout the season, which usually runs about nine months, from June through February. Also, there have been attempts to establish the repertory principle of production in Washington, D.C., New York, and Cleveland.

Nonetheless, there is a depressing sameness to the theater and opera picture in America. Employment is meager, performance standards vary wildly from good to bad, and the people of the large cities of the country do not possess a high opinion of the theater as a cultural or educational institution. It is hard to avoid the conclusion that the American theater is in a state of severe stagnation, both artistically and economically.

The fact that there are no public theaters in the country—theaters that receive 50 percent or more of their annual budgets from tax subsidies—surprises foreigners. The principle of tax support for the performing arts has been established for so long in so many countries that it is hard to imagine a civilized republic in the western world a large proportion of the population of which has never heard of such a thing.

It is true that there are signs of change. The National Endowment for the Arts received $149.0 million from Congress in 1978, and what little can be done with this sum of money will be welcome to those who receive modest portions of it. But the Endowment is handicapped by being in Washington, far away from the realities of theater, opera, and ballet production in Chicago, Los Angeles, and Houston. Some Congressmen have been studying a plan that would reorganize federal support in such a way that the funds would be sent to the cultural departments of the executive branches of the larger cities on a per capita basis. It would be up to the mayor's office, through a cultural administrator, to assist the performing arts companies already established in a city to grow into true national theaters—repertory companies performing drama, opera, operetta, and ballet 40 to 46 weeks per year in modern theater complexes—by providing tax subsidies in amounts equal to 50 percent or more of the annual budgets.

Before Congressmen will consider voting subsidies for national theaters, however, the people must make clear to them, by word and by mail, that they want such educational institutions and that they wish their tax dollars spent to support them. Our present institutions of higher learning provide exceptional facilities for the education of the intellect and of the body, but the education of feeling is neglected. Perhaps only professional theaters, opera and ballet companies, and art museums can successfully address this aspect of human education. But the question constantly arises, what is meant by the "education of feeling" and why is it valuable?

Susanne Langer has tried to provide an answer to these questions. In an article entitled "The Cultural Importance of Art" (included in her *Philosophical Sketches* of 1962), she discusses the influences of art on life and notes that "a wide neglect of artistic education is a neglect in the education of feeling. Most people are so imbued with the idea that feeling is a formless, total organic excitement in men as in animals that the idea of educating feeling, developing its scope and quality, seems odd to them, if not absurd. It is really, I think, at the very heart of personal education." And further: "Art education is the education of feeling, and a society that neglects it gives itself up to formless emotion . . . This is a large factor in the irrationalism which dictators and demagogues exploit."

APPENDIX

A. THEATER COLLECTIONS AND RESEARCH INSTITUTES IN GERMANY AND AUSTRIA

BAYREUTH

Richard-Wagner-Gedenkstätte der Stadt Bayreuth
Städtisches Museum und Archiv
858 Bayreuth, Neues Schloss
    Pictures and manuscript documents on the life and works of Richard Wagner as well as the history of the Bayreuth Festivals. Library of 10,000 volumes, recording archive, and collection of stage settings and models.

BERLIN

Freie Universität Berlin
Institut für Theaterwissenschaft
1 Berlin 37, Riemeisterstrasse 21/23
    Library of volumes on the contemporary history of the German theater and the library of Walter Unruh.

Archive, Sammlungen und Bibliotheken der Akademie der Künste
1 Berlin 21, Hanseatenweg 10
    Manuscripts, prompt books, press notices, monographs, dissertations, scene design sketches, photos, recordings, posters, and programs in connection with the work of many of the most important figures of the German theater, among them Lovis Corinth, George Grosz, Käthe Kollwitz, Ferruccio Busoni, Alfred Einstein, Herman Scherchen, Gottfried Benn, Lion Feuchtwanger, Carl Hauptmann, Ödön von Horváth, Georg Kaiser, Ernst Toller, Julius Bab, Ernst Deutsch, Jürgen Fehling, Heinz Hilpert, Alfred Kerr, Fritz Kortner, Erwin Piscator, Max Reinhardt, Heinz

Tietjen, Paul Wegener, Mary Wigman, and many others. There are also large special collections of books, manuscripts, and records from the history of the German theater.

BERN

Schweizerische Theatersammlung
CH-3000 Bern, Hallwylstrasse 15
   Pictures, photographs, costumes, marionettes, model settings, recordings, and books on the Swiss theaters. Materials on the life and work of Adolphe Appia.

BOCHUM

Ruhr-Universität Germanistisches Institut
Institut für Theaterwissenschaften
463 Bochum-Querenburg, Universitätsstrasse 150, Gebäude GB
   Seminars in theater history, film, and television.

DARMSTADT

Theatersammlung der Hessischen Landes- und Hochschulbibliothek
61 Darmstadt, Schloss
   Stage designs, figurines, drawings, sketches, scene photos, documents, posters, and programs of the Darmstadt theaters from the 18th century to the present.

ERLANGEN

Universität Erlangen-Nürnberg
Theaterwissenschaftliche Abteilung am Deutschen Seminar
852 Erlangen, Bismarckstrasse 1, Haus B
   Library on the contemporary history of the German theater. Seminars in theater history and dramaturgy; practical work in radio and television and in an experimental theater.

ESSLINGEN a.N.

Ostdeutsches Theater-Archiv der Künstlergilde e.V.
Esslingen am Neckar, Webergasse 1
   Documents, programs, stage designs, portraits, and photographs together with a large library of books in connection with the history of the 80 German theaters in the lost eastern provinces.

FRANKFURT AM MAIN

Stadt- und Universitätsbibliothek

Abteilung Musik, Theater und Medien
Sammlung F. N. Manskopf
6000 Frankfurt am Main, Bockenheimer Landstrasse 134–138
    Collections of manuscripts, prompt books, musical scores, programs, stage designs, portraits, photographs, and books on the Frankfurt theaters from the 18th century to the present. Also available are the papers of Engelbert Humperdinck.

GÖTTINGEN

Dramaturgische Abteilung des Seminars für deutsche Philologie
34 Göttingen, Nikolausberger Weg 15
    Seminars in the history of theater and drama.

HAMBURG

Theatersammlung der Freien und Hansestadt Hamburg
2 Hamburg 13, Rothenbaumchausee 162
    Theater collection of more than 30,000 volumes, programs, critical writings, pictures, photographs, and manuscripts concerned principally with the history of the theater in Hamburg from the 17th century to the present.

Otto-Ackermann-Archiv e.V.
    Large personal theater collection of the director Otto Ackermann.

KÖLN

Institut für Theaterwissenschaft der Universität Köln
5 Köln 1, Meister-Ekkehart-Strasse 11
    Library of about 3,000 volumes on the contemporary theater, radio, television, and film. Study space in connection with the materials in the Museum in the Wahn Schloss, described below.

Theatermuseum
verbunden mit dem Institut für Theaterwissenschaft der Universität zu Köln
505 Porz-Wahn, Burgallee 2, Schloss
    The Niessen collection is the basis for this contemporary theater library of over 75,000 volumes, many programs, newspaper clippings, scene and costume designs, photographs, slides, recordings, and model stages.

Tanzarchiv
Institut für Bühnentanz
5 Köln 41, Stadion-Aachener-Strasse
    Collection and library of materials pertaining to dance art.

MANNHEIM

Theatersammlung des Städtischen Reiss-Museums
68 Mannheim 1, C 5, Zeughaus
Large collection of books, documents, manuscripts, figurines, oil paintings, sketches, watercolors, photos, and autographs pertaining to the history of the Nationaltheater Mannheim from its founding in 1779 to the present.

MÜNCHEN

Institut für Theaterwissenschaft an der Universität München
8 München 22, Ludwigstrasse 25
Library on the current history of the German theater. Seminars and lectures in German theater history and criticism.

Theatermuseum
(früher Clara-Ziegler-Stiftung)
8 München 22, Galeriestrasse 4a, Hofgartenarkaden
Large theater collection from many countries and periods of the history of the theater. Established in 1910.

Theaterwissenschaftliches Archiv Dr. Steinfeld
8 München 40, Schraudolphstrasse 13b
The archives are divided into departments of opera, plays, operettas, dances, authors, and actors. Large collection of documents, reviews, biographical materials, programs, posters, and photographs.

WIEN

Institut für Theaterwissenschaft an der Universität Wien
A-1010 Wien I. Hofburg, Batthyanystiege
Seminars and lectures on the history of the theater. Library of materials on the contemporary theater.

Theatermuseum
A-1010 Wien I, Hanuschgasse 3
Theater collection of the Austrian National Library: manuscripts, programs, documents, scene and costume designs, paintings, sketches, and autographs pertaining to the history of the theater in Vienna and Austria. Over 1,200,000 items—the largest theater collection in the world.

B. THEATRICAL AND MUSICAL AGENTS IN GERMANY AND AUSTRIA

West Germany

Dr. Germinal Hilbert
8000 München 22, Maximilianstrasse 22

Cornelius Hom
6000 Frankfurt am Main 1, Steinweg 4

Friedrich Paasch
4000 Düsseldorf-Oberkassel, Drakestrasse 2

Hans Schmid (Walter Meyer Nachfolger)
8000 München 80, Cuvilliésstrasse 31

Harry Schmidt
Franz Siebenlist
8000 München 40, Leopoldstrasse 44/VI

Wolfgang Stoll (Robert Schulz Nachfolger)
8000 München 40, Martiusstrasse 3

Ilse Zellermayer
8000 München 40, Artur-Kutscher-Platz 1

Die Zentrale Bühnen-, Fernseh- und Filmvermittlung der Bundesanstalt für Arbeit
    Generalagentur Frankfurt
        6000 Frankfurt am Main, Feuerbachstrasse 42

    Agentur Berlin
        1000 Berlin 15, Kurfürstendamm 206

    Agentur Hamburg
        2000 Hamburg 13, Mittelweg 41
        2000 Hamburg 70, Tonndorfer Hauptstrasse 90

    Agentur München
        8000 München 40, Leopoldstrasse 19

Austria

Ioan Holender
Theateragentur Starka

A-1060 Wien, Mariahilferstrasse 3

Österreichische Internationale Künstlervermittlung
A-1090 Wien, Maria-Theresien-Strasse 11

Österreichische Künstleragentur
Austroconcert
A-1010 Wien, Ruprechtsplatz 4–5

"Opera" Vladarski
A-1190 Wien, Reithlegasse 12

Dr. Rudolf Raab
A-1010 Wien, Plankengasse 7

BIBLIOGRAPHY

A. PERIODICALS

Autor, Der
1 Berlin 31, Bundesallee 23
   Publication of the Dramatiker-Union: Writers and composers for stage, film, radio, and television.

Bühne und Parkett
1 Berlin 12, Wilmersdorfer Strasse 94
   Publication of the Verband der deutschen Volksbühnenvereine e.V.

Bühnentechnische Rundschau
Friedrich Verlag
3016 Seelze 6, Im Brande 15
   Zeitschrift für Theatertechnik, Bühnenbau und Bühnengestaltung.

Deutsche Bühne, Die
5 Köln 1, Quatermarkt 5
   Publication of the Deutscher Bühnenverein. The society also publishes an annual *Theaterstatistik,* covering performances, attendance, personnel, income, subsidies, expenses, and seat prices in connection with the activities of all the national theaters in West Germany and Austria.

Deutscher Musikrat
53 Bonn-Bad Godesberg, Michaelstrasse 4a
   Publication of the Präsidium des Deutschen Musikrates.

Deutsches Bühnen-Jahrbuch
2 Hamburg 13, Feldbrunnenstrasse 74
   Publication of the Genossenschaft Deutscher Bühnen-Angehörigen im Verlag Bühnenschriften-Vertriebs, G.m.b.H.

dg-Nachrichtenbrief
1 Berlin 41, Sarrazinstrasse 10
    Publication of the Dramaturgische Gesellschaft.

Hörfunk-Fernsehen-Film
8 München 19, Klarastrasse 19
    Publication for the Mitglieder der Rundfunk-Fernseh-Film-Union im DGB.

Kunst, Freie Berufe (KFB)
A-1090 Wien IX, Maria-Theresien-Strasse 11
    Publication of the Gewerkschaft Kunst und Freie Berufe.

Maske und Kothurn
A-1010 Wien, Hofburg, Batthyanystiege
    Internationale Beiträge zur Theaterwissenschaft. Eigentümer und Herausgeber: Institut für Theaterwissenschaft an der Universität Wien.

Musica
Bärenreiter Verlag
3500 Kassel, Postfach 100 329
    Zweimonatsschrift für alle Gebiete des Musiklebens.

Mykenae
Mykenae Verlag
61 Darmstadt, Ahastrasse 9
    Theater-Korrespondenz und Theater-Feuilletondienst.

Nordwestdeutscher Theaterbrief
2 Hamburg 13, Hartungstrasse 12
    Nachrichten und Kommentare für Rundfunk, Fernsehen, Presse.

Opera
6 Woodland Rise, London N 10 3UH
    Reports and reviews covering the international opera scene. Edited by Harold Rosenthal.

Opernwelt
Erhard-Friedrich-Verlag
3016 Seelze 6, Im Brande 15
    Nachrichten und Kommentare für Oper. Herausgeben von Erhard Friedrich und Imre Fabian.

Orpheus
1 Berlin 31, Bundesallee 56
    Informationzeitschrift über Oper, Konzert, Bühne, Ballet, Schallplatte.

Schweizer Theater-Jahrbuch
CH-8002 Zürich, Richard-Wagner-Strasse 19
    Publication of the Schweizerische Gesellschaft für Theaterkultur.

Der Spielplan
Spielplan Verlag
33 Braunschweig, Kastanienallee 2a
    Die monatliche Theatervorschau. Herausgeben von Paul-Albrecht Schmückking.

Tanzarchiv, Das
5 Köln 41, Stadion-Aachener-Strasse
    Deutsche Zeitschrift für Tanzkunst und Folklore.

Theater heute
Friedrich Verlag
3016 Seelze 6, Im Brande 15
    Nachrichten und Kommentare für Bühne, Oper und Ballet.

Theater der Zeit
Henschelverlag, Kunst und Gesellschaft
X-104 Berlin, Oranienburger Strasse 67/68
    Organ des Verbandes der Theaterschaffenden der DDR.

Theater-Rundschau
53 Bonn, Bonner Talweg 10
    Blätter fur Bühne, Film, Musik und Literatur.

B. A SELECTION OF RECENT BOOKS ON THE GERMAN THEATER

Abert, Anna Amalie, ed. *Richard Strauss—Die Opern.* Seelze: Friedrich Verlag, 1977.

Barz, Paul. *Götz Friedrich. Abenteuer Musiktheater—Konzepte, Versüche, Erfahrungen.* Bonn: Keil Verlag, 1978.

Benn, Maurice B. *The Drama of Revolt: A Critical Study of Georg Büchner.* Anglica Germanica Series 2. Cambridge and New York: Cambridge University Press, 1976.

Besci, Kurt. *Das galaktische Weltbild des künftigen Theaters.* Wien: Herder Verlag, 1978.

Best, Alan. *Frank Wedekind.* London: Oswald Wolff, 1975.

Biba, Otto. *Die Unvergleichlichen: Die Wiener Philharmoniker und Salzburg.* Wien: Herder Verlag, 1977.

Bing, Sir Rudolf. *Five Thousand Nights at the Opera.* New York: Doubleday, 1972.

Braulich, Heinrich. *Die Volksbühne. Theater und Politik in der deutsche Volks-bühnenbewegung.* Ost Berlin: Henschelverlag, 1976.

Carlson, Marvin A. *German Theater History of the Nineteenth Century.* Metuchen, N.J.: Scarecrow Press, 1972.

Crosby, Donald H. and George C. Schoolfield, eds. *Studies in the German Drama: a Festschrift in Honor of Walter Silz.* Chapel Hill: University of North Carolina Press, 1974.

Curjel, Hans. *"Experiment Kroll Oper" 1927–1931.* München: Prestel-Verlag, 1975.

Daiber, Hans. *Deutsches Theater seit 1945.* Stuttgart: Philip Reclam jun., 1976.

Davies, Cecil W. *Theater for the People. The Story of the Volksbühne.* Manchester: Manchester University Press, 1977.

Deutscher Bühnenverein, ed. *Was spielten die Theater?* Remagen-Rolandseck: Verlag Rommerskirchen, 1978.

Dierig, Klaus. *Schauspieler ohne Maske.* München: Nymphenburger Verlagsan-stalt, 1977.

Fetting, Hugo. *Max Reinhardt: Schriften.* Ost-Berlin: Henschelverlag, 1976.

Fontana, Oskar Maurus. *Das grosse Welttheater. Theaterkritiken 1909–1967.* Wien: Amalthea-Verlag, 1976.

Friese, Wilhelm, ed. *Ibsen auf der deutschen Bühne. Texte zur Rezeption.* Tübin-gen: Max Niemeyer Verlag, 1976.

Garland, Mary. *Hebbel's Prose Tragedies: An Investigation of the Aesthetic Aspect of Hebbel's Dramatic Language.* London: Cambridge University Press, 1973.

Graham, Ilse. *Goethe and Lessing: The Wellsprings of Creation.* New York: Barnes and Noble, 1973.

———. *Schiller's Drama: Talent and Integrity.* New York: Barnes and Noble, 1974.

Gray, Ronald. *Brecht the Dramatist.* New York: Cambridge University Press, 1976.

Goltschnigg, Dietmar, ed. *Materialen zur Rezeptions- und Wirkungsgeschicte Georg Büchners.* Kronberg, Ts.: Scriptor Verlag, 1974.

Hacks, Peter. *Die Massgaben der Kunst—Gesammelte Aufsätze.* Düsseldorf: Claa-sen Verlag, 1978.

Hadamowsky, Franz. *Die Wiener Hoftheater (Staatstheater) 1776–1966.* Wien: Pra-chner, 1966. 2 vols.

Harding, Lawrence V. *The Dramatic Art of Ferdinand Raimund and Johann Nes-troy: A Critical Study.* The Hague: Mouton, 1974.

Hartmann, Otto Julius. *Die geistigen Hintergründe der Musikdramen Richard Wagners.* Schaffhausen: Novalis Verlag, 1976.

Hartmann, Rudolf. *Das geliebte Haus. Mein Leben mit der Oper.* München: R. Piper & Co., 1976.

———. ed. *Oper—Regie und Bühnenbild heute.* Stuttgart: Verlag W. Kohlhammer, 1978.

Hausenstein, Wilhelm. *Die Masken des Komikers Karl Valentin.* München: Süddeutscher Verlag, 1977.

Hayman, Ronald, ed. *The German Theater.* London: Oswald Wolf and New York: Harper & Row, 1975.

Heer, Hannes, ed. *Dario Fo über Dario Fo.* Köln: Prometh Verlag, 1978.

Hildebrandt, Dieter. *Ödön von Horváth in Selbstzeugnissen und Bilddokumenten.* Reinbeck: Rowohlt Taschenbuch Verlag, 1975.

Hilzinger, Klaus Harro. *Die Dramaturgie des dokumentarischen Theaters.* Tübingen: Max Niemeyer Verlag, 1977.

Honolka, Kurt. *Dreitausend Mal Musik. Stars und Premieren in Stuttgart und anderswo.* Stuttgart: Konrad Theiss Verlag, 1978.

Innes, C. D. *Erwin Piscator's Political Theater. The Development of Modern German Drama.* London: Cambridge University Press, 1972.

Ismayr, Wolfgang. *Das politische Theater in Westdeutschland.* Meisenheim am Glan: Verlag Anton Hain, 1977.

Izenour, George. *Theater Design.* New York: McGraw-Hill, 1977.

Janz, Curt Paul, ed. *Friedrich Nietzsche: Der Musikalische Nachlass.* Kassel: Bärenreiter, 1976.

Karasek, Hellmuth. *Bertolt Brecht—Der jüngste Fall eines Klassikers.* Zürich/München: Kindler Verlag, 1978.

Karbaum, Michael. *Studium zur Geschichte der Bayreuther Festspiele (1876–1976).* Regensburg: Gustav Bosse Verlag, 1976.

Kessler, Sinah, ed. *Giorgio Strehler: Für ein menschlicheres Theater.* Frankfurt am Main: Suhrkamp Verlag, 1976.

Kilian, Hannes. *Marcia Haydée—Porträt einer grossen Tänzerin.* Sigmaringen: Jan Thorbecke Verlag, 1975.

Koegler, Horst, ed. *Friedrichs Ballet-Lexikon von A–Z.* Seelze: Friedrich Verlag, 1977.

Kosch, Wilhelm. *Deutsches Theater-Lexikon.* Klagenfurt und Wien: Verlag Ferd. Kleinmayr, 1960. 3 vols.

Kothes, Franz-Peter. *Die theatralische Revue in Berlin und Wien.* Wilhelmshaven: Heinrichshofen Verlag, 1977.

Krause, Ernst. *Oper von A–Z.* Leipzig: VEB Deutscher Verlag für Musik, 1961.

Kutsch, K. J. and Leo Riemans. *Unvergängliche Stimmen, Sängerlexikon.* München: Francke Verlag, 1976.

Lacis, Asja. *Revolutionär im Beruf.* München: Verlag Rogner und Bernhard, 1978.

Liebermann, Rolf. *Opernjahre.* Bern und München: Scherz Verlag, 1978.

Löb, Ladislaus. *From Lessing to Hauptmann: Studies in German Drama.* London: University Tutorial Press, 1974.

Loose, Hans-Dieter and others. *Dreihundert Jahre Oper in Hamburg.* Hamburg: Hans Christians Verlag, 1977.

Loup, Kurt. *Die Wohlbrücks, Eine deutsche Theaterfamilie.* Düsseldorf: Claasen Verlag, 1976.

Maack, Rudolf. *Tanz in Hamburg.* Hamburg: Hans Christians Verlag, 1975.

Mack, Dietrich. *Der Bayreuther Inszenierungstil.* München: Prestel Verlag, 1978.

Mayer, Hans. *Richard Wagner in Bayreuth.* Stuttgart: Belser Verlag, 1976.

Mews, Siegfried and Herbert Knust, eds. *Essays on Brecht: Theater and Politics.* Chapel Hill: University of North Carolina Press, 1974.

Molinari, Cesare. *Theater. Die faszinierende Geschichte des Schauspiels.* Freiburg: Verlag Herder, 1976.

Pahlen, Kurt. *Oper der Welt.* Zürich: Schweizer Verlagshaus, 1974.

Patterson, Michael. *German Theater Today.* London: Pitman, 1976.

Prodhoe, John. *The Theatre of Goethe and Schiller.* Oxford: Blackwell, 1973.

Quadflieg, Will. *Wir spielen immer. Erinnerungen.* Frankfurt am Main: S. Fischer Verlag, 1976.

Raabe, Paul, ed. *The Era of German Expressionism.* London: Calder, 1974. Tr. by J. M. Ritchie.

Richards, David G. *Georg Büchner and the Birth of the Modern Drama.* Albany: State University of New York Press, 1977.

Richter, Horst, Karl Ruhrberg and Wieland Schmied, eds. *Das Kunstjahrbuch 77/78.* Mainz: Alexander Baier Presse, 1978.

Riess, Curt. *Gustaf Gründgens, eine Biographie.* Hamburg: Hoffman und Campe, 1965.

Rühle, Günther. *Theater in unserer Zeit.* Frankfurt am Main: Suhrkamp Verlag, 1976.

Ruppel, K. H. *Grosse Stunden der Musik.* München: List-Verlag, 1976.

Schäfer, Walter Erich. *Bühne meines Lebens—Erinnerung.* Stuttgart: Deutsche Verlags-Anstalt, 1976.

Scharberth, Irmgard. *Musiktheater mit Rolf Liebermann—ein Bericht über 14 Jahre Hamburgische Staatsoper.* Hamburg: Hans Christians Verlag, 1976.

Schleyer, Winifred. *Die Stücke von Peter Hacks. Tendenzen—Themen—Theorien.* Stuttgart: Ernst Klett, 1976.

Schröder, Ernst. *Das Leben verspielt.* Frankfurt am Main: S. Fischer Verlag, 1978.

Schuh, Willi. *Richard Strauss—Jugend und frühe Meisterjahre, 1864–98.* Frieburg: Atlantis Verlag, 1977.

Schumacher, Ernst. *Berliner Kritiken. Ein Theater Dezennium 1964–1974.* Ost Berlin: Henschelverlag, 1975. 2 vols.

Schütze, Peter. *Peter Hacks—Ein Beitrag zur Ästhetik des Dramas.* Kronberg, Ts.: Scriptor Verlag, 1975.

Thomas, R. Hinton and Keith Bullivant. *Literature in Upheaval: West German Writers and the Challenge of the 1960's.* Manchester: Manchester University Press, 1976.

Unruh, Walther. *Theatertechnik.* Berlin und Bielefeld: Verlag Klasing und Co., 1970.

Urbach, Reinhard. *Arthur Schnitzler.* New York: Ungar, 1973. Tr. Donald Daviau.

Valois, Ninette de and others. *John Cranko und das Stuttgarter Ballet.* Pfullingen: Verlag Günther Neske, 1969. (German, French, and English.)

Völker, Klaus. *Bertolt Brecht—Eine Biographie.* München: Hanser Verlag, 1976.

———. *Brecht Chronicle.* New York: Seabury Press, 1975. Tr. Fred Wieck.

Voss, Egon. *Die Dirigenten der Bayreuther Festspiele.* Regensburg: Bosse-Verlag, 1976.

Wagner, Cosima. *Die Tagebücher, 1869–1883,* ed. by Martin Gregor-Dellin and Die- trich Mack. München: Piper Verlag, 1978. 2 vols. Tr. Geoffrey Skelton. London: Collins, 1978.

Wekwerth, Manfred. *"Brecht?" Berichte—Erfahrungen—Polemik.* München: Carl Hanser Verlag, 1976.

Witt, Herbert, ed. *Brecht as They Knew Him.* London: Lawrence and Wishart, 1975. Tr. John Peet.

Zelinsky, Hartmut. *Richard Wagner—ein deutsches Thema. Eine Dokumentation zur Wirkungsgeschichte Richard Wagners 1876 bis 1976.* Frankfurt am Main: Zweitausendeins, 1976.

GLOSSARY

Abonnement   Subscription
Al gran sole carico d'amore   Nono's opera *Burdened by Love under the Great Sun*
Alle Reichtümer der Welt   O'Neill's *More Stately Mansions*
Allgemeine   General
Amt   Office
Angelegenheiten   Services
Antrieb   Drive
Arbeitsgalerie   Work gallery, fly gallery
Arzt   Doctor
Aufstieg und Fall der Stadt Mahagonny   Brecht/Weill's *Rise and Fall of the City of Mahogany*
Aufwand   Expenditure
Ausbezahlte   Payments
Ausflüge des Herrn Brouček's, Die   Janáček's *The Excursions of Mr. Brouček*
Ausgaben   Expenses
Ausstattung   Scene and costume design department of a national theater
Bajazzo, Der   Leoncavallo's *Pagliacci*
Bauangelegenheiten   Building services
Baumeister Solness   Ibsen's *The Master Builder*
Begleiter   Attendant, chaperone
Belagerungszustand, Der   Keleman's opera *The Siege* (after Camus)
Beleuchterbrücke   Lighting bridge
Beleuchtung   Lighting
Bericht   Report
Besuch der alten Dame, Der   Dürrenmatt's *The Visit of the Old Lady*
Besucherorganisation   Block booking organization
Bestellbüro   Reservation office
Beträge   Monetary amounts
Betriebsbüro   Office of the day-to-day operations of a national theater

Betriebsdirektion   Direction of the routine operations of a national theater

Biografie—Ein Spiel   Frisch's *Biography—a Play*

Blick zurück im Zorn   Osborne's *Look Back in Anger*

Buchhaltung   Bookkeeping

Bühne   Stage

Bühnen   Stages

Bühnenhöhe   Stage level

Bühnenkapellmeister   Conductor of off-stage soloists and choruses

Bühnenwagen   Wagon stage used for shifting large settings

Bundestheaterverband   Federal Theater Association (Vienna)

Burg   Castle

Clownspielen   *Clown plays*

Darsteller   Male theatrical performer

Darstellerin   Female theatrical performer

Dekorationswerkstatt   Scene shop

Deutsch   German

Deutsches Bühnen Jahrbuch   Yearbook of the German national theaters

Dirigent   Orchestra conductor

Disponent   The official in a repertory company who schedules all performances and rehearsals

Dornröschen   Tschaikowsky's ballet *Sleeping Beauty*

Doppelstock   Double deck, double floor

Dramaturg   Literary adviser to the management of a national theater

Dramaturgie   The literary department of a national theater

Drehbühne   Turntable, revolving stage

Drehbühnenzylinder   Revolving stage cylinder

Einen Jux will er sich machen   Nestroy's *He'll Have Himself a Fling*

Einer flog über das Kuckusnest   Wassermann's *One Flew over the Cuckoo's Nest*

Eingang   Entrance

Einnahmen   Income, cash receipts

Eintrittspreis   Entrance price, ticket price

Eiserner Vorhang   Iron safety curtain

Eismann kommt, Der   O'Neill's *The Iceman Cometh*

Eleven   Male students

Elevinnen   Female students

Erstaufführung   First performance, local premiere

Feuervogel, Der   Strawinsky's ballet *The Firebird*

feurige Engel, Der   Prokofieff's opera *The Fiery Angel*

Florentinerhut, Ein   Labiche's *An Italian Straw Hat*

Frau ohne Schatten, Die   Strauss' opera *The Woman without a Shadow*

Frau vom Meer, Die   Ibsen's *The Lady from the Sea*

Frühlings Erwachen   Wedekind's *Spring's Awakening*

Garderobe   Cloakroom, dressing room

Gast   Guest

Gastspiel   Performance on tour
Gebäude   Buildings
Geliebter Lügner   Kilty's *Dear Liar*
Generalintendant   Director of a national theater
Gerettet   Bond's *Saved*
Gesang   Song
Geschichten aus dem Wienerwald   Horváth's *Tales from the Vienna Woods*
geschlossen   Closed
Gespenster   Ibsen's *Ghosts*
grosse Gott Brown, Der   O'Neill's *The Great God Brown*
Grosses Haus   Large theater, usually used for opera, operetta, and ballet performances
Grundriss   Ground plan (architectural drawing)
Handzug   Hand-operated batten
Hauptkassa   Principal cash receipts
Hausmeister, Der   Pinter's *The Caretaker*
Hebebühne   Freight elevator that can lift a loaded truck
Heftgebühr   Program charge, theater magazine charge
heilige Johanna, Die   Shaw's *Saint Joan*
heilige Johanna der Schlachthöfe, Die   Brecht's *Saint Joan of the Stockyards*
Herr Puntila und sein Knecht Matti   Brecht's *Herr Puntila and his Servant Matti*
Herrenhaus   Thomas Wolfe's *Manor House*
Hinterbühne   Rear stage
Hochzeit des Figaro, Die   Mozart's *The Marriage of Figaro*
Hochzeit des Papstes, Die   Bond's *The Pope's Marriage*
Hofburg   The Imperial palace in Vienna
Hoffman's Erzählungen   Offenbach's *The Tales of Hoffmann*
Hofkapellmeister   Court conductor
Hoftheater   Court theater
Horizont   Cyclorama
Horizontbeleuchtungsbrücke   Cyclorama lighting bridge
Hubpodium   Stage lift
Hubpodien   Stage lifts
Inspizient   Stage manager
Intendant   Manager of a national theater
Intendanz   The collective management department of a national theater
Irre, Der   Bond's *The Fool*
Jacabowsky und der Oberst   Werfel's *Jacabowsky and the Colonel*
Jeppe vom Berge   Holberg's *Jeppe from the Hill*
Johanna auf der Scheiterhaufen   Honegger's *Saint Joan at the Stake*
Josef Lang, k.u.k. Scharfrichter   Dorfer/Zettel's *Josef Lang, Imperial and Royal Execu-
    tioner*
junge Lord, Der   Henze's opera *The Young Lord*
jüngste Tag, Der   Horváth's *Judgment Day*
Kabale und Liebe   Schiller's *Love and Intrigue*

Kamelindame   Chopin/Neumeier's ballet *The Lady of the Camellias*

Kammersänger   Concert singer (title)

Kammerspiel(e)   Chamber theater, experimental theater

Kammertheater   Chamber theater, experimental theater

Kantine   Company restaurant or cafeteria

Karte   Theater ticket

Kleines Haus   Small theater, usually used for plays and chamber operas

Klimaanlage   Air conditioning equipment

Kluge, Die   Orff's opera *The Wise Woman*

Komiker   Griffith's *The Comedians*

König Ottokars Glück und Ende   Grillparzer's *King Ottokar, His Rise and Fall*

Korrepetitor   Opera or ballet coach

Kulissen   Wings, scenery

Künst   Art

Künstler   Artist

Kupplungseinrichtung   Hydraulic connecting units for stage lifts

Landestheater   State theater

Landschaftschule   State school

Längschnitt   Section (architectural drawing)

Lastenaufzug   Freight elevator

Lehrer   Teacher

Leitung   Leadership

Loge   Box in a theater

lustige Witwe, Die   Lehár's *The Merry Widow*

Macht des Schicksals, Die   Verdi's *La forza del destino*

Magazin   Storage area

Malsaal   Painting studio

Mantel, Der   Puccini's *Il tabarro*

Maschinenzug   Winch or hydraulic controlled batten

Maske   Makeup

Mass für Mass   Shakespeare's *Measure for Measure*

Meisterpult   Master control station

Mord   Renfranz's *Murder*

Möwe, Die   Chekhov's *The Sea Gull*

Nachmittag   Afternoon

Neuinszenierung   New production

Normans Eroberungen   Ayckbourn's *The Norman Conquests*

Nussknacker, Der   Tchaikowsky's ballet *The Nutcracker*

Oberlicht   Border light, overhead strip light

Oberösterreich   Upper Austria

Österreich   Austria

Parkett   Orchestra seating area in a theater (British: stalls), main-floor seats

Paulus unter den Juden   Werfel's *Paul among the Jews*

Personalangelegenheiten   Personnel services

Personalaufwand   Personnel expenditures

Pique Dame   Tschaikowsky's opera *The Queen of Spades*

Platz der Opfer des Fascismus   Square in Memory of the Victims of Fascism

Platzmiete   Season ticket, subscription

Plebejer proben den Aufstand, Die   Grass's *The Plebians Rehearse the Uprising*

Podien   Plural of Podium

Podium   Stage lift, orchestra lift

Portalbrücke   Main lighting bridge over the proscenium area

Portalturm   Tormentor, vertical masking unit in the proscenium area

Preisermässigung   Price saving when buying a season ticket

Preisgruppe   Price group, group of seats at the same price

Pressebüro   Press and public relations office

Probebühne   Rehearsal stage

Prospekt   Backdrop

Prospekthebebühne   Backdrop lift used in a backdrop storage pit

Prospektmagazin   Backdrop storage pit

Prospektzug   Batten used to raise and lower a backdrop

Raff-vorhang   Draw or tab curtain

Rang   Balcony, gallery, dress circle in a theater

Raten   Installment payments

Rauchklappen   Smoke lid that opens automatically in case of fire to let smoke escape
     through the roof over the stage

Rauchschieber   Smoke ventilator

Referent   Advisor

Regenmacher, Der   Nash's *The Rainmaker*

Regie   Stage direction

Regisseur   Stage director

Reihe   Row of seats in a theater

Reinigung   Cleaning

Rollenboden   Upper gridiron

Rollstuhl   Wheelchair

Rundhorizont   Cyclorama that can be rolled up on a large vertical spindle at the
     side of the stage

Sachaufwand   Materials expenditure

Schalldämmvorhang   Sound absorption curtain

Schauspiel   Drama, serious play

Schauspieler   Actor

Schauspielerin   Actress

Schauspielhaus   Playhouse, theater for spoken drama

Scheinwerfer   Spotlight

schlaue Füchslein, Das   Janáček's *The Cunning Little Vixen*

Schloss   Castle

schmutzigen Hände, Die   Sartre's *Dirty Hands*

Schneider   Tailor

Schnürboden   Lower gridiron

Schrägstellbar   Slantable, rakable (in connection with a stage floor)

Sech Personen suchen einen Autor   Pirandello's *Six Characters in Search of an Author*

seidene Schuh, Die   Claudel's *The Silken Slipper*

Seitenbühne   Side stage

Sessel   Chair

Sicherheitsdienst   Security service

sieben Todsünden der Kleinbürger, Die   Brecht/Weill's *Seven Deadly Sins of the Middle Class*

Sonderabgaben   Special tax

Souffleur   Prompter

Souffleurraum   Prompter's box

Sozialversicherung   Social security

Spiel   Play

Spielleiter   Stage director

Spielplan   Performance schedule

Spielzeit   Theatrical season

Staatsoper   State opera

Staatstheater   State theater

Stadt   City

Städtische Bühnen   City theaters

Stehplatz   Standing room

Stellvertreter   Deputy

Stelwarte   Lobby with statuary in a theater

Steuerpult   Control platform

Strasse, Die   Rice's *Street Scene*

Sturm, Der   Shakespeare's *The Tempest*

Tantiemen   Royalties

Tanz   Dance

Tänzer   Dancer

Tänzerin   Female dancer

Termin   Fixed day, fixed date

Theaterkeller   Basement theater

Tischlerei   Carpentry shop

Tischversenkung   Table elevator, used to raise or lower a performer to or from the stage

Traumspiel   Strindberg's *A Dream Play*

Trommeln in der Nacht   Brecht's *Drums in the Night*

Uraufführung   World premiere

Verbotsgebarung   Forbidden behavior

verlorene Paradies, Das   Penderecki's opera *Paradise Lost* (after Milton)

Verriegelungseinrichtung   Locking units for stage lifts

Versuchung, Die   Tal's opera *The Temptation*

Verwaltung   Administration

Verwandlungen Tabori's *Metamorphosis* (after Kafka)
Vorhang Curtain
Vorstand Management
Vorstellung Performance
Wahrer Held, Ein Synge's *Playboy of the Western World*
Warten auf Godot Beckett's *Waiting for Godot*
Was ihr wollt Shakespeare's *Twelfth Night or What You Will*
Werbung Advertising
Widerspenstigen Zähmung, Der Shakespeare's *The Taming of the Shrew*
Wildente, Der Ibsen's *The Wild Duck*
Wintermärchen, Das Shakespeare's *The Winter's Tale*
Zerissene, Der Nestroy's *A Man Full of Nothing*
Zofen, Die Genet's *The Maids*
Zoogeschichte Albee's *Zoo Story*
Zufälliger Tod eines Anarchisten Fo's *Accidental Death of an Anarchist*
Zuschauerraum Auditorium, seating area for the audience in a theater

INDEX

Play, opera, operetta, and ballet titles and authors are indicated in the following manner:

Plays: *Title* (author)
Operas and operettas: *Title* (composer) or *Title* (author of text/composer)
Ballets: *Title* (composer/choreographer) or *Title* (composer/arranger of the music/choreographer)